HOW TO WRITE A FINANCIAL REPORT

HOW TO WRITE A

COMMUNICATING CRITICAL FINANCIAL

WILEY

FINANCIAL REPORT

SIGNS FROM THE NUMBERS

TAGE C. TRACY

Published by John Wiley & Sons, Inc., Hoboken, New Jersey.
Published simultaneously in Canada.

For general information on our other products and services or for technical support, please contact our Customer Care Department within the United States at (800) 762-2974, outside the United States at (317) 572-3993 or fax (317) 572-4002.

Wiley also publishes its books in a variety of electronic formats. Some content that appears in print may not be available in electronic formats. For more information about Wiley products, visit our web site at www.wiley.com.

Library of Congress Cataloging-in-Publication Data

Names: Tracy, Tage C., author.
Title: How to write a financial report / Tage C. Tracy.
Description: Hoboken, New Jersey : Wiley, [2025] | Includes index. |
  Summary: "Improve your ability to write and produce financial reports
  and analyses that are more effective, better understand where
  information comes from, and obtain a deeper understanding of how
  financial reports are prepared and how they are used"—Provided by
  publisher.
Identifiers: LCCN 2024017350 (print) | LCCN 2024017351 (ebook) | ISBN
  9781394263349 (paperback) | ISBN 9781394263363 (adobe pdf) | ISBN
  9781394263356 (epub)
Subjects: LCSH: Financial statements. | Report writing.
Classification: LCC HG4028.B2 T74 2025 (print) | LCC HG4028.B2 (ebook) |
  DDC 658.15/12—dc23/eng/20240514
LC record available at https://lccn.loc.gov/2024017350
LC ebook record available at https://lccn.loc.gov/2024017351

Cover Design: Wiley
Cover Image: © John Wiley & Sons, Inc.

SKY10082732_082724

CONTENTS

List of Exhibits   *vii*

Preface   *xi*

*Part One—Financial Report Writing Basics – What
You Absolutely Must Know!*   *1*

1   Communicate or Die!   3

2   Target Audience "E" – External Users   15

3   Target Audience "I" – Internal Consumers   27

4   Introducing CART – To Start, the Big "C,"
    Completeness   37

5   Embracing CART – Accuracy, Reliability,
    and Timeliness, the Best of Friends   49

*Part Two—Financial Statements – The Economic
Heartbeat of a Company*   *61*

6   Understanding the Income Statement   63

7   Trusting the Balance Sheet   73

8   Relying on the Statement of Cash Flows   85

9   Connecting the Financial Statement Dots   97

10 The Significance of Financial Forecasts   107

Part Three—The Types and Targets of Financial Reports   *123*

11 The Role of Accounting   125

12 Preparing Financial Reports from Company
Financial Statements – External Users   137

13 Preparing Financial Reports from Company
Financial Statements – Internal Consumers   151

14 Preparing Financial Reports from Company
Financial Information   165

15 Revisiting Our Example Company
with a Slight Twist   179

About the Author   *197*

Index   *199*

LIST OF EXHIBITS

Exhibit 3.1   **Internally Prepared Income Statement – Company Level** — 30

Exhibit 3.2   **Internally Prepared Income Statement – By Primary Operating Division** — 33

Exhibit 3.3   **Sales Revenue By Product Type Flash Report – Software/Saas Operating Division** — 34

Exhibit 4.1   **Local Sample Service Company – Simple Internally Prepared Balance Sheet** — 41

Exhibit 4.2   **Local Sample Service Company – Simple Internally Prepared Income Statement** — 42

Exhibit 4.3   **Top Half of Income Statement – Presented in Complete Format** — 46

Exhibit 5.1   **Local Sample Service Company – Income Statement, Accuracy versus Reliability** — 52

Exhibit 6.1   Audited Financial Statements – Income
             Statement   66

Exhibit 6.2   Internally Prepared Income Statement –
             Company Level   71

Exhibit 7.1   Audited Financial Statements – Balance
             Sheet   76

Exhibit 7.2   Internally Prepared Balance Sheet –
             Company Level   81

Exhibit 8.1   Audited Financial Statements – Statement
             of Cash Flows   88

Exhibit 8.2   Unaudited – Revenue & Expense
             Comparison, Cash versus Accrual   90

Exhibit 8.3   Sources & Uses of Funds   95

Exhibit 9.1   Connecting Annual Income Statement
             with Year-End Balance Sheet   99

Exhibit 9.2   Connecting Balance Sheet Changes with
             Statement of Cash Flows   100

Exhibit 9.3   Calculating Change in Balance Sheet
             Accounts Between Two Years   102

Exhibit 10.1 High, Medium, & Low Case Forecasts –
             Income Statement   117

Exhibit 10.2	High, Medium, & Low Case Forecasts – Balance Sheet	119
Exhibit 10.3	High, Medium, & Low Case Forecasts – Statement of Cash Flows	121
Exhibit 12.1	Audited Financial Statements – Balance Sheet	141
Exhibit 12.2	Audited Financial Statements – Income Statement	142
Exhibit 12.3	Audited Financial Statements – Statement of Cash Flows	142
Exhibit 12.4	Company Expanded Income Statement	146
Exhibit 12.5	Company Expanded Balance Sheet	147
Exhibit 13.1	Internally Prepared Income Statement – Base Case	155
Exhibit 13.2	Internally Prepared Income Statement – Preferred Case	157
Exhibit 13.3(A)	Internally Prepared Balance Sheet – Preferred Case (Top Half)	159
Exhibit 13.3(B)	Internally Prepared Balance Sheet – Preferred Case (Bottom Half)	161

Exhibit 14.1   **Sales Flash Financial Report**   171

Exhibit 14.2   **Product Division P&L Financial Report & Analysis**   176

Exhibit 12.2   **Audited Financial Statements – Income Statement**   182

Exhibit 13.2   **Internally Prepared Income Statement – Preferred Case**   185

Exhibit 15.1   **Alternative Ending – Income Statement Comparison**   189

Exhibit 15.2   **Alternative Ending – Balance Sheet Comparison**   190

PREFACE

The original concept for this book originated with, of all parties, Wiley, the publisher of this book as well as countless other books I've written or co-authored with my late father, John A. Tracy (who passed away in 2022). As we were discussing revising the latest edition of *How to Read a Financial Report* (with the latest 10th edition of the book set for release in the spring of 2024), Wiley inquired about what it would take to produce a book on how to write a financial report. My first response was, wow, what a great idea, and then my second response shifted to finding a way to tie these two books together to provide an even deeper and more complete understanding of how companies produce, report, and present financial information, financial statements, and financial reports. Thus, the idea was born and launched to produce the first edition of this book, *How to Write a Financial Report*.

This book represents a companion or sister book to *How to Read a Financial Report*, but tackles financial and accounting topics from a different perspective. That is, *How to Read a Financial Report* takes the reader on a journey from the perspective of how a party would evaluate a company or business from the outside looking in. *How to Write a Financial Report* takes our reader on a new and exciting journey of how individuals within a company or business produce and communicate financial information and financial statements to both external and internal parties. Or more simply put, this book helps readers understand the opposite side of the process by gaining significant insight from the inside looking out.

This book has been structured along the same lines as *How to Read a Financial Report* in terms of its base architecture and primary financial and accounting concepts covered but does so with a shift in focus from external financial statement and report analysis to internal production, presentation, and communication of critical financial information, financial statements, and financial reports. In fact, you will find that our fictious example company utilized in *How to Read a Financial Report* is used in this book again, but with a focus on presenting far more detailed, informative, and valuable financial information.

Critical concepts covered in this book include:

- The art of communicating to both internal and external parties, in a complete, accurate, reliable, and timely manner (i.e., CART), and why differences exist. Included is an overview of key accounting and financial terminology to help build your verbiage and master this unique language.

- The all-important and overriding concept of making sure you completely know and understand your target audience before writing a financial report.

- Why financial information, statements, and reports are prepared with different levels of detail, analysis, and confidential information for eventual distribution to both internal and external parties.

- Diving deeper into our fictious example company's financial performance, financial statements, and analyses to further your understanding of how business economic decisions are made and how financial operating results are communicated.

- Continuing to focus on essential accounting and financial concepts introduced in *How to Read a Financial Report* by expanding our discussions on the importance of understanding and managing *cash flows* (a hallmark and focal point in all the books I've published) as well as providing a refresher course on further mastering your knowledge of financial statement *connections* (i.e., how the big three financial statements are interconnected with one another).

- Offering multiple real examples of financial reports prepared from different sources of company financial information that is directed toward external parties and multiple levels of internal company personnel, ranging from the "C" suite and Board of Directors down to managers and even staff.

- And finally, offering a few twists and turns along the way with our fictious example company and how its financial outcome could have changed and how a financial report represents an essential part of communicating its business plan.

Countless financial statements and related financial exhibits are presented in this book, which are basically spreadsheets. All exhibits in the book are prepared as Excel spreadsheets. If you would like a copy of the Excel workbook of the exhibits, please contact me at my email address: tagetracy@cox.net.

I cannot thank my late father and John Wiley & Sons enough for providing me the opportunity to write this book that communicates essential, must-know concepts and strategies on how to effectively communicate financial information, reports, and statements. As with all the books I've written, an emphasis is placed on accounting being just as much of an art form as science, which will be on full display in this book. While it's one thing to master the art of accounting, it's something completely different learning how to master the art of the financial report story, spin, pitch, and for lack of a better term, BS that is so often produced and distributed in this day and age of financial engineering. My sincere hope is not just that you learn how to write a financial report but just as importantly, how to read through a financial report and separate fact from the art of the spin.

TAGE C. TRACY

Anthem, Arizona
March 2024

Part One

FINANCIAL REPORT WRITING BASICS – WHAT YOU ABSOLUTELY MUST KNOW!

Part One

FINANCIAL REPORT WRITING BASICS – WHAT YOU ABSOLUTELY MUST KNOW!

1

COMMUNICATE OR DIE!

Let me be as frank and blunt as possible to start this book, keeping in mind that the following statement is coming from an accounting and financial professional that has spent the better part of his entire career, almost 40 years, primarily "crunching numbers" (for lack of a better term) and on occasion, writing a book or two.

Writing a financial report cannot be achieved unless you can effectively communicate. Period!

When I mean communicate, I mean it in the broadest sense possible as communication skills extend far beyond what a typical financial or accounting professional may view as representing essential communication skills such as simply stating that 2 plus 2 equals four. What you will quickly learn from this book is that in order to effectively communicate, you must be able to speak, listen, observe, write, read, calculate, educate, lead, interpret, analyze, and direct, all equally well, and be able to package and present your financial report and deliver it via a story to your target audience in a format that they can understand, trust, and believe.

As you work through this book, a primary goal will be to find the proper balance between helping you (in the role of producing a financial report) understand how to prepare best in class financial reports as well as assisting you (in the role of student attempting to learn more about financial reports and financial statements) to expand and improve your knowledge of accounting and financial concepts and topics.

To start, I'll warn you that I tend to emphasize using acronyms to remember key concepts, so out of the gate keep in mind the acronym FIK, which stands for fundamentals, interest, and knowledge. That is, you must have the proper *f*undamentals to write and communicate (e.g., can you structure a sentence?), have an appropriate level of passion and *i*nterest in the subject matter

(nothing more painful than reading content that the author has limited interest in), and have advanced *k*nowledge in the subject matter (to ensure your target audience understands the financial report and the conclusions you're drawing).

To help you navigate the book, I have prepared this simple summary of the book's structure that covers the how, who, what, where, and why of preparing financial reports:

- Chapter 1, How to Communicate Financial Information: To start, I dive into the subject matter of How to Write a Financial Report, focusing on strategies, techniques, etc. that are essential to the process of communicating financial information in financial reports. Further, I expand on the "how" to communicate concept by diving deeper into a simple but powerful acronym CART (covered in Chapters 4 and 5). This stands for providing Complete, Accurate, Reliable, and Timely financial reports.

- Chapters 2 and 3, Who Are You Communicating Financial Information To?: Next up, I then turn the book's attention to gaining a better understanding of your target audience, both between external users of financial reports and information and internal parties such as board members, the management, and others. If you don't have a clear understanding of who you are communicating to, not only do you run the risk of having your financial report get lost in translation but more importantly, you may be preparing financial reports that contain vital and confidential financial information that falls into the wrong hands.

- Chapters 6 through 10, What Financial Information Are You Communicating?: An entire section of the book has been dedicated to gaining a better understanding of what financial information you will be communicating by providing a thorough understanding of the big three financial statements (i.e., the income statement, balance sheet, and statement of cash flows), why developing best in class financial forecasts should always be a priority, and closing out our discussion on revisiting the importance of gaining a handle on how financial statements and financial information are connected.

- Chapter 11, Where Does Financial Information Come From?: In this chapter, I move my attention to gaining a better understanding of where critical financial information comes from that will be presented in a financial report. Simply put, I spend some time helping you as a reader understand basic concepts associated with accounting and financial reporting systems, basic accounting principles and concepts, and other critical information.

- Chapters 12 through 15, Why Are You Communicating Financial Information?: Finally, I cover the subject of why you are communicating financial information. Of course, this should be obvious as any type of business, organization, governmental entity, etc. needs to ensure it has CART financial reports on which to base sound economic decisions. In these chapters I offer real-life examples of different internal and external financial reports, as well as tips and tidbits on making sure your financial statements are more effective in delivering the Why!

Finally, I would like to mention that throughout this book, I sometimes will use the phrases of financial information and financial reports interchangeably. To be clear, financial information really represents the source accounting and financial data that needs to be communicated in a financial report. Or thinking of it differently, you cannot produce a reliable financial report without having quality financial information and vice versa; having quality financial information unto itself does not mean a business will have access to a reliable financial report. Both are highly connected and are dependent on one another, but it is important to not confuse these two concepts as one does not automatically produce the other.

Remember the Basics

To master the art of preparing the most effective financial reports, you will gain a new appreciation of just how important developing communication skills is and why, in all the books I've written by myself and/or in partnership with my late father, five critical concepts should be kept in mind at all times:

- *Accounting – Art vs. Science:* Accounting is just as much an art form as it is a science. I, along with my late father, have driven home this concept, time and time again, in the books we've published including our sister book to *How to Write a Financial Report, How to Read a Financial Report* (10th edition), *Accounting for Dummies* (7th edition), and others. As you will discover reading this book, writing a financial report is often even more of an art form than having to apply generally accepted accounting principles (i.e., GAAP) to produce financial statements. Examples will be provided throughout this book.

- *Financial Report Range:* The concept of a financial report is extensive, broad, and extremely diverse. Financial reports range from something as big and complex as preparing an annual financial report for a publicly traded company such as Microsoft (most recent, 83 pages for 2023) read by thousands of external parties to something as small and simple to understand as an e-commerce company selling products online and trying to understand how much they can spend on advertising and promotional expenses (one page of information, read by two executives). Which brings me to the third critical concept.

- *Financial Report Audience:* Similar to understanding just how broad the range of financial reports is, the audience for financial reports is even broader. Financial reports are read by all types of parties, ranging from some of the most sophisticated financial professionals in the country to small business owners, managers, sales professionals, staff, lenders, lawyers, students, etc., etc., etc. that are on the opposite end of the technical spectrum. That is, these parties are not experts in financial and accounting matters and as such, need to be treated in a completely different manner (when financial reports are prepared) than the top financial minds and experts spread across the financial centers around the world. Translation – you better be keenly aware of and know your target audience for the financial report (a topic covered throughout this book). A much deeper dive on this topic is provided in Chapter 2, "Target Audience 'E' – External Users."

- *Never Assume:* Being direct as possible again, assumption is the mother of all f-ups. Don't just assume that after you've produced a financial report that you deliver old school via paper or new school in an electronic file, your job is done. This represents an absolute fatal error as after a financial report is produced, delivered, and discussed, you will almost always need to respond in a follow-up fashion that encompasses verbal discussions, listening attentively, reading feedback, observing reactions, etc. For example, if you provide a financial report to a party that is not professionally trained in the field of accounting and finance, assuming that this party understands the financial report and its primary financial message or critical output, without discussing the financial report with them, often represents a significant mistake. To combat this potential problem, direct discussions should be held with the target audience to walk through the financial report (line by line if needed), help educate the party(s) as to the structure and findings of the financial report, and confirm that they understand the output. From a factual standpoint, confirming without a doubt that you provided a financial report to the target audience and discussed it with them is always a much better path to pursue than assuming the target audience received, read, and understands the financial report.

◆ ***Always the Storyteller:*** As a storyteller, you must remember to be confident, credible, focused, and clear when communicating financial information. Just as important, the financial story presented must flow in an easy to follow and efficient manner that includes using the proper report format, structure (i.e., ensure the report conclusion is easily identified), level of detail, information, and data and is delivered with a style that is effortlessly digested. To expand on the concept of being an effective storyteller, I'm often drawn to a quote from the movie *Caddyshack* that Judge Smails delivers – "It's easy to grin when your ship comes in and you have the market beat, but the man who is worthwhile is the man who can smile when his shorts are too tight in the seat." The reason I offer this quote is to remind everyone about the critical importance of delivering bad, challenging, and difficult news (as part of the financial reporting process). It's even more important than being the hero when providing good news. Mastering the art of communicating difficult news (and providing possible solutions) is a skill set that very few have, and which is desperately needed. Always provide full disclosure (to the right parties), especially with bad news.

It Always Helps to Speak the Language

If you're heading to France or Italy, it goes without saying that you should brush up on the basics of French and Italian as, let's face it, being able to communicate in the local dialect can really improve your trip's experience. Same goes for accounting and finance; if you can at least master some basic terminology and begin to speak the "language," you will be well ahead of the game. This section of the chapter covers two buckets of terminology, basic and advanced.

Basic Terminology

Basic terminology is primarily associated with communicating the results of financial statements (from an accounting perspective), with a heavy weighting toward the income statement. Below, I've provided a sampling of the most commonly used basic accounting and financial terminology (which I will use frequently through this book):

- Top Line: A company's net sales revenue generated over a period of time (e.g., for a 12-month period).

- COGS or COS: Pronounced like it is spelled; stands for costs of goods sold (for a product-based business) and costs of sales (for a service-based business). COGS or COS tend to vary directly (or in a linear fashion) with the top-line sales revenue.

- Gross Profit and Margin: Sometimes used interchangeably, gross profit equals your top line less your COGS or COS. The gross margin (a percentage calculation) is determined by dividing your gross profit by the top line.

- Op Ex: Is a broad term that is short for operating expenses, which may include selling, general, administrative, corporate overhead, and other related expenses. Unlike COGS or COS, Op Ex tends to be fixed in nature and will not vary directly with the top-line sales revenue.

- SG&A: Selling, general, and administrative expenses. Companies may distinguish between Op Ex and SG&A to assist parties with understanding the expense structure of its operations in more detail.

- Bottom Line: A company's net profit or loss after all expenses have been deducted from net sales revenue. Being in the "black" indicates that a net profit is present and being in the "red" indicates that a net loss was generated.

- Breakeven: The operating level where a company generates zero in profit or loss as it "broke even." Or, conversely, it is the amount of sales revenue that needs to be generated to cover all COGS/COS and Op Ex.

- Contribution Margin: You may hear companies reference the term *contribution margin*. What this generally refers to is the profit generated by a specific operating unit or division of a company (but not for the company as a whole). Most larger companies have multiple operating units or divisions, so the profit (or loss) of each operating unit or division is calculated to determine how much that specific unit or division "contributed" to the overall performance of the entire company.

- Cap Ex: While Op Ex is associated with the income statement, Cap Ex stands for capital expenditures and is a calculation of how much a company invested in tangible or intangible assets during a given period (for equipment, machinery, new buildings, investments in intangible assets, etc.).

- YTD, QTD, MTD: These are simple and stand for year to date, quarter to date, or month to date. For example, a flash report may present QTD sales for the period of 10/1/20 through 11/15/20 (so management can evaluate sales levels through the middle of a quarter).

- FYE and QE: These two items stand for fiscal year-end and quarter-end. Most companies utilize a fiscal year-end that is consistent with a calendar year-end of 12/31/xx (which would make their quarter-ends 3/31/xx, 6/30/xx, 9/30/xx, and 12/31/xx). Please note that several companies utilize FYEs that are different than a calendar year-end to match their business cycle with that of a specific industry. For example, companies that cater to the education industry may use a FYE of 6/30/xx to coincide with the typical operating year for schools or colleges (which tend to run from 7/1/xx through 6/30/xx).

Advanced Terminology

Advanced terminology tends to be centered in references to financial concepts that are focused on cash flows, forecasts, projections, and financing topics (i.e., raising capital such as securing loans or selling equity in a company). With that said, here's a summary listing of advanced terminology to reference.

- EBITDA: This is one of the most used (and abused) terms in finance today and stands for earnings before interest, taxes, depreciation, and amortization. A shorter version that is also used frequently is EBIT or earnings before interest and taxes. The reason for EBITDA's popularity is that capital sources want to clearly understand just how much earning a company can generate in the form of operating cash on a periodic basis. EBITDA strips out interest, taxes, and depreciation and amortization expense (both noncash expenses) to calculate what is perceived to be a company's ability to generate internal positive cash flow (which is widely used when evaluating the value of a company and its ability to service debt).

- Free Cash Flow: FCF is closely related to EBITDA but takes into consideration numerous other factors or adjustments such as the need for a company to invest in equipment or intangible assets on a periodic basis (to remain competitive), the required or set debt service the company is obligated to pay each year (for interest and principal payments), any guaranteed returns on preferred equity, and other similar adjustments. FCF can be a highly subjective calculation based on the estimates and definitions used by different parties.

- YOY and CAGR: YOY stands for a year-over-year change in a financial performance (e.g., sales change for the current 12-month period compared to the prior 12-month period). CAGR stands for compounded annual growth rate and represents a financial calculation that evaluates a financial performance over a number of periods (e.g., sales increased at a CAGR of 15.5% for the five-year period of 2016 through 2020).

- Sustainable Growth Rate: This calculation estimates a company's maximum growth rate it can achieve by using internal operating capital (i.e., positive cash flow) only. When a company exceeds its sustainable growth rate, external capital such as loans or equity from new investors may need to be secured to support ongoing operations.

- Debt Service: Total debt service includes both required loan interest and principal payments due over a period of time.

- B2B and B2C: A company that sells primarily to other businesses is B2B (business-to-business) whereas a company that sells primarily to consumers is B2C (business-to-consumer).

- Burn Rate and the Runway: A burn rate is generally used for newer businesses or starts-up that have not achieved profitability and are "burning" a large amount of cash. The burn rate calculates the amount of cash burn a company is incurring over a specific period, such as a month or a quarter. If a company has a burn rate of $250,000 a month (before generating any sales), then an investor could quickly calculate that this company would need $3 million of capital to support it for one year. The runway calculates how much time a company has before it runs out of cash. In our example, if the company has $1 million of cash left and is burning $250,000 per month, it has a remaining runway of four months.

- TTM and FTM: TTM stands for trailing twelve months and FTM stands for forward twelve months. These figures are often used by parties to help understand a company's annual operating results that are not in sync with its FYE (e.g., how much sales revenue was generated for the period of the QE 9/30/19 through the QE 6/30/20, 12 months of operating history). TTM and FTM can be especially useful when evaluating companies that are growing rapidly or have experienced a recent significant change in business.

Throughout the remainder of this book, I will reference these concepts frequently so you may want to bookmark this section to help refresh your memory as needed. There's no harm in reading and re-reading this section of Chapter 1, as when you're swimming with the financial sharks out in the open water, there's nothing worse than becoming the "chum" (or chump) and looking overmatched when you can't even understand basic accounting and financial terminology.

A Friendly Reminder About the Era of Technology

As I write this book and prepare it for distribution with my publisher, I would be remis if a discussion on technology was not included. And oh, what a world of high technology we live in as over the past two decades, we've graduated from the web and internet, to data mining/big data and the cloud, to all the promise associated with the Metaverse to the latest buzz words, yes, artificial intelligence ("AI"). So with this in mind, I would offer you these pieces of advice as it relates to the interface, or some may refer to it as more of a collision, of financial reporting and technology.

- Significant risks and dangers are present when using artificial intelligence to produce a financial report. The first question that you must ask is do you, as the author (of the financial report), even understand the output and conclusion drawn? If you trust and rely on the output generated, your target audience that trusts you will rely on it. As such, the entire information flow runs the risk of becoming polluted if AI incorporates what it deems as facts into the financial report that lead to an incorrect conclusion. I'm not debating that AI can be a useful resource or tool. It certainly can be but in the same breath, AI must be controlled, understood, and managed to produce CART financial reports.

- Furthering our discussion on AI, you must ask another important question related to if AI is even producing an appropriate response or output in the financial report. If you are not educated and/or familiar with the financial topics of primary importance in the financial report, how would you know if AI is producing accurate information? My point here is that relying on AI, without having a complete and thorough understanding of the issues, can be a fatal error.

- Moving past AI, I would note that accounting and ERP systems (enterprise resource planning systems) range from relatively simple platforms such as QuickBooks to extremely complex ERP systems, such as SAP/Oracle. From easy-to-use platforms such as QuickBooks (but a platform that lacks proper controls so financial transaction recording risks tend to be elevated) to complex systems that require far more knowledge and technical experience, these systems are great but if they are not properly implemented, managed, and controlled, the risk of DIGO (data in, garbage out) can be significantly increased.

- And just to complicate this matter further, it's worth chewing on this concept. Most companies utilize multiple data sources and systems that feed into their ERP systems and flow through to financial reporting. It is important to remember that invaluable financial data and information comes from not just an accounting or ERP system, but data and information located elsewhere such as customer relationship management systems (CRM), third-party payroll providers, and proprietary database management systems, just to name a few. It's incredibly important to manage the flow of digital financial information, from multiple sources, with proper policies, procedures, and controls to avoid the often fatal virus of DIGO (data in, garbage out).

There is simply no way I can cover the topic of technology and its impact on financial reporting and financial analysis in just one section of this chapter, let alone an entire book. There are just too many moving parts, elements, and facets associated as technology has without question infiltrated just about every aspect of accounting and financial information systems (not to mention our entire lives). Rather, what you need to remember about technology and its influence in financial reporting comes down to two key concepts. First, technological advancements have greatly improved financial reporting and analysis, and should be viewed as a critical tool to improve the efficiency and accuracy of financial reporting. Second and in the same breath, never, ever rely solely on technology to produce financial reports. You should always complete a thorough review of any financial report, whether produced with the assistance of technology or not, prior to distributing to the intended audience.

A Final Word About This Book

For those of you anticipating/expecting a technical book designed around how to write a financial report in a step-by-step fashion, such as preparing an annual report for a publicly traded company, drafting an audit report for a private company, or preparing a 10-K for a company that is required to provide periodic information to the Securities and Exchange Commission (i.e., SEC), I'm sorry to disappoint you as this is not the book's primary objective. While I will reference a wide range of standard financial reports throughout the coming chapters (often used as examples), the book's real goal is to educate you, as a reader, with understanding how to more effectively communicate critical financial and operating information, data, and results to a broad range/target audience in the most efficient manner possible.

In summary and a thought to keep in mind with not only reading this book but in your day-to-day professional career, if a financial report looks, smells, feels, tastes, reads, etc. like BS, then it probably is BS. If a financial report is logical, defendable, understandable, easily digested, and draws appropriate conclusions, then you've done your job and have helped produce valuable internal company intellectual knowledge and property that will benefit your company in more ways than you can imagine.

2

TARGET AUDIENCE
"E" – EXTERNAL USERS

You can't possibly write a financial report without understanding who your target audience is. That is, you must always have a clear line of sight as to who will be the end user of the financial report, financial information embedded in the financial report, and conclusion(s) drawn. Think of this like a professional sports organization that puts their team on the field not knowing who the customers or audience is. While the sports organization may get lucky and deliver exactly what the audience is looking for, more times than not, this will fail. In the world of sales and marketing, you must know your target customers to ensure your selling process is as efficient as possible. The same holds true for financial reporting, as knowing your customer or audience is of paramount importance.

Basically, two target audiences are present when preparing financial reports – external users covered in this chapter and internal consumers (covered in Chapter 3).

- External Users: This group of users is very broad based and includes parties such as financial analysts, investors, creditors or lenders, regulatory bodies (e.g., the SEC or IRS), compliance groups, and the list goes on and on and on. The general rule of thumb when issuing financial reports to external users is to provide these parties with exactly the information they want and need, but no more or no less. The real art to this process is to present the proper balance between disclosing relevant financial information (for an external party to be able to complete a proper analysis) but at the same time, not disclosing confidential or secretive financial information that "bad actors" may use against the business. Trust me when I say, this is much easier said than done.

- Internal Consumers: Internal users (which I refer to as consumers) include a wide range of parties that are directly employed, retained (such as board members, consultants, advisors), and/or engaged with a business or organization. These would include executive management team members, the company's board of directors or advisors, the mid-level management team, and also specific staff members. More times than not, it is important to remember that the recipient of a financial report will not be an accounting or financial professional but rather other key management team members that are essential to a company's success such as human resource managers, the technology team (e.g., developers, data analysts, etc.), "C" level team members (e.g., the CTO or Chief Technology Officer, the COO or Chief Operating Officer, etc.) and similar parties. For the internal team, a delicate balance is present between providing too much and overly complex financial and accounting reports (that a non-accounting or financial employee has no idea what it means) with making sure just the right amount of financial information is presented to properly educate the target audience. Remember, the goal is to empower the team, improve their knowledge of financial information, and to assist them with creating incremental value in a business.

When thinking of the target audience, you must be prepared to take on different roles. That is, you must be prepared to be an educator, a storyteller, a knowledge builder, a messenger, a leader, and sometimes, even a student, as you would be amazed at how much you can learn, and subsequently improve your financial report writing skills, by simply listening to what your target audience is saying and needs to understand better. External parties must feel satisfied that the financial report received allows them to undertake their jobs in a confident and credible manner. Internal parties must be able to act on the financial information provided in the financial report and be able to make appropriate/proper business decisions. This chapter focuses our discussion on external users of financial reports, whereas Chapter 3 turns our attention to internal users of financial reports.

The Role and Importance of External Financial Reporting

Before I dig deeper into our discussion explaining the primary differences between internally generated financial information and externally prepared financial reports and statements, an overview of the role and importance of externally prepared financial reporting is warranted. In the context of this chapter, when the term *financial information* is used, it is with the broadest meaning and includes reports, statements, analyses, evaluations, assessments, and so on (i.e., basically any type of internally generated financial data or information). This compares to externally produced financial information, which, for ease of understanding, includes financial statements and financial reports. Or, from a different perspective, internally generated financial information is all-encompassing whereas externally produced financial reports and statements represent a selection or fraction of the financial information that management has elected to provide to external parties (either by choice or due to regulatory requirements).

As with internally generated financial information, the main purpose of external financial reporting is to provide up-to-date, complete, accurate, reliable, and timely financial information from a business to shareholders, investors, lenders, analysts, governmental agencies, credit bureaus, and the like. In fact, an efficiently functioning accounting and financial information system, one that leverages both software/technology and company personnel resources, can achieve the dual mandate of producing financial information for both external and internal consumption (in a cost-effective manner).

It should be obvious that investors and lenders are straightforward examples of external parties requiring access to financial information as they represent potential sources of capital (equity and debt) to support a business's ongoing operations. As such, they have a right to and need for financial information. Other parties are also interested in the financial affairs of a business – for example, its employees, other creditors, analysts (who provide independent assessments of a business), regulatory groups, governmental agencies, and so on. When external parties read financial reports that are made public, they should keep in mind that these communications are primarily directed at the owner-investors of the business and its lenders (i.e., the primary capital sources). External financial reporting standards that are utilized to prepare and provide financial information to the public have been developed with this primary audience in mind.

A quick word of caution as it relates to the term *public*: When I use this term, any financial information that is provided to the public can be accessed by basically any third party. This could be a financial analyst, a governmental entity, a competing business, or an investor or day trader plying their trade on Robinhood. If they know where to access the information, any party can gain rather detailed insight into a business.

According to estimates, there were more than 8,000 publicly traded companies on the U.S. stock exchanges in the mid-1990s. Since then, by 2022, this number had decreased to just 3,750 publicly owned businesses in the United States. Their capital stock shares and other securities are traded in public markets. The dissemination of financial information by these companies is governed by federal law, which is enforced mainly by the Securities and Exchange Commission (SEC). The New York Stock Exchange, Nasdaq, and Internet securities markets also enforce rules and regulations over the communication of financial information by companies whose securities are traded on their markets.

Securities of foreign businesses are traded in stock markets around the world. Many countries, including the United States, have been attempting to develop a set of *international financial reporting and accounting standards*. This process has not gone as smoothly as many had hoped for. Indeed, at the time of this writing (2023), the SEC has not yet given its formal endorsement of international standards. U.S. businesses are not yet required to adopt the global standards.

In the United States and other countries, public companies cannot legally release information to some stockholders or lenders but not to others, nor can a business tip off some of them before informing the others. The laws and established standards of financial reporting are designed to ensure that all stockholders, analysts, and lenders have equal access to a company's financial information and financial reports.

A company's financial report may not be the first source of information about its profit performance. In the United States, most public corporations issue press releases of their most recent earnings results, but it is important to remember that the releases of the earnings may not have been audited by an independent CPA firm. These press releases precede the mailing of hard copies of the company's financial report to its stockholders, lenders, and other parties. Most public companies put their financial reports on their websites at the time of or soon after the press releases. Private businesses do not usually send out letters to their owners and lenders in advance of their financial reports, although they could. As a rule, private companies do not put their financial reports on publicly accessible websites.

Primary External Reporting Drivers

Basically, the need for external reporting comes down to one of two primary drivers – *taxation and compliance* and *capital sources*:

1. *Taxation and compliance:* Most people realize that there is a significant demand for financial reporting because of income taxes. Whether it is at the federal (i.e., IRS) or state (e.g., the Franchise Tax Board in California) level, it goes without saying that financial reporting of operating results to tax authorities is generally not the most eagerly anticipated task on an annual basis. It is important to remember that beyond income tax reporting, a vast requirement is present to report financial information to other organizations (primarily governmental) that involve many different taxes and financial data needs. Quite honestly, income tax reporting often is the least worrisome tax compliance requirement, as once a business expands and begins to operate in multiple states and foreign countries, a bevy of additional tax reporting is required, including payroll (for both employees and consultants), sales and use taxes (a hot issue because of e-commerce business models), property taxes, excise taxes, and others. But let us not stop here as, in addition to reporting financial information for different types of business taxes, there is a large demand for financial data from other regulatory organizations as well. Any business operating in government contracting realizes this, as having to validate prevailing wage compensation (remitted to

employees) or adhering to product or service pricing that is governed by strict agreements is par for the course. The list of potential nontaxation financial reporting requirements is endless and tends to vary by industry but the point that needs to be made is simple. Governmental data and financial reporting requirements are extensive and, without a properly functioning accounting and financial reporting system (refer to Chapter 5 on accuracy and reliability), businesses will undoubtedly waste time, effort, and money.

2. *Capital sources:* Throughout this book, I will dive into a deeper discussion on different forms, types, and structures of business financial capital sources but to start, external business financial capital basically comes from one of two sources – equity or debt. When thinking of equity, public companies are the obvious reference here given the slew of financial reporting that needs to be made available publicly. This includes the need to report financial results on an annual (referred to as a 10K) or quarterly (referred to as a 10Q) basis via issuing reports to the Securities and Exchange Commission (SEC). These reports are required reporting for public companies, but the need for external financial reporting does not stop with public companies. Most private businesses and organizations must also report financial results to investors, analysts (that perform important independent financial analyses on businesses), owners,

lenders (such as banks, private credit, non-bank lenders, or leasing companies), board members, and other similar parties. The sheer volume of the different types of financial reports and statements that may be requested make it impossible to list them in this book, but the basic premise is simple: If a third party is going to invest financial capital in your business (equity or debt), then you can be assured that external financial reporting will be required.

In trying to simplify our discussion as to the parties requiring external financial reporting and main drivers demanding business financial information, I might leave you with these three tidbits of advice:

- First, basically every government entity, including states, counties, and cities, is hungry for tax receipts in the current economic environment (which is being amplified by the post COVID-19 pandemic world). It would be wise to become familiar with the acronym SALT (state and local taxation) as, while the federal government presents enough challenges with taxation, just wait until you must deal with 20+ states, all with different rules, regulations, and reporting requirements. And if you need any proof with just how daunting this can be, please brief yourself on *South Dakota v. Wayfair*, which basically paves the way for states to require businesses, even without establishing a nexus or having a physical place of business in the state, to charge, collect, and remit sales tax for the sale of specific goods and services. Given the shift toward e-commerce and the demise of traditional retail, it does not take a genius to figure

out how much sales tax revenue states have been losing over the past decade.

- Second, remember this all-important statement – Less is more! What I mean by this is that when reporting to external parties, for whatever need, focus on providing the external party with the specific information requested, in the desired preferred report format, no more or no less. The reason for this is simple. If you provide any type of excess information, reports, data, and so on, you are only going to open up Pandora's box, as not only are you going to confuse the requesting party but even more problematic, you are going to potentially invite them into areas of your business that they do not have any reason to be involved with. So, in the spirit of Less is more, also remember this all-important acronym – KISS (keep it simple, stupid), as keeping the information as simple as possible for the receiving party will make both your and their lives much easier.

- Third, understand the difference between public information and public entities demanding financial information. I previously noted that publicly traded companies are required to prepare financial reports to be made available to the general public. This should not be confused with preparing financial information for public entities (e.g., taxing authorities) that should remain confidential and not available to the general public. Unlike an annual report issued by Apple, Inc., which is readily available to all interested parties, Apple's annual federal income tax return is confidential and should remain private (under the control of the IRS).

Types of Externally Prepared Financial Statements

This section of the chapter centers around the external financial statement reporting options that are most frequently utilized by company management to present financial statements to external parties. I should note that in some cases, these options by themselves represent a basic type of financial report as when a company has audited financial statements prepared, the full audit report includes an audit opinion, the audited financial statements, and accompanying audited footnotes to the financial statements. As you will learn later in this book, providing this base level financial report is a commonly used strategy and one that is widely accepted by external parties. However (and explained later in this book), other and more robust external reporting strategies are available that may better serve a company in terms of communicating financial statements and financial results in a clearer, more concise, and more informative manner that helps further build credibility and confidence with external users (a critical element when raising and managing external capital sources such as banks and investors).

To start, I would like to drive home an important concept related to externally prepared financial statements versus reports. That is, for many private companies, there is no need to prepare and issue an entire financial report (as required by the SEC), as providing just the financial statements (along with financial footnotes when appropriate as well as a simple MDOR, management discussion of operating results, or MD&A, management

discussion & analysis) is considered adequate. It should be obvious that providing financial statements with some supplemental information is usually much quicker and cheaper than going to the trouble of providing a complete financial report (such as Microsoft, Inc.'s annual financial report monstrosity); even for the external parties, it represents a more efficient process, as everyone can simply cut to the chase when analyzing a company's financial results.

Issuing external financial statements basically comes down to one of four choices, three of which are most often produced from retaining an independent CPA firm to prepare the financial statements (and include the following):

1. *Compiled financial statements:* Compiled financial statements are really nothing more than a CPA firm's taking company-prepared financial statements, formatting the information for external presentation, and then slapping the report on the CPA firm's letterhead; that's about it. Further, the CPA firm will not attest to the reliability of the compiled financial statements (being prepared in accordance with GAAP) and almost never attach or include financial statement footnotes. If it hasn't already occurred to you, compiled financial statements are basically a farce, as almost no serious business utilizes this type of financial statement reporting.

2. **Reviewed financial statements:** For smaller to medium-sized businesses, reviewed financial statements are frequently prepared and utilized for external reporting purposes (as they are much lower in cost, easier to produce, and often satisfy external capital source reporting requirements). Reviewed financial statements are usually prepared by an independent CPA firm and involve the CPA's completing a more thorough evaluation of a company's financial performance using various analytical and financial analysis procedures. The CPA firm will attempt to present the financial statements in accordance with GAAP and generally will attach and include financial statement footnotes. It should be noted that the CPA firm will issue a review report that clearly states that they have not audited the company's financial information and, as such, do not guarantee compliance with GAAP (or other similar accounting frameworks). However, the review report will often make a statement that provides limited assurance that the company's financial statements are in compliance with GAAP without knowledge of any material modifications. Reviewed financial statements are much better than compiled financial statements but are not at the same level as audited financial statements.

3. **Audited financial statements:** Independent CPA firm–audited financial statements are without question the most reliable and comprehensive but also are the most time-consuming to prepare, expensive, and often the most complex. Audited financial statements generally include an audit report, the audited financial statements, audited footnotes, and in some cases, supplemental schedules or exhibits (if requested by the company). As previously noted, all publicly traded companies must have audited financial statements prepared and issued at least annually but it should be noted that countless other private businesses, governmental organizations, not-for-profit entities, and so on also have audited financial statements prepared. The reason for this is simple. The larger and more complex the reporting entity, the greater the demand for independent CPA firm audits to be completed. For example, a not-for-profit that receives $5 million a year in annual contributions may get by with having reviewed financial statements prepared, as the financial risks are relatively small compared to a group such as the Salvation Army, which raised approximately $150 million in 2019 and makes statements as to how much of each dollar raised is dedicated to program services (something large donors absolutely want verified).

If you recall, I referred to four types of financial statements being available for external presentation, which I have not forgotten about. The fourth type of financial statement is internally prepared financial statements (formatted or structured for external distribution). That is, a company can issue internally prepared financial statements that have not been reviewed, audited, evaluated, or analyzed by any third party or CPA firm. Rather, the company simply prepares the financial statements and issues them to the various third parties requesting the financial information.

In the private sector, you would be amazed (especially with smaller and medium-sized businesses) how often internally prepared financial statements are issued and accepted by external parties such as banks, investors, other lenders and creditors, and so on. There are several reasons why internally prepared financial information is the preferred route; they include cost (reviews and audits can be expensive), speed or timeliness (much quicker to produce and issue), simplicity (complex accounting issues are limited), and management credibility (third parties have a high degree of trust in the management team), to name a few. Whatever the reason, issuing internally prepared financial information to external parties is a quite common practice in the private sector, and if this is indeed the path chosen, two key disclosures should always be made:

- First, a clear reference needs to be made stating that the financial information is unaudited and has been prepared by company management.

- Second, equally important, is that the following statement should always appear on this financial information: "Confidential, Property of XYZ Corporation."

By the way, I cannot pass on the opportunity to take a shot at the IRS and comment on the fact that many small companies often rely on issuing just their income tax returns (which technically represents a type of financial report, just not a great one) to external parties for review (when requested). For many small companies, annual income tax returns often represent the only financial statements or information prepared on a periodic basis. In effect, this strategy represents the same concept as issuing internally prepared financial information to external parties but uses IRS forms and guidelines to report operating results.

There is a plethora of problems with providing income tax returns to external parties for review (to report financial information), including that the information is poorly structured, the IRS format is sorely outdated, there is no statement of cash flows presented, the method of reporting operating results may be misleading (e.g., cash basis of reporting is utilized, which is generally worthless), income tax returns may take more than six months to prepare, income tax returns may contain highly confidential information, and the list goes on and on. But above all, it should be noted that taxing authorities request financial information in a structure and format that meets their needs (for compliance and governmental use) and not yours or any of your capital partners.

Relying on annual income tax returns (to support business decisions) is not recommended and is clearly not a prudent financial reporting strategy, as all businesses need to develop and implement proper financial information and reporting strategies on which to evaluate operating results – period!

The Financial Report versus Financial Statements

To further our discussion on externally prepared financial reports and statements, I would like to clarify the difference between the purpose and function of financial statements versus a company financial report. In this context, I'm referring to a publicly traded company that is required, by regulatory bodies such as the SEC, to issue a quarterly or annual financial report.

Company financial statements (excluding footnotes, which is a topic covered in our sister book, *How to Read a Financial Report*) include the income statement (covered in Chapter 6), the balance sheet (covered in Chapter 7), and the statement of cash flows (covered in Chapter 8). Together, these financial statements are referred to as the big three financial statements throughout this book as every business should, without question, produce these financial statements on a periodic basis such as monthly, quarterly, and/or annually.

It is important to keep in mind that while a company's financial statements represent the backbone for analyzing and evaluating its financial performance, financial reports include extensive additional financial, business, legal, and regulatory material that accompany the financial statements. The actual financial statements may take up anywhere from three to six pages of an external business financial report. But the complete financial report may often exceed 100 pages (compliments of management providing their discussion/assessment of operating results, along with the required financial statements' footnotes that accompany audited financial statements).

Although the remainder of the book is focused on producing and analyzing internally generated financial information, understanding what additional content and data are presented in financial reports (and why) makes sense, with our focus being on two primary tranches of additional information, including management discretionary disclosures and financial statement footnotes.

1. **Management discussion of operating results (MDOR):** The MDOR, sometimes referred to as the MD&A (management discussion and analysis), is a section of a business's financial report that is generally reserved for management to provide an assessment or overview of key operating results, market trends, industry data, strategies, and so on that management believes would be beneficial to external parties to help them more fully understand the operating results of a business. The MDOR is usually located at the front of the periodically prepared externally distributed financial report and quite often starts with a shareholder or investor letter prepared by the company's chairman of the board or CEO, for example. There is no doubt that the MDOR can provide useful information to external parties, but it should be noted that generally speaking, the information provided in

the MDOR has not been audited by the independent CPA firm (but rather represents information being presented by a company's management team). Translation: The MDOR tends to include a broader range of business information that has been internally prepared by the company and incorporates more "opinions" and "perspectives" than audited financial statements (which tend to stay factual in nature).

2. **Financial statement footnotes:** In contrast to MDOR disclosures, financial statement footnotes are part of the audited financial statements, prepared by an independent CPA firm (with support from company financial executives and legal counsel), and are most often located toward the back of the externally prepared financial report, just after the financial statements. The goal of financial statement footnotes is to provide additional clarity, support, and detail to validate and substantiate the information provided in the financial statements. For example, if a company has established a reserve for a potential liability due to uncertain legal actions brought against the company, the footnote will help shed additional light on the nature of the legal action and potential damages. Financial statement footnotes tend to avoid presenting management opinions and rather are more focused on sticking to the facts. Yet even here I must again point out an irony in the accounting and financial reporting world; that is, while the purpose of audited financial statements and associated footnotes is to present external financial reports, prepared by independent third-party CPAs, that are factual in nature, almost all audited financial statements and associated footnotes rely heavily on the use of estimates when calculating operating results. This concept underscores the importance of remembering that accounting is often just as much an art form as a science! In short, footnotes are the fourth essential part of every CPA prepared or audited financial report. Financial statements would be naked without their footnotes. Studying a financial report should always include reading the footnotes to the financial statements.

In summary, it is important to remember that this chapter refers to information as presented in *external* financial reports – those that circulate outside the business. These financial reports and communications are designed mainly for use by outside business shareowners, analysts, company lenders, governmental agencies, and the like, with the business shareowners and lenders representing the two primary *stakeholders* in the business. Inside business executives, managers, and staff have access to significantly more information than that released in the company's external financial reports. This information is incredibly detailed in nature and is usually highly confidential, so external disclosure is tightly guarded. Diving into a more thorough discussion on internal business information will represent the balance of this book and is supported by the words of wisdom bestowed on us by Mr. Warren Buffett (when analyzing financial information) – the devil is in the detail – so it goes without saying that invaluable internal financial information is both highly sought after and closely guarded, given its importance.

3

TARGET AUDIENCE "I" – INTERNAL CONSUMERS

In Chapter 1, I focused on the importance of being able to communicate effectively, which was followed in Chapter 2 by providing an overview of external target audiences and an explanation of the importance and role of external financial reporting. With these topics out of the way and assuming you understand the importance of being able to communicate effectively and the role of external financial reporting, let us turn our attention to generating internal financial information.

Notice the broad reference to financial information, as for internal purposes it is not necessary to prepare complete financial statements for each specific management need or request. In fact, while complete financial statements should always be prepared, the distribution of these financial statements is generally reserved for the senior or executive management team (i.e., the parties who are responsible for all financial operating results of the company).

The norm for most companies is to prepare key financial information based on the needs or requirements of their internal audience. For example, a division manager may only see a sales flash report or a "short" P&L that captures the financial performance for this operating division (as opposed to the entire company's financial results). Thus, this represents the rifle approach as the goal is to deliver specifically tailored financial information to a targeted or narrow audience.

The reason for using this rifle strategy is twofold – focus and confidentiality. Businesses want to ensure that key management team members remain focused on achieving their targeted performance objectives and avoid distracting them with other business operations that they have no control or influence over. In addition, business financial information can be just as confidential inside a company or when distributed to external parties. A perfect example of this is centered in how key management team members are compensated, including any potential bonuses earned on achieving performance objectives. If bonus plans were made available to all management team members, you can imagine the potential problems that might arise within an organization from everyone wanting the best compensation plan available.

The purpose of this chapter is to pivot our discussion and focus on generating, presenting, and evaluating financial information for internal management use and analysis. I will pass along one spoiler alert, which should be both obvious and logical. The result of a financial statement, whether it be a balance sheet, income statement, or statement of cash flows, will be the exact same; that is, total assets reported in the balance sheet will be the same, the net profit or loss reported in the income statement will be the same, and the ending cash balance reported in the statement of cash flows will be the same. What will be different basically boils down to understanding five key items – format, detail, confidentiality, timeliness, and completeness.

The Basics of Generating Internal Financial Information

The best way to gain an understanding of the difference between external and internal financial reporting is to dive right in and view our example company's internally generated income statement, presented in Exhibit 3.1. When reviewing Exhibit 3.1, please compare it to Exhibit 6.1 (not presented here to avoid duplication of material) which shows our example company's income statement that would be presented to external parties.

For ease of presentation with Exhibit 3.1, I have included just the income statements for the FYE 12/31/22 and 12/31/23, but similar income statements should be available for all company operating periods. As you can see comparing Exhibit 3.1 versus Exhibit 6.1, there are significant differences in the presentation of the financial information, which, as I noted earlier, boils down to five primary areas:

1. Format: The format should be much more user- and management-friendly (to drive home key points) as dictated by the company and not driven by external guidelines such as those of the IRS or SEC. We want to strike a proper balance between providing too much information (pushing the user toward "getting lost in the forest") versus not enough, as the idea is to give the reviewing party what they ask for and need (based on their level of responsibility). Further, we do not want to divulge data that a party does not need or understand, that will confuse them, and/or is confidential (translation – above their security clearance, so to speak).

Remember that most readers are not sophisticated accounting and financial professionals but are parties that do understand basic math and business logic (i.e., yes, I understand that the company needs to make a profit), so the goal with the format is to provide financial information in the easiest-to-understand and reliable manner.

2. Detail: Obviously, the level of detail presented is far greater. In Exhibit 3.1, you can see that marketing, selling, advertising, branding, and promotional expenses have been split between direct operating expenses and corporate costs. The difference between these two expense groups is that direct operating advertising and selling expenses capture what are commonly referred to as "call to action" expenses that are designed to turn a prospect into an actual customer (by placing an order). Corporate marketing and branding expenses represent a broader range of costs designed to help build awareness of the business and enhance its brand. For most businesses, understanding the difference between these two expense groups is especially important.

3. Confidentiality: The information presented in Exhibit 3.1 is highly confidential and needs to be controlled and safeguarded from not just external parties and prying eyes (e.g., a competitor) but also from internal parties (who may not understand the financial information and accidently disclose it to an unwanted party). Companies are always

EXHIBIT 3.1—INTERNALLY PREPARED INCOME STATEMENT – COMPANY LEVEL

Unaudited – Prepared by Company Management

Income Statement for the Fiscal Years Ending	12/31/2022	% of Net Rev.	12/31/2023	% of Net Rev.
Sales Revenue:				
Software Platform & SAAS Sales	$36,400,000	67.15%	$48,533,321	81.58%
Product Sales	$19,200,000	35.42%	$13,440,000	22.59%
Other Sales, Discounts, & Allowances	$ (1,390,000)	-2.56%	$ (2,479,000)	-4.17%
Net Sales Revenue	$54,210,000	100.00%	$59,494,321	100.00%
Costs of Sales Revenue:				
Direct Product Costs	$11,040,000	20.37%	$ 7,392,000	12.42%
Wages & Burden	$12,012,000	22.16%	$13,589,000	22.84%
Direct Overhead	$ 800,000	1.48%	$ 700,000	1.18%
Other Costs of Sales Revenue	$ 70,000	0.13%	$ 85,000	0.14%
Total Costs of Sales Revenue	$23,922,000	44.13%	$21,766,000	36.59%
Gross Profit	$30,288,000	55.87%	$37,728,321	63.41%
Gross Margin	55.87%		63.41%	
Direct Operating Expenses:				
Advertising, Promotional, & Selling	$ 3,659,000	6.75%	$ 3,867,000	6.50%
Personnel Wages, Burden, & Compensation	$10,300,000	19.00%	$11,899,000	20.00%
Facility Operating Expenses	$ 1,219,725	2.25%	$ 1,264,254	2.13%
Other Operating Expenses	$ 375,000	0.69%	$ 450,000	0.76%
Total Direct Operating Expenses	$15,553,725	28.69%	$ 17,480,254	29.38%
Contribution Profit	$14,734,275	27.18%	$20,248,067	34.03%
Contribution Margin	27.18%		34.03%	
Corporate Expenses & Overhead:				
Corporate Marketing, Branding, & Promotional	$ 2,134,575	3.94%	$ 2,751,500	4.62%
Research, Development, & Design	$ 5,692,000	10.50%	$ 7,139,000	12.00%
Corporate Overhead & Support	$ 4,878,900	9.00%	$ 5,057,017	8.50%
Depreciation & Amortization Expense	$ 1,571,429	2.90%	$ 1,642,857	2.76%
Total Corporate Operating Expenses	$14,276,904	26.34%	$16,590,374	27.89%
Operating Income (EBIT)	$ 457,371	0.84%	$ 3,657,692	6.15%
Operating Margin (EBIT Margin)	0.84%		6.15%	
Other Expenses (Income):				
Other Expenses, Income, & Discontinued Ops.	$ 0	0.00%	$ 2,000,000	3.36%
Interest Expense	$ 339,000	0.63%	$ 407,000	0.68%
Total Other Expenses (Income)	$ 339,000	0.63%	$ 2,407,000	4.05%
Net Income (Loss) Before Income Taxes	$ 118,371	0.22%	$ 1,250,692	2.10%
Income Tax Expense (Benefit)	$ 41,000	0.08%	$ 438,000	0.74%
Net Income (Loss) After Income Taxes	$ 77,371	0.14%	$ 812,692	1.37%

Notice inclusion of a analytical ratio analysis.

We now have far more detail related to the primary types of sales and costs of goods sold are split between major categories.

Look at the level of detail now as we can understand exactly how much is being spent on different types of company selling & marketing expenses as well as facility versus corporate overhead.

attempting to manage the delicate balance between disclosing extremely sensitive information (that is confidential and valuable) to external parties who help them accurately assess the operating results but at the same time not provide too much detail. I might also draw your attention to the confidentiality statement provided at the bottom of Exhibit 3.1, which I generally recommend is included in financial reports and statements and acts as a "friendly reminder" as to the confidential nature of the financial information being presented.

4. Timeliness: With internal financial information, quick is not an option; it is a necessity, including for full financial statements as, for company management team members, financial statements are generally prepared, distributed, and analyzed well in advance of issuing external financial statements and reports. This is done for two reasons. First, it gives key management team members an opportunity to evaluate the results and identify any potential errors, mistakes, or omissions. Second, if either good or bad news needs to be delivered to external parties, it provides the management team an opportunity to prepare for the inevitable "grilling" that will be forthcoming. It should be noted that speed in reporting goes well beyond the financial statements as different types of flash reports (covered in Chapter 14) are produced daily, hourly, and even to the minute as heavily data-dependent businesses (e.g., retailers) can now, thanks to digital information and technology, literally monitor the effectiveness of a new advertising campaign within minutes of its being launched. Finally, I also would like to emphasize that strength in accuracy (refer to Chapter 5) is critical, as speed in reporting is dependent on highly accurate information.

5. Completeness: The concept of completeness really lies in the eye of the beholder or rather, is based on the specific needs of the target audience. For example, a general manager of a manufacturing plant will need a complete income statement for that plant, but not necessarily for the entire company. Further, the income statement should also include all relevant financial information including prior-year comparisons, a budget-to-actual-variance analysis, key performance indicators (KPIs), and so on. Another example would be a sales team manager that is focused on top-line sales for a region through the gross profit or margin generated, which may be compared against the budget or even other regions' performances. If that party does not have bottom-line responsibility, then there is no need to provide a complete income statement.

In a nutshell, internally produced financial information needs to be presented in a manner that assists your target audience with efficiently and effectively interpreting critical financial data and results. I cannot emphasize enough the importance of this function, the ability for accountants and financial types to effectively communicate complex information to other professionals and management team members, is often the Achilles heel of the so-called numbers people. Do the numbers people know debits, credits, GAAP, FASB, and how to communicate to external numbers people? Yes. But what really separates the best-in-class companies from the pack is having their numbers people be extremely strong communicators and educators as well.

A Deeper Dive and Example of Internal Financial Information

To assist readers, two additional examples of internal financial information have been provided in Exhibits 3.2 and 3.3.

Exhibit 3.2 breaks down the company's operations (through the contribution margin) between its two main operating divisions, product sales and software/SaaS sales. What is clear is that the product division is struggling and has been for years, as is shown in Exhibit 3.1, product sales have declined on a year-over-year basis whereas software and SaaS sales have rocketed higher. Further, you can see that most sales discounts and allowances are centered in the product division (because of having to use aggressive discounts to move old products) and that the product division barely breaks even at the contribution income level. With this additional level of information, we can see in more detail that the company's business strategy associated with transitioning from a product-centric business to a software/SaaS model is starting to pay dividends in 2023 as both top-line (increased from $54,210,000 for the FYE 12/31/22 to $59,494,321 for the FYE 12/31/23) and bottom-line (increased from a small profit of $77,371 for the FYE 12/31/22 to a more reasonable profit of $812,692, for the FYE 12/31/23) growth have been solid.

Another point of note with Exhibit 3.2 is that I have elected to cut off the presentation of the financial information at the contribution profit level. The reason for this is simple: This report is designed to focus management's attention on contributed earnings for each primary division (as the audience for the purposes of this report does not have control or authority over corporate overhead expenses).

Taking this analysis one step further, I would direct your attention to Exhibit 3.3, which represents a specific sales flash report for the software/SaaS operating division. For those of you wondering, SaaS is a commonly used acronym in the technology industry and stands for Software as a Service. The target audience for this report is the sales team that has management responsibility for software and SaaS sales. Exhibit 3.3 reports sales financial information for the entire year but it could just as easily report sales covering a monthly or quarterly period. As you can see in Exhibit 3.3, the total sales figure of $47,562,655 agrees with the division income statement total sales figure of $47,562,655 in Exhibit 3.2.

What you might notice in Exhibit 3.3 is that although the year-over-year sales revenue growth for the software division has been impressive, it has fallen short of the forecast. Even more interesting is that the main shortfall was centered in the SaaS Platform Expert product line whereas a positive variance was realized in the SaaS Platform Basic product line. There could be any number of reasons for these variances,

EXHIBIT 3.2—INTERNALLY PREPARED INCOME STATEMENT – BY PRIMARY OPERATING DIVISION

Unaudited – Prepared by Company Management

Income Statement - By Division for the Fiscal Year Ending	Product Div. 12/31/2023	% of Net Rev.	Software Div. 12/31/2023	% of Net Rev.	Total 12/31/2023
Sales Revenue:					
Software Platform & SAAS Sales	$ 970,666	7.81%	$47,562,655	101.05%	$48,533,321
Product Sales	$13,440,000	108.15%	$ 0	0.00%	$13,440,000
Other Sales, Discounts, & Allowances	$ (1,983,200)	-15.96%	$ (495,800)	-1.05%	$ (2,479,000)
Net Sales Revenue	$12,427,466	100.00%	$47,066,855	100.00%	$59,494,321
Costs of Sales Revenue:					
Direct Product Costs	$ 7,392,000	59.48%	$ 0	0.00%	$ 7,392,000
Wages & Burden	$ 1,358,900	10.93%	$12,230,100	25.98%	$13,589,000
Direct Overhead	$ 350,000	2.82%	$ 350,000	0.74%	$ 700,000
Other Costs of Sales Revenue	$ 42,500	0.34%	$ 42,500	0.09%	$ 85,000
Total Costs of Sales Revenue	$ 9,143,400	73.57%	$12,622,600	26.82%	$21,766,000
Gross Profit	$ 3,284,066	26.43%	$34,444,255	73.18%	$37,728,321
Gross Margin	26.43%		73.18%		
Direct Operating Expenses:					
Advertising, Promotional, & Selling	$ 580,050	4.67%	$ 3,286,950	6.98%	$ 3,867,000
Personnel Wages, Burden, & Compensation	$ 1,784,850	14.36%	$10,114,150	21.49%	$11,899,000
Facility Operating Expenses	$ 632,127	5.09%	$ 632,127	1.34%	$ 1,264,254
Other Operating Expenses	$ 225,000	1.81%	$ 225,000	0.48%	$ 450,000
Total Direct Operating Expenses	$ 3,222,027	25.93%	$14,258,227	30.29%	$17,480,254
Contribution Profit	$ 62,039	0.50%	$20,186,028	42.89%	$20,248,067
Contribution Margin	0.50%		42.89%		34.03%

Confidential - Property of QW Example Tech, Inc.

Notice large discounts in the Product division. This division is dying with large discounts needed to move old products.

Software division has much higher gross margin and contribution margin as this represents the growth segment of the business. Old product business is struggling to even breakeven.

ranging from customer preference to the company not having the right resources dedicated to the selling cycle supporting the Expert product line but whatever the cause, this result warrants a deeper management review and analysis to implement corrective action.

Countless other examples of internally generated financial information and reports could be provided but no matter what information is generated, the same concept holds. Deliver the right information to the right party in the right format at the right time to support business decisions.

EXHIBIT 3.3—SALES REVENUE BY PRODUCT TYPE FLASH REPORT – SOFTWARE/SAAS OPERATING DIVISION

Unaudited – Prepared by Company Management

Sales by Product Type for the Fiscal Year Ending	Forecast 12/31/2023	% of Net Rev.	Actual 12/31/2023	% of Net Rev.	Variance
Sales Revenue:					
Software Installation Platform	$ 7,425,000	15.00%	$ 7,212,655	15.16%	$ (212,345)
SaaS Platform Basic	$ 9,900,000	20.00%	$10,850,000	22.81%	$ 950,000
SaaS Platform Advanced	$ 17,325,000	35.00%	$16,850,000	35.43%	$ (475,000)
SaaS Platform Expert	$13,365,000	27.00%	$11,500,000	24.18%	$(1,865,000)
Other Software Sales	$ 1,485,000	3.00%	$ 1,150,000	2.42%	$ (335,000)
Total Sales Revenue	$49,500,000	100.00%	$47,562,655	100.00%	$(1,937,345)

Notice the negative variances with installation and expert and positive variance with basic.

Confidential - Property of QW Example Tech, Inc.

In Summary – Don't Make These Rookie Mistakes!

First, do not ever confuse internal financial information with external financial reporting. If it is not clear by now, these two have vastly different uses, purposes, and audiences.

Second, never just hit the send bottom. Although tempting, any financial information distributed to external parties should always be reviewed and approved by all appropriate personnel and management.

Third, a word of caution to aspiring entrepreneurs: Assumption is the mother of all you-know-whats; that is, if financial statements are requested, by internal or external parties (especially external), your policy should be loud and clear. The financial information is always reviewed, scrubbed, approved, and authorized by the appropriate company personnel before it is distributed. Do not assume that you can push a couple of buttons and print a report from accounting systems such as QuickBooks, Sage 50, or NetSuite and then distribute this information. This can be a fatal mistake and almost always leads to far more questions and problems than it solves.

Fourth, all financial information distributed, whether to external parties or for internal use, should clearly note two key items. First is that the financial information is either audited or unaudited and second is that the financial information is confidential and the property of the company. Even for companies that have the best safeguards installed to protect their internal financial information, at some point this information is going to end up outside the organization, so it is always helpful (from a legal perspective) to have clear disclosures as to the confidential nature of the information.

4

INTRODUCING CART – TO START, THE BIG "C," COMPLETENESS

As the old saying goes, you should never put the cart before the horse. This represents a wise statement as basically it means doing things in the wrong order. However, in the case of preparing financial reports and statements, the CART (in this case) should always be put before the horse. What CART stands for is preparing complete, accurate, reliable, and timely financial reports before the financial reports are distributed to external or internal parties. You always want to make sure that the financial reports prepared are as complete, accurate, reliable, and timely as possible.

This chapter will introduce you to the concept of CART with a specific focus on the C portion of CART, completeness. Then in Chapter 5, we will turn our attention to the ART portion of the acronym as we explore the importance of accuracy, reliability, and timeliness.

Essential to Understanding the Big Picture

Let me start with a simple analogy. If a doctor completed an annual physical medical examination and only administered a limited number of tests and provided even fewer results, most people would find this unacceptable. What is needed (and expected) is a full examination with all results made available and, ideally, comparisons against key benchmarks for similar demographics (e.g., what should the cholesterol level be for a man my age?). The concept of completeness is no different for a business than a person, as to gain a full understanding of a company's operating results, potential risks, and opportunities, complete financial reporting is essential.

To better understand the concept of completeness, I provide examples of internal and external financial information reporting, starting with relatively weak or poor information through what at a minimum would be considered essential to successfully operate a business in today's challenging and fiercely competitive economic environment. For ease of presentation, our examples are focused on the big three financial statements (which we learned in previous chapters have a limited internal audience), but the concept holds for any internal financial information distributed. Also, the concept of completeness should always include presenting financial information against some type of benchmark or target, such as internally prepared forecasts, prior-year results, industry averages or standards, and so on. It should go without saying that it is one thing to present the financial results of a company, but without having something to measure these financial results against, gaining a complete understanding of the company's operating results would be next to impossible.

Barely Acceptable (the World of Small Businesses)

I start our discussion with what would be considered the bare minimum in terms of providing financial information to either internal or external parties; that is, single-year financial statements that really boil down to providing just the current-year income statement and balance sheet (as the cash flow statement is not provided). For any serious business owner, investor, or manager, this bare minimum approach is not acceptable, but you would be absolutely amazed at how often companies can get by with providing such limited financial information. Even more amazing is how often external parties such as banks, investors, government agencies, and the like are willing to accept this limited level of information for analysis purposes and then to base a decision upon it.

Whatever the reason or logic, Exhibit 4.1 presents what would be considered the bare minimum when providing a balance sheet and Exhibit 4.2 shows an income statement. In these exhibits, I do not present our example company but rather offer the basic financial statements of a small professional service company operating in a local market.

Taking a closer look at the financial statements presented in Exhibits 4.1 and 4.2, the following should jump out at you:

- Our sample company is a small professional service business operating out of a single office in a large city. Like most smaller companies, audited or reviewed financial statements are not available, as these types of businesses generally rely heavily on internally prepared financial information. Further, you will almost never see footnotes attached to internally generated financial statements.

- Notice the different reporting format used for the income statement compared to Exhibit 3.1. It not only provides too much detail (as some of the expenses should probably be grouped together when reported) but, in addition, it uses a standard reporting technique that lists all expenses in alpha order (that is common when preparing income tax returns). Note: I presented this reporting format to not only highlight the fact that small businesses often utilize this type of reporting but, in addition, to emphasize that while this reporting format may be accurate, it doesn't present information in a reliable manner (refer to Chapter 5).

- The lack of information, including not providing comparable prior-year results, not including a statement of cash flows, and offering no ratio analysis, indicates that the company's internal accounting and financial management resources may be limited. This format does not help the reader understand much other than the basics.

- You may also note that this company has only $800 of income tax expense compared to taxable income of more than $300,000. How is this possible? The answer lies in the fact that

EXHIBIT 4.1 – LOCAL SAMPLE SERVICE COMPANY – SIMPLE INTERNALLY PREPARED BALANCE SHEET

Unaudited – Prepared by Company Management

Balance Sheet
as of the Fiscal Year Ending — **12/31/2023**

Current Assets:	
Cash Accounts, Operating, Payroll & MM	$ 284,521
Accounts Receivable, Net	$ 531,453
Prepaid Expenses	$ 42,100
Total Current Assets	$ 858,074
Long-Term Operating & Other Assets:	
Office Equipment, Furniture, & Computers	$ 178,250
Company Vehicles	$ 135,000
Accumulated Depreciation	$ (147,500)
Net Fixed Assets	$ 165,750
Other Assets:	
Other Assets & Deposits	$ 15,000
Total Long-Term Operating & Other Assets	$ 180,750
Total Assets	**$1,038,824**

(Callout: No prior year information is provided. Also, note the added descriptions offered with the cash accounts, a common presentation format with smaller companies.)

(Callout: Added information provided related to company assets including reference to vehicles.)

Balance Sheet
as of the Fiscal Year Ending — **12/31/2023**
Liabilities

Current Liabilities:	
Accounts & Professional Fees Payable	$ 42,200
Accrued Payroll & Compensation	$ 68,412
Line of Credit, Outstanding Balance	$ 106,291
Other Current Liabilities & Customer Deposits	$ 18,875
Total Current Liabilities	$ 235,778
Long-Term Liabilities:	
Note Payable Bank, Vehicles	$ 75,000
Total Liabilities	**$ 310,778**
Owners' Equity	
Common Stock	$ 150,000
Distributions of Earnings	$ (777,089)
Retained Earnings	$1,055,105
Current Year Net Income (Loss)	$ 300,030
Total Stockholder's Equity	**$ 728,047**
Total Liabilities & Stockholders Equity	**$1,038,824**

(Callout: Again, added detail provided with account descriptions as small companies generally lack sophistication when presenting financial information.)

(Callout: Usually a much more simplistic capital table with only common equity, distributions of earnings, retained earnings, and current year income (loss).)

Confidential – Property of Local Sample Service Co, Inc.

Unaudited – Prepared by Company Management

Income Statement For the Fiscal Year Ending	12/31/2023
Sales Revenue:	
Professional Fees Billed	$3,955,000
Direct Expense Reimbursement	$ 296,625
Total Sales Revenue	$4,251,625
Costs of Sales:	
Personnel Wages & Burden	$1,381,778
Subcontractors & Consultants	$ 850,325
Third Party Fees Incurred	$ 393,275
Total Costs of Sales	$2,625,378
Gross Profit	$1,626,247
Selling, Operating, & Administrative Expenses:	
Advertising	$ 78,450
Dues & Subscriptions	$ 25,680
Insurance, General	$ 42,500
Insurance, Health, Life, & Disability	$ 42,000
Marketing & Promotional	$ 30,000
Office Expenses & Supplies	$ 20,525
Payroll	$ 497,500
Payroll Taxes	$ 47,263
Professional Fees, Legal & Acctg.	$ 27,500
Rent	$ 260,013
Telecommunications	$ 18,750
Travel, Lodging, Meals, & Entertainment	$ 124,500
Utilities	$ 37,702
Website Maintenance	$ 18,000
Total Selling, Operating, & Admin. Expenses	$1,270,382
Operating Profit	$ 355,864
Other Expenses:	
Charitable Contributions	$ 5,000
Depreciation Expense	$ 39,156
Interest Expense	$ 10,877
Income Tax Expense	$ 800
Total Other Expenses	$ 55,834
Net Income (Loss)	$ 300,030

This company has elected to provide additional levels of detail in the income statement as they are using the financial statement for both internal and external presentation purposes.

Notice a number of items including the level of detail (indicates inexperienced team releasing the income statement), all expenses listed in alpha order (simple order used for tax reporting), and some rather large expenses (travel fairly high, most likely owners running through auto expenses).

Income tax expense lumped in with other as this entity uses a tax passthrough structure as is formed as a Sub Chapter S corporation.

Confidential - Property of Local Sample Service Co, Inc.

this entity is structured as a Subchapter S corporation, which means that all taxable profits and losses are passed through to the individual owners of the company (who are then responsible for remitting income taxes on the profits passed through at the personal level). Also, you will note the reference to distributions of earnings in the owners' equity section of the balance sheet as opposed to the company issuing dividends. In tax pass-through entities, distributions of earnings are made (and not dividends) to return excess profits to the owners that are commonly used to cover personal income tax obligations (from the pass-through of profits).

Needless to say, the financial statements presented in Exhibits 4.1 and 4.2 are nowhere near being best in class so you may ask why I went to the trouble. Well, the answer is simple. Based on the data available for October 2020, there are approximately 17.6 million businesses operating in the United States, of which almost 90% generate less than $10 million a year in sales revenue and have less than 100 employees. And the financial reporting norm for much of the 90% business group will most likely be something akin to Exhibits 4.1 and 4.2 so for any party that spends a fair amount of time dealing with small businesses, this reporting format will most likely be the par for the course.

Better and Appropriate for the External Audience

Progressing up the food chain to the next tranche of businesses, that is, the 10% that are much larger and more sophisticated, I would direct your attention to Chapters 6, 7, and 8 and refer you to Exhibits 6.1, 7.1, and 8.1. I'm not going to re-present these exhibits but will emphasize that the next leg up when presenting complete financial statements includes the following:

- The financial statements will have a much higher likelihood of being audited or, at a minimum, reviewed (by external CPA firms) and should include financial statement footnotes; translation, the financial information is more reliable.

- The financial statements will be presented in a more technical accounting structure in a format adhering to GAAP. This compares to financial information prepared for internal evaluation and use that may not always be in accordance with GAAP.

- For public companies and extremely large private companies, full financial reports should also be available. The additional financial reports will most likely include an overview of the company's financial performance, key milestones met, benchmark comparisons, and other selected results (to help educate or, should I say, sway the external audience).

- Comparable and complete financial information is provided, as multiple years of data should be presented along with ensuring that the statement of cash flows is included.

This middle-of-the-road level of completeness is the minimum or standard level expected for distribution to external parties by both public companies and larger, private businesses – that is, full disclosure as required by GAAP with select additional information provided but always, and I mean always, with the understanding that this financial information is targeted for use by external parties (and available publicly). You will note that I make the reference to larger, private businesses using this standard external reporting structure in a similar fashion to publicly traded companies. While there is no legal requirement that larger, private companies use this reporting structure, most do, as external parties including investors, lenders, banks, and so on will demand the same information. Their logic is simple: When the stakes are raised (i.e., significantly higher loans and investments being made), the level and quality of financial information distributed is also raised.

Let's Take It Up a Notch to Best in Class

Finally, our discussion on completeness will evolve to a level designed for use primarily by internal company management team members. Here, I will refer back to our example company as I'm going to present just the top half of the income statement through the calculation of gross profit (in Exhibit 4.3). To avoid overkill, it should be noted that the type of completeness disclosed in Exhibit 4.3 can similarly be applied to the entire income statement, balance sheet, and statement of cash flows, as well as countless other internal financial reports and information prepared for a company's management team. For anyone interested, a complete Exhibit 4.3 and Exhibits 4.4 and 4.5 (which cover the balance sheet and statement of cash flows) are available in the Excel workbook file, which you can request and will be sent to you free of charge.

Okay, there is a hell of a lot more financial and even operational information presented that is significantly more robust than what was provided to the external users. As we dig in deeper to the financial information presented in Exhibit 4.3, I call your attention to the following items:

♦ The financial statement variance analysis presented in Exhibit 4.3 is designed for internal use only and for select executive management. The financial information, while consistent with the externally audited financial statements (as the net sales revenue for the FYE 12/31/23 is the exact same at $59,494,321), is confidential and has not been audited (but rather prepared internally).

♦ Prior-year operating comparisons are helpful (which I have done with 2022 and 2023) but comparing actual results to forecast results is usually much better. The goal with most companies is to reach or exceed the financial performance targets established in the business plan and forecasts, so this is where management tends to focus their attention (i.e., what went right and what went wrong).

♦ I have included a select few key performance indicators (KPIs) in the financial analysis as, for the target internal audience, the KPIs selected are critical to understanding the business performance. There are countless KPIs that could be incorporated into the financial analysis but those included should be critical to quickly and efficiently understanding the company's performance.

♦ Far more information and detail has been provided, which generally requires additional management attention, analysis, and support to verify. Although it was not provided in Exhibit 4.3 (because of space limitations), a management overview and explanation of the positive and negative variances should be attached. For example, a negative sales variance of roughly $3,685,679 was realized between actual FYE 12/31/23 results

EXHIBIT 4.3—TOP HALF OF INCOME STATEMENT – PRESENTED IN COMPLETE FORMAT

Unaudited - Prepared by Company Management

Income Statement for the Fiscal Years Ending	Actual 12/31/2022	% of Net Rev.	Actual 12/31/2023	% of Net Rev.	Forecast 12/31/2023	% of Net Rev.	Variance FYE 12/31/2023
Key Performance Indicators:							
Net Sales Revenue Per Full Time Employee	$ 542,100		$ 487,658		$ 505,440		$ (17,782)
Product Sales, Avg. Order Value (net)	$ 23,747		$ 15,659		$ 18,240		$ (2,581)
Software Platform & SAAS Sales:							
SAAS Sales, Total Customer Accounts	400		525		500		25
SAAS Sales, Total Earned Avg. Per Account	$ 81,900		$ 74,667		$ 81,180		$ (6,513)
Sales Revenue:							
Software Platform & SAAS Sales	$36,400,000	67.15%	$48,533,321	81.58%	$49,500,000	78.35%	$ (966,679)
Product Sales	$19,200,000	35.42%	$13,440,000	22.59%	$15,200,000	24.06%	$(1,760,000)
Other Sales, Discounts, & Allowances	$ (1,390,000)	-2.56%	$ (2,479,000)	-4.17%	$ (1,520,000)	-2.41%	$ (959,000)
Net Sales Revenue	$54,210,000	100.00%	$59,494,321	100.00%	$63,180,000	100.00%	$(3,685,679)
Costs of Sales Revenue:							
Direct Product Costs	$11,040,000	20.37%	$ 7,392,000	12.42%	$ 7,600,000	12.03%	$ 208,000
Wages & Burden	$12,012,000	22.16%	$13,589,000	22.84%	$15,575,000	24.65%	$ 1,986,000
Direct Overhead	$ 800,000	1.48%	$ 700,000	1.18%	$ 750,000	1.19%	$ 50,000
Other Costs of Sales Revenue	$ 70,000	0.13%	$ 85,000	0.14%	$ 100,000	0.16%	$ 15,000
Total Costs of Sales Revenue	$23,922,000	44.13%	$21,766,000	36.59%	$24,025,000	38.03%	$ 2,259,000
Gross Profit	$30,288,000	55.87%	$37,728,321	63.41%	$39,155,000	61.97%	$(1,426,679)
Gross Margin	55.87%		63.41%		61.97%		n/a

Confidential - Property of QW Example Tech, Inc.

and forecast FYE 12/31/23 results. As shown in the exhibit, the company exceeded its target number of SaaS customers by 25 (forecast of 500 compared to actual of 525). So, what's the problem? Well, customers ended up purchasing a higher number of Basic SaaS software products compared to the Expert SaaS software platform (at a lower price point). Management will certainly want to understand this customer preference and how to better prepare in the coming years.

- You will notice the highlighted areas, which at a macro level are the root cause of why the company "missed" its forecasted gross profit operating results. Sales revenue across all primary product and service segments came in below forecasts by roughly 5.8% or $3,685,679. As previously discussed in this chapter, the under performance with sales revenue is based in the type of software products the customers are purchasing, which is a key issue the company's management will want to further understand and address to ensure corrective action is taken in future years.

I do want to pass along one additional key concept, as it relates to the distribution of this level of financial information. In certain cases, critical external parties such as strategic partners or large capital sources may be provided access to this financial information as it can help build credibility and confidence with these partners, knowing that management is on top of their financial and accounting game.

Completeness Revisited

Preparing complete financial information represents an integral part of developing and maintaining best-in-class financial reporting systems, for both internal management review and business decision-making and external analysis. Completeness is a broad subject that is heavily influenced by the financial information reporting needs of the target audience. But remember that completeness represents just the first letter in CART, as without accurate, reliable, and timely financial information, the effectiveness of providing complete financial information is often muted.

Also note that providing complete financial information does not magically originate from business "day one" as companies will need to develop, over time, their financial information reporting systems to find that ideal and reliable format, with just the proper balance of detail versus summary information, all packaged and delivered in a timely manner. Operating a business in today's economic environment requires a keen focus on ensuring that complete financial information is available to adjust business plans on the turn of a dime.

5

EMBRACING CART – ACCURACY, RELIABILITY, AND TIMELINESS, THE BEST OF FRIENDS

In Chapter 4, I covered the importance of producing complete financial information as a critical component to the business evaluation and decision-making process. What is important to remember about producing complete financial information is that it is 100% dependent on a properly functioning accounting information system that produces both accurate and reliable financial information. Or, stated differently, you cannot prepare complete financial information without having the assurance that your accounting system generates both accurate and reliable information. Although the concepts of accuracy and reliability are closely connected, it is important to remember to not confuse the two as being one and the same (as they each serve different and very important roles).

As I dive further into our discussion on this topic, let's first provide definitions for both accuracy and reliability, starting with Webster's Dictionary and then expanding on the definitions within the context of an accounting environment.

♦ Accuracy: Webster's Dictionary defines accuracy as "freedom from mistake or error" and further "conformity to a truth or to a standard or model." This is an excellent starting point but to expand on this from an accounting perspective, the reference to "freedom from mistake or error" needs to be understood, keeping in mind the all-important concept of materiality (discussed later in this chapter). In my travels of 35+ years, I have never seen an accounting and financial reporting system produce 100% accurate information, as there is always some number of small differences, mistakes, rounding errors, and so on. The key with an accounting system producing accurate information is that "material" errors, mistakes, omissions, and so on are avoided or eliminated with a tolerance level established for minor mistakes or errors (that do not distort the financial information produced by a business).

♦ Reliability (i.e., reliable): Again, I turn to Webster's Dictionary, which defines being reliable as "suitable or fit to be relied upon" and further, "giving the same result on successive trials." This makes perfect sense as the goal with producing reliable financial information is to enable a company's management team to rely on this information to make sound economic and business decisions (in a consistent manner, regardless of number of analyses completed). Further, what will become clear in our discussion on producing reliable financial information is how critically important it is to properly format, structure, and present this information so that a company's management team can efficiently understand the information, draw effective conclusions, and make important business decisions (in a timely and assured manner).

I provide examples in this chapter of just how important preparing reliable financial reports and information is. As for accuracy, I've reserved Chapter 11 for discussing the role of accounting in generating accurate financial data.

Producing Reliable Financial Information

To close out our discussion on the "what" and "when" of producing CART financial information, I will turn our discussion to the final two components – reliability and timeliness. What should be remembered with these two concepts is that for financial information to be reliable, it must be presented in not only the proper format and structure but, in addition, needs to be provided the ideal time frame with the assurance of accuracy. Managing businesses in today's hyper-data-driven economy no longer affords companies the opportunity to delay producing and distributing financial information, as management cannot wait on critical data. Rather, management must be provided certain financial information in real time to assess operating results and, if needed, implement corrective business actions.

The second section of this chapter focuses on the timeliness of financial information reporting, both as dictated by external parties and required by internal management, but I start by diving into the topic of financial information reliability and direct you to Exhibit 4.2 presented in Chapter 4. This exhibit provides a crash course in understanding the importance and difference between accuracy and reliability.

Exhibit 4.2 presents the income statement of a small local professional service company that realized $4,251,625 in sales revenue for the FYE 12/31/23, resulting in a net profit of $300,030. Okay, this seems reasonable as generating a profit of roughly 7% on sales revenue is probably not out of the ordinary and it is assumed that the accuracy of the information is sound. As previously discussed,

Exhibit 4.2 offers a look at a standard reporting format used by small businesses for income statements that displays sales revenue first, costs of sales second, and then provides a detailed listing of operating expenses followed by disclosing other expenses. While this format of an income statement is widely used (by small businesses), it will drive home the key concept of accuracy versus reliability.

Exhibit 5.1 takes the income statement presented in Exhibit 4.2 and reformats the information into a more useful and easier-to-understand layout. As you can see, 2023 was not kind to this company when compared to 2022, but as you work through financial information presented, it will become evident as to why the year-over-year performance was so poor. Items of interest and focus are the following:

- The income statement presented in Exhibit 4.2 was structured using a descriptive format with expense accounts listed in alphabetical order (and providing too much detail). Exhibit 5.1 presents the income statement using a functional format that groups or combines like expenses to help third parties understand relationships and ratios more efficiently (removing excess detail and confidential information).

- Completeness is on full display with the income statement presented in Exhibit 5.1 as not only is the prior-year information presented, but analytical analyses have been included, such as

EXHIBIT 5.1—LOCAL SAMPLE SERVICE COMPANY – INCOME STATEMENT, ACCURACY VERSUS RELIABILITY

Unaudited - Prepared by Company Management

Income Statement For the Fiscal Years Ending	12/31/2022	% of Sales	12/31/2023	% of Sales	Notes/Comments ->
Sales Revenue:					
Professional Fees Billed	$7,750,000	88.89%	$3,955,000	93.02%	Large project did not recur in 2023.
Direct Expense Reimbursement	$ 968,750	11.11%	$ 296,625	6.98%	
Total Sales Revenue	$8,718,750	100.00%	$4,251,625	100.00%	
Costs of Sales:					
Personnel Wages & Burden	$2,615,625	30.00%	$1,381,778	32.50%	Sacrificed margin to maintain staff.
Subcontractors & Consultants	$1,612,969	18.50%	$ 850,325	20.00%	
Third Party Fees Incurred	$ 632,109	7.25%	$ 393,275	9.25%	
Total Costs of Sales	$4,860,703	55.75%	$2,625,378	61.75%	
Gross Profit & Gross Margin	$3,858,047	44.25%	$1,626,247	38.25%	Decrease anticipated.
Selling, Operating, & Administrative Expenses:					
Payroll, Wages, & Burden	$1,040,400	11.93%	$ 586,763	13.80%	Owners took 50% reduction in comp.
Advertising, Marketing, & Promotional	$ 395,400	4.54%	$ 126,450	2.97%	Low hanging fruit to cut/but need to increase.
Corporate Overhead & Professional Fees	$ 647,722	7.43%	$ 432,670	10.18%	Successfully subleased 30% of space.
Other Company Operating Expenses	$ 170,600	1.96%	$ 129,500	3.05%	Owners "travel" bucket reduced.
Total Selling, Operating, & Admin. Expenses	$2,254,122	25.85%	$1,275,382	30.00%	
Operating Profit	$1,603,925	18.40%	$ 350,864	8.25%	
Other Expenses:					
Depreciation Expense	$ 39,156	0.45%	$ 39,156	0.92%	
Interest Expense	$ 9,790	0.11%	$ 10,877	0.26%	
Income Tax Expense	$ 800	0.01%	$ 800	0.02%	
Total Other Expenses	$ 49,746	0.57%	$ 50,834	1.20%	
Net Income (Loss)	$1,554,179	17.83%	$ 300,030	7.06%	
Additional Analysis & KPIs:					
Current Ratio	4.15		3.64		Well above minimum level of 2.5x.
Owners Distributions (exhibit 4.1 balance sheet)	$ 777,089		$ 777,089		Large distributions related to prior year profits.
Current Year Distributions % of Net Income	50.00%		259.00%		
Number of Professional Associates	16		10		Cut excess/inefficient staff. Maintained core.
Average Revenue Earned Per Prof. Associate	$ 544,922		$ 425,163		Need minimum prod of $500k per. Should return.
Average Wages & Bonus Per Prof. Associate	$ 125,751		$ 106,291		

Confidential - Property of Local Sample Service Co, Inc.

calling out employee KPIs and even capturing balance sheet data. One item I would draw your attention to is the distribution of earnings analysis. As can be seen from Exhibit 5.1, the $777,089 of earnings distributions is reasonable (at 50%) compared to the prior-year net profit of $1,554,179. Distribution of earnings on a delayed or lagged basis is common with smaller companies, as they often defer distributions for three to six months after the previous fiscal year-end (to finalize the financial results and individual income tax obligations). If you were to simply evaluate the distributions of earnings against the current-year net profit of $300,030, you might think the company was crazy to distribute so much cash in excess of profitability.

- I opted not to include the actual variance analysis as presented in Exhibit 4.3 but rather elected to include a notes or comments section as an example (which I previously alluded to in Chapter 4) to assist with understanding the financial results. The simple notes and comments now offer better insight into the company's financial performance; even though 2023 was a difficult operating year, the company was able to pivot and implement business decisions to proactively adjust and still generate a small profit (with management being fully aware of the new economic reality).

I cannot emphasize enough that preparing and distributing reliable financial information is highly dependent on the target audience. In our example, the target audience is the ownership group of the company along with senior management. The ownership group needs to understand the company's financial results in an efficient and effective manner, without providing excessive amounts of detail or "noise." In one page or a simple snapshot, the owners need to clearly understand the company's financial performance or "story" with confidence so that executive-level business decisions can be made. In our example, the owners may implement a financial performance objective that average earned revenue per professional associate must reach $500,000 in 2024, or further headcount reductions will be made (as this represents one of the company's critical KPIs).

For all businesses, it is imperative to remember who your audience is or will be when preparing financial information. Clearly understanding the business management chain of command is essential as senior- or executive-level parties will demand one type of financial information (i.e., macro-level and critical KPIs that really drive the financial results) versus mid-level or even lower managers who require more granular financial information to assess and manage a specific function.

Better Late Than Never, Okay for External Parties

Timely financial information reporting has an entirely new meaning and value in today's rapid-fire economic environment. The ability to accumulate and analyze data, prepare financial information reports, and implement business decisions is more important today than ever before. Honestly, the topic of timely financial information reporting should not even be a discussion – if there was ever a no-brainer, this is it – but I would be remiss if I did not provide a bit more depth on the subject of timely financial information reporting as it relates to our two main audiences – external and internal parties.

Externally, reporting timelines are governed by regulatory or compliance requirements or by specific demands placed on a company by capital sources, investors, strategic partners, and similar parties. At a macro level, here are some of the more significant financial reporting timelines:

- *Taxation:* Filing dates for federal income tax returns are set by the IRS and vary by type of legal entity. For example, Subchapter S corporation returns are due on the 15th day of the third month following the fiscal year reporting period (e.g., March 15th, 2024), whereas regular C corporation income tax returns are due 30 days later. However, companies may request an extension, which may provide as much as six more months of added time to file the income tax returns. Further, states generally adhere to the federal guidelines for filing business income tax returns but may implement their own policies. Confused yet? Well to be quite honest, income tax returns are just the tip of the iceberg as, between other federal, state, city, county, and local tax reporting (think payroll taxes, sales and use, property, excise, etc.), trying to keep track of all the reporting deadlines requirements can quickly become overwhelming. So, keep in mind the following three tips in understanding and managing tax reporting requirements.

- First, retain the services of a quality CPA firm or third-party tax specialty management company to assist with and administer tax reporting requirements. These groups have significant resources and experience to ensure that tax reporting requirements are responsibly managed.

- Second, the simpler or more specifically focused the tax, the quicker the filing requirement generally is. For example, sales taxes are generated on the sale of tangible goods, which are easy to calculate (what was the sales price and what is the tax rate?). Therefore, sales tax returns are often required to be filed every month, within 30 days of the previous month close of business.

- Third, and hugely important, understand the difference between a tax that is an expense of a business (e.g., property tax or income taxes) and taxes that are held in trust by the business and must be remitted to the taxing authority (e.g., sales tax and payroll tax withholdings). For taxes that are held in trust, the taxing authorities can get very nasty and aggressive when collecting and may pursue the officers, board members, and/or executives of a company at a personal level, if these taxes are not paid. This is known as "piercing the corporate veil," as not remitting taxes you have collected on behalf of a third party is an extremely sensitive issue.

- *Public Companies:* Financial information reporting timelines have been established by the SEC. A company's annual report (the 10-K), including audited financial statements, is due within 60 or 90 days of the end of its fiscal year (depending on the size of the company). Similarly, a company's quarterly report (the 10-Q), including unaudited financial statements, is due within 35 to 45 days of the previous quarter end (depending on size). The SEC has established other reporting timelines as well for miscellaneous business activity that must be communicated to the public in a timely fashion. Basically, all public companies secure the best CPA firms and legal counsel to support this effort.

- *Private Companies:* The banks, lenders, and investors of private companies will almost always demand that financial information be reported within set time frames. Unlike public companies (that have specific rules established by the SEC), the financial information reporting time frames for private companies are established in specific agreements executed between two parties. For example, a bank may require that a company provide internal financial statements or covenant compliance calculations within 120 days of the fiscal year-end, a borrowing base certificate within 30 days of the month end, or a business valuation within 180 days of a specific date (e.g., the original loan date). The list of potential financial information reporting and associated timelines is endless, but the general rule of thumb is that the higher the perceived risk of investment loss from a third party, the quicker and more complete the financial reporting.

You may ask why I went to this effort to overview various external reporting requirements, as it should be evident that timeliness for external reporting requirements is really not all that timely. And that is the point, as external reporting timelines are based more on compliance than business management and planning needs. External parties seem to be forever behind the curve, as by the time these groups receive the financial information, 30 to 180 days after the fact, the industries in which they operate or even the world (e.g., the COVID-19 outbreak in 2020) may have changed with all eyes now focused on the future rather than the past.

Better Late Than Never Does Not Fly Internally!

Speed is everything in today's fast-paced business world, but let us take a moment to remember the all-important acronym DIGO (which, if you have forgotten, stands for data in – garbage out). Simply put, if your accounting system has failed and cannot be relied on to produce accurate information, then the timeliness of your financial information reporting will be all for naught. I wanted to emphasize this point as while timely financial information reporting is critical, it should not be undertaken at the expense of producing accurate, reliable, and complete financial information. All businesses must find that right balance between speed, accuracy, and reliability when producing internal financial information and reports.

With this said, let us turn our attention to better understanding how companies produce timely financial information in somewhat of a chronological order (fastest to slowest).

- Hourly (or even more frequent): You would be amazed at how many companies now produce internal financial information and reports on an hourly or even more frequent basis. For example, during the critical holiday selling season for retailers, sales data can be accumulated on demand, thanks to advancements in technology. The effectiveness of an advertising campaign can almost immediately be evaluated by companies selling products direct to consumers (DTC) as they can literally monitor, in real time, consumer reactions to different promotions (and make changes as needed). This type of financial information is generally reported via "flash reports" (refer to Chapter 14) and is centered on accumulating data that is more efficiently obtained and deciphered (e.g., total sales, total units sold, and average unit selling price). The idea is to not overwhelm the user with excessive amounts of data, calculations, and so on, but rather "flash" three to five pieces of key financial information that relays the message (loud and clear).

- Daily: Daily reporting is now the norm in several industries and once again, you can thank technology for making this happen. Here, certain data points or key operating metrics are accumulated for a day or similar period to take a snapshot of the operating performance. A perfect example of daily reporting resides in the restaurant industry, as companies can evaluate total sales by type, costs of sales, personnel expenses, and key efficiency ratios to monitor like-period performances or determine whether staffing levels are too high or too low. Unlike the flash reports noted above, daily reporting requires more data or source inputs to support a management evaluation of operating results so the reporting timelines, instead of an hour, are often reviewed one day in arrears (to provide a small window for a scrubbing by the accounting team).

- Weekly: Moving down the reporting timeline food chain I arrive at weekly financial reporting. Similar to daily reporting requiring more data inputs than hourly, weekly follows the same logic. A couple of prime examples of weekly reporting are centered in a production manager analyzing the prior week's manufacturing targets or quotas (based on volume, product type, and quality assurance) or a weekly cash flow analysis that reports beginning cash, total inflows, total outflows, and ending cash. Data or source inputs are more voluminous, volatile, and tend to be somewhat more complex, so a company may elect for weekly reporting to smooth out certain variances or ensure that a set of transactions scheduled for once a week are captured (e.g., a company may only pay its vendors once a week, on each Friday). By the way, the reason I referenced weekly cash flow reporting is that for companies that may be operating under elevated business stress levels, with limited financial capital and tight cash balances, weekly monitoring of available cash is essential. Companies often utilize a 13- or 26-week rolling cash flow report to monitor cash inflows, outflows, and to determine exactly when cash stress will be at its peak. This helps the company's management team look forward and plan accordingly including tapping vendors that can be "leaned on" to defer payments (helping free up cash for a short window) or identify customers who might be able to accelerate payments.

- Monthly: The big three financial statements offer a perfect example of monthly financial information reporting. When I discuss financial statement reporting throughout this book, annual or quarterly financial statement reporting is generally being referenced, but it should be noted that almost all companies produce financial statements monthly (given the importance of the financial results to the owners, management team,

capital sources, etc.). Given the added complexity of the financial statements along with the large number of data or source inputs, monthly financial statements are the norm (as producing more frequently is difficult). Also, internally prepared financial statements are usually produced in a much quicker time frame than financial statements prepared for external distribution. This provides management with plenty of time to review, analyze, scrub, adjust (if needed), prepare, and present to external parties.

- Quarterly and Annual: Financial statements represent an example of quarterly and annual financial information reporting in addition to a wide range of other requirements, including preparing quarterly or annual operating budgets and financial forecasts (refer to Chapter 10) or specialized financial analyses that require large amounts of data accumulated over a long time period (such as auto companies evaluating the amount of a warranty reserve for a new product line or a distribution company analyzing slow-moving inventory). If you had not noticed moving down our financial reporting timeline, the less frequent the reporting requirement usually is associated with a higher likelihood that the financial information will be distributed to external parties. It is both pointless and foolish to distribute frequently prepared financial information and reports (i.e., hourly, daily, and weekly) to external parties that may confuse the external party, are confidential in nature, and that have not been properly vetted by management.

Additional examples of the types of business financial information reporting could be provided, as the potential list of reports is endless. The primary concept to remember is that it is up to the company's management team to determine what financial information is needed, for whom, and when it is needed to ensure that critical information is provided to executives and managers on which to base sound business decisions.

I should also note that effective business reporting is just as important in evaluating operational or qualitative matters as with financial results. Employee turnover (critical to the hospitality industry), customer service requests and complaints, and average customer response times offer just a few examples. It is beyond the scope of this book to dig deeper into these types of business reporting requirements, but I did want to mention them as, in some capacity, they all will have an impact on a company's financial results.

Reliability, Timeliness, and the Financial Story

A subject matter that is near and dear to our hearts warrants a brief discussion as I close out this chapter; that is, how does reliability and timeliness translate into assisting the executive management team with properly relaying and communicating the business and economic financial story and opportunity to a target audience?

As an example, a company that is growing rapidly and wants to specifically call attention to a segment of the business that has perceived high value by external parties will want to structure or format its external financial reports and statements to help "tell (or sell) the story." Management may specifically tailor or structure the financial information to support the business story in the most attractive manner possible and then deliver the information at the opportune time. For the ideal external audience, the reliability and timeliness of the financial information is strategically prepared and distributed to achieve an optimum outcome. If you need further insight on this concept just think about the large number of IPOs that took place in late 2020, riding on the tailwinds of very robust public markets and the impact on business models resulting from COVID-19. The story fit perfectly as did the timing of the IPO.

Internally, the company should be just as motivated to ensure that reliable and timely financial information is prepared for management review and analysis. But here, the audience is different so the financial story (at a micro level) will need to be tailored as necessary, keeping in mind just how confidential the financial information can be and the need to tightly control sensitive data.

In either case, the goal remains the same, as the focus is to assist your audience with understanding financial information and operating results in an efficient, effective, and controlled manner and that the financial information story aligns with the macro-level business opportunity story. You will better understand just how important it is to effectively communicate a business opportunity, in a reliable and timely fashion, if and when you ever attempt to raise capital to launch a new business venture.

Part Two

FINANCIAL STATEMENTS –
THE ECONOMIC HEARTBEAT
OF A COMPANY

6

UNDERSTANDING
THE INCOME STATEMENT

Part One of this book was dedicated to helping you understand critical concepts related to ensuring you can effectively communicate financial information to the intended audience. While I took the opportunity in Part One to provide selected exhibits that presented various financial information, I have reserved the "meat and potatoes" of understanding actual financial information and more importantly, financial statements, to Part Two of this book. For those of you that have read our companion book, *How to Read a Financial Report* (now in its 10th edition), Chapters 6 through 10 of this book will be somewhat of a refresher course for you. However, I would like to emphasize two important thoughts as we move through the next five chapters:

- First, in every book produced by myself and/or with my dad, we emphasize the importance of understanding the big three financial statements including the income statement, balance sheet, and statement of cash flows, along with how these financial statements are connected. The big three financial statements represent absolutely critical must know financial information (for every type of business, organization, or government entity) as eventually, every piece of financial information or transaction will flow through one of these three financial statements. Thus, the reason I present this information again.

- Second, in this book, we'll expand on our discussion of financial statements to take a deeper look at the level of detail provided and the structure of financial statements when comparing external prepared financial statements to internally prepared financial statements and information. One of the most common rookie mistakes made when preparing financial reports and statements is treating all parties in the same light and forwarding the same financial reports to both internal consumers and external users. Wrong, very wrong as if you retain only one concept from this book it should be to understand the difference between internal consumers and external users of financial reports.

Every business needs to produce financial information for both internal and external parties to assess, analyze, review, and base business decisions on. Financial information comes in many different shapes, sizes, and forms which can range from generating a simple sales report (e.g., displaying sales by different product types generated over a three-month period) to preparing periodic financial statements to producing a complete year-end financial report. For the purposes of this book, we will focus our attention on the production and analysis of financial statements and select financial information as both are absolutely essential to internal and external parties, not to mention that financial statements represent the core financial information of a company's annual financial report.

The next two chapters are going to focus on the two most commonly understood and referenced financial statements that people are generally familiar with – the income statement (covered in Chapter 6) and the balance sheet (covered in Chapter 7). I want to emphasize that this is in no way, shape, or form disrespecting the statement of cash flows (covered in Chapter 8) as I have already emphasized the importance of this financial statement. However, when it comes to diving into financial statements, it is almost without fail that everyone wants to first (and often only) understand how much sales revenue a company generates and what profit or loss is being realized on a periodic basis, two critical pieces of information located in, you guessed it, the income statement.

The Income Statement – A Closer Look

So why do I start with the income statement? It's simple, as this is where most people first look when evaluating a company's financial performance. But a word of caution and advice as you proceed through this chapter and the remainder of the book. Understanding the income statement also means that you will begin to have a clearer picture on how this financial statement is often the easiest to manipulate (for lack of a better term) and lends itself to being the most efficiently engineered for the purposes of swaying perspectives.

To start, it's worth repeating that business managers, lenders, and investors need to know and understand the operating performance of a company such as the total sales revenue generated, the direct costs associated with the sales revenue generated, the expenses of a business, and whether or not a company realized a profit or loss. All of this information is presented in the income statement (the focus of this chapter) which is also commonly referred to as the P&L (short for profit & loss statement).

The income statement for our example company was initially introduced in Chapter 3, and is presented here again in Exhibit 6.1, but in a format designed for external users. The format and content of the income statement presented in Exhibit 6.1 apply to manufacturers, wholesalers, tech companies, and retailers – businesses that make or buy *products and services* that are sold to their customers. Although the financial statements of service businesses that do not sell products (e.g., a law firm) differ somewhat, Exhibit 6.1 illustrates the basic framework and content of income statements for all businesses.

EXHIBIT 6.1—AUDITED FINANCIAL STATEMENTS – INCOME STATEMENT

Dollar Amounts in Thousands

Income Statement For the Fiscal Years Ending	12/31/2022	12/31/2023
Net Sales Revenue	$ 54,210	$ 59,494
Costs of Sales Revenue	$(23,922)	$(21,766)
Gross Profit (aka Gross Margin)	$ 30,288	$ 37,728
Operating Expenses:		
Selling, General, & Administrative	$ 22,567	$ 25,289
Research & Development	$ 5,692	$ 7,139
Depreciation & Amortization	$ 1,571	$ 1,643
Total Operating Expenses	$ 29,831	$ 34,071
Operating Income (Loss)	$ 457	$ 3,658
Other Expenses (Income):		
Other Expenses or (Income)	$ 0	$ 2,000
Interest Expense	$ 339	$ 407
Total Other Expenses (Income)	$ 339	$ 2,407
Net Income (Loss) Before Income Taxes	$ 118	$ 1,251
Income Tax Expense (benefit)	$ 41	$ 438
Net Income (Loss) After Income Taxes	$ 77	$ 813

See Notes to Financial Statements

Sales revenue (AKA the "top line") is always reported first with costs of sales revenue then reported to calculate gross profit.

Operating expenses are reported after gross profits and capture general company business expenses.

Finally, after all expenses are reported the company reports its net profit (or loss) often referred to as the "bottom line."

The Income Statement – for External Users

The first question on most everyone's mind is usually whether a business made a profit (i.e., net income) or suffered a loss (i.e., net loss) and how much. Also, people are interested in the *size* of the business, which usually refers to the annual sales revenue. The income statement summarizes sales revenue and expenses for a period of time (one year in Exhibit 6.1). To help with your understanding of the income statement, I elected to include two years of comparable financial operating results. All the dollar amounts reported in this financial statement are cumulative totals for the 12 months of operating results for each year.

The top line identifies the total amount of proceeds or gross income from sales to customers, and is generally called *sales revenue*. The bottom line reflects *net income* (also sometimes called *net earnings*, but seldom *profit* or *net profit* in formally issued external financial reports). Net income is the final profit after all expenses are deducted from sales revenue. The business in this example earned $813,000 net income on its sales revenue of $59,494,000 for the FYE (remember, fiscal year ending) 12/31/23. In other words, after deducting all expenses, only a smidgeon more than 1% of the company's sales revenue remained as final profit (net income). Thin, to say the least.

The income statement is read in a step-down manner, like walking down stairs. Each step down is a deduction of one or more expenses. The first step deducts the cost of sales revenue (products, services, software, and other items) sold from the sales revenue of goods and services sold, which gives *gross profit*. (Note that *gross profit* is also called *gross margin*, which is one of the few terms on an income statement that contains the word *profit*.) This measure of profit is called *gross* because many other expenses have not yet been deducted. At this point, I would like to stop and clarify an important distinction in financial statements as follows:

- Costs of Sales Revenue: When a company sells multiple items including products, services, software, and/or a wide range of other items (e.g., Microsoft), you will most often see it reference the direct costs associated with the sales revenue as "Costs of Sales Revenue" or simply "Costs of Revenue." This represents a broader term and includes not only the costs of products sold to customers, but also other direct costs such as compensation paid to employees (that are being billed to a customer for services rendered). For our sample company presented throughout this book, I use the term Costs of Sales Revenue as our sample company sells products, software, and services to its customers.

- Costs of Goods Sold: When a company primarily sells only products to its customers, you will generally see a reference made to Costs of Goods Sold as only goods or products are being sold.

In both cases, the same purpose is present as the general idea is to report all the expenses incurred that are directly connected and associated with the sales revenue generated.

Next, three additional expense deductions are made. The first is selling, general, and administrative expenses, which is a broad category of operating expenses. The second is research & development expenses as this company wanted to "call out" just how much it is spending on research and development related efforts (a critical piece of information for technology based companies). The third is the depreciation & amortization expense (a unique expense). All three of these are deducted from gross profit, giving *earnings before interest and income tax*. This measure of profit is also called *operating income or earnings* (which sometimes goes by a slightly different name). Next, interest expense on debt is deducted along with other expenses, which gives earnings before income tax. You may be asking yourself what would other expenses include and the answer generally lies in a company attempting to call out or segregate expenses that are one-time or non-recurring in nature. For example, if the company incurred a large loss associated with a natural disaster that was not covered by insurance, they would tend to disclose this loss below operating income to help the reader understand the unique nature of this expense.

The last step is to deduct income tax expense, which then gives us net income, which appears on the bottom line on the income statement. Undoubtedly, you have heard the term "bottom line," and the placement of net income on the income statement is where it comes from. (However, this slang is not used in financial reports.)

As an aside, note that you may hear the income statement called a *profit and loss* or *P&L statement*. This title is not used in external financial reports released outside the business.

Publicly owned business corporations are required to report *earnings per share* (EPS), which is basically the annual net income divided by the number of capital stock shares. Privately owned businesses do not have to report EPS, but this figure may be useful to their stockholders. For further information on calculating EPS, please refer to our companion book, *How to Read a Financial Report*.

In our income statement example (Exhibit 6.1) you see seven different expenses (costs of sales revenue, SG&A, R&D, depreciation & amortization, other, interest, and income tax). You may find more expense lines in an income statement, but there would seldom be more than 10 or so, as a general rule. (There can be exceptions if a business has a very unusual year.) One expense that companies are required to report is costs of sales revenue or sometimes referred to as simply costs of sales. Depreciation & amortization, two other expenses, are so unique that I prefer to report it on a separate line (to help illustrate the unique nature of this expense throughout this book), but some companies do not do this. However, depreciation and amortization can be included in another operating expense in the income statement instead of being reported separately.

Other than depreciation and amortization, Exhibit 6.1 includes two broad, all-inclusive operating expenses lines including Selling, General, and Administrative Expenses and Research & Development. A business has the option of disclosing two or more operating expenses, and many do. Marketing, promotional, and selling expenses often are separated from general and administration expenses as are research and development expenses. The level of detail for expenses in income statements is flexible; financial reporting standards are somewhat loose on this point.

The sales revenue and expenses reported in income statements follow generally accepted conventions, which I briefly summarize here:

◆ **Sales revenue:** The total amount received or to be received from the sales of products (and/or services) to customers during the period. Sales revenue is *net*, which means that discounts off list prices, prompt payment discounts, sales returns, and any other deductions from original sales prices are deducted to determine the sales revenue amount for the period. Sales taxes are not included in sales revenue, nor are excise taxes that might apply. In short, sales revenue is the amount the business should receive to cover its expenses and to provide profit (bottom-line net income).

- *Costs of Sales Revenue expense (aka Costs of Revenue or Costs of Goods Sold):* The total cost of goods and services (products and services) sold to customers during the period. This is clear enough. What might not be so clear, however, is the expense of goods that were shoplifted or are otherwise missing, and write-downs due to damage and obsolescence. The cost of such *inventory shrinkage* may be included in cost of goods sold expense for the year (or, this cost may be put in another expense account instead).

- *Selling, general, and administrative expenses (operating expenses):* Broadly speaking, every expense other than cost of sales revenue, interest, unique or non-recurring, and income tax. This broad category is a catchall for every expense not reported separately. In our example, depreciation & amortization are broken out as a separate expense instead of being included with other operating expenses. Some companies report advertising and marketing costs separately from administrative and general costs, and some report research and development expenses separately (which is the case in our example company). There are hundreds, even thousands, of specific operating expenses, some rather large and some very small. They range from salaries and wages of employees (large) to legal fees (small, one hopes).

- *Depreciation & Amortization expense:* The portions of original costs of tangible long-term assets including buildings, machinery, equipment, tools, furniture, computers, and vehicles that is recorded to expense in one period. Depreciation is the "charge" for using these so-called tangible *fixed assets* during the period. Amortization expense is similar to depreciation expense; however, it is usually associated with intangible assets such as patents, goodwill, software development costs, etc. Similar to depreciation, amortization is the "charge" for using these so-call intangible fixed assets during the period. These expense amounts are not a cash outlay in the period recorded, which makes it a unique expense compared with other operating expenses.

- *Interest expense:* The amount of interest on debt (interest-bearing liabilities) for the period. Other types of financing charges may also be included, such as loan origination fees.

- *Income tax expense:* The total amount due to the government (both federal and state) on the amount of taxable income of the business during the period. Taxable income is multiplied by the appropriate tax rates. The income tax expense does not include other types of taxes, such as unemployment and Social Security taxes on the company's payroll. These other, non-income taxes are included in operating expenses.

A business may present a two- or three-year comparative income statement in its financial report. Indeed, public corporations are required to provide historical information. I elected to provide two years of financial information to help explain the income statement.

The Income Statement – for Internal Consumers

Now I turn your attention to Exhibit 6.2, which presents the same income statement as with Exhibit 6.1 but for use by internal business parties (e.g., owners, management team members, etc.). You will notice that this is the same information as presented in Exhibit 3.1, but I wanted to include here again to highlight the key differences between internal and external income statements as follows:

- First, notice the reference to audited financial statements in Exhibit 6.1 versus the reference to unaudited financial statements in Exhibit 6.2. Even though the figures are the same in each Exhibit, the internally prepared income statement has technically not been audited by an external party, thus the reference to unaudited.

- Second, the format is much more user- and management-friendly (to drive home key points) as dictated by the company and not driven by external guidelines such as those of the IRS or SEC. A proper balance needs to be struck between providing too much information (pushing the user toward "getting lost in the forest") versus not enough, as the idea is to give the reviewing party what they ask for and need (based on their level of responsibility).

- Third, it should be obvious that far more detail is provided in the internally prepared income statement presented in Exhibit 6.2 compared to Exhibit 6.1. This is done to provide internal consumers with much more visibility and transparency with key financial information, figures, ratios, and trends that external users do not necessarily need or should not have access to (as the information is confidential).

- Fourth, inclusion of basic trend and ratio analysis has been provided to assist internal consumers with gaining a better understanding of key operating metrics. For example, if you refer to the line titled Other Sales, Discounts, & Allowances, you will notice that this ratio increased from 2.56% of gross sales during the FYE 12/31/22 to 4.17% during the FYE 12/31/23. This "jump" or increase in this ratio is significant enough to warrant management's attention and gain a better understanding as to what is driving the increase. Is it related to having to discount the selling price of older, slow-moving products to get rid of these items or are more aggressive selling discounts needed to obtain new customers to purchase the company's software products? Whatever the case, this should attract management's attention.

Additional differences could be presented but the basic idea between internal and externally prepared financial statements, and in this case the income statement, should be obvious. The format, level of detail, analysis provided, and disclosure of confidential information need to be proactively managed to ensure external users and internal consumers receive the appropriate financial reports.

EXHIBIT 6.2—INTERNALLY PREPARED INCOME STATEMENT – COMPANY LEVEL

Unaudited – Prepared by Company Management

Income Statement for the Fiscal Years Ending	12/31/2022	% of Net Rev.	12/31/2023	% of Net Rev.
Sales Revenue:				
Software Platform & SAAS Sales	$36,400,000	67.15%	$48,533,321	81.58%
Product Sales	$19,200,000	35.42%	$13,440,000	22.59%
Other Sales, Discounts, & Allowances	$ (1,390,000)	-2.56%	$ (2,479,000)	4.17%
Net Sales Revenue	$54,210,000	100.00%	$59,494,321	100.00%
Costs of Sales Revenue:				
Direct Product Costs	$11,040,000	20.37%	$ 7,392,000	12.42%
Wages & Burden	$12,012,000	22.16%	$13,589,000	22.84%
Direct Overhead	$ 800,000	1.48%	$ 700,000	1.18%
Other Costs of Sales Revenue	$ 70,000	0.13%	$ 85,000	0.14%
Total Costs of Sales Revenue	$23,922,000	44.13%	$21,766,000	36.59%
Gross Profit	$30,288,000	55.87%	$37,728,321	63.41%
Gross Margin	55.87%		63.41%	
Direct Operating Expenses:				
Advertising, Promotional, & Selling	$ 3,659,000	6.75%	$ 3,867,000	6.50%
Personnel Wages, Burden, & Compensation	$10,300,000	19.00%	$11,899,000	20.00%
Facility Operating Expenses	$ 1,219,725	2.25%	$ 1,264,254	2.13%
Other Operating Expenses	$ 375,000	0.69%	$ 450,000	0.76%
Total Direct Operating Expenses	$15,553,725	28.69%	$ 17,480,254	29.38%
Contribution Profit	$14,734,275	27.18%	$20,248,067	34.03%
Contribution Margin	27.18%		34.03%	
Corporate Expenses & Overhead:				
Corporate Marketing, Branding, & Promotional	$ 2,134,575	3.94%	$ 2,751,500	4.62%
Research, Development, & Design	$ 5,692,000	10.50%	$ 7,139,000	12.00%
Corporate Overhead & Support	$ 4,878,900	9.00%	$ 5,057,017	8.50%
Depreciation & Amortization Expense	$ 1,571,429	2.90%	$ 1,642,857	2.76%
Total Corporate Operating Expenses	$14,276,904	26.34%	$16,590,374	27.89%
Operating Income (EBIT)	$ 457,371	0.84%	$ 3,657,692	6.15%
Operating Margin (EBIT Margin)	0.84%		6.15%	
Other Expenses (Income):				
Other Expenses, Income, & Discontinued Ops.	$ 0	0.00%	$ 2,000,000	3.36%
Interest Expense	$ 339,000	0.63%	$ 407,000	0.68%
Total Other Expenses (Income)	$ 339,000	0.63%	$ 2,407,000	4.05%
Net Income (Loss) Before Income Taxes	$ 118,371	0.22%	$ 1,250,692	2.10%
Income Tax Expense (Benefit)	$ 41,000	0.08%	$ 438,000	0.74%
Net Income (Loss) After Income Taxes	$ 77,371	0.14%	$ 812,692	1.37%

Confidential - Property of QW Example Tech, Inc.

Notice inclusion of a analytical ratio analysis.

We now have far more detail related to the primary types of sales and costs of goods sold are split between major categories.

Look at the level of detail now as we can understand exactly how much is being spent on different types of company selling & marketing expenses as well as facility versus corporate overhead.

7

TRUSTING THE BALANCE SHEET

Business managers, lenders, investors, analysts, and a slew of other parties need to know the *financial condition* of a business at a point in time. They need a report that summarizes the business entity's assets, both current and long term, and liabilities, both current and long term, as well as the ownership residual of its assets in excess of liabilities (often referred to as owners' equity). The financial condition of a business is reported in the second of the two bedrock financial statements – the balance sheet (which will be the focus of this chapter).

Similar to the income statement, I would offer a word of caution about the balance sheet before you dive deeper into its purpose and structure by making this somewhat bold statement:

The balance sheet is where losses go to hide, cash goes to die, and the bullshit goes to lie. Conversely, you must always assess the balance sheet from the perspective of whether the assets are lying to you and/or are the liabilities telling you the truth.

You may ask yourself what in the hell am I talking about to start this chapter, to which I would offer this simple case study related to a common asset on businesses' balance sheets – inventory.

Inventory represents goods and products that are owned by a business that are available for sale but that have not been sold (as of the date the balance sheet financial statement is prepared). As such, inventory represents an asset of the business. But looking closer at inventory, you should pay attention to these three potential issues:

- First, if the inventory asset continues to increase in value, this indicates higher levels of goods and products are available for sale. Inventory doesn't magically appear out of thin air, as a business needs to buy or manufacture inventory (for eventual sale). Thus, cash is needed to buy or manufacture inventory, which underscores the statement – "cash goes to die."

- Second, if relatively elevated levels of inventory are present, this all-important question must be asked. That is, can all this inventory even be sold to customers (or has it become obsolete or worthless)? You would think that all business executives are honest and auditors competent, but this may not always be the case. Thus, you should now understand our statement – "losses go to hide" as obsolete, slow moving, and worthless inventory should always be written-off when losses are known and measurable (but let's just say more than a few companies and executives have bent the rules with this concept over the years).

- Third, our executive management team members have assured its investors and lenders that its elevated inventory levels are not only valuable but have been increased due to anticipated increased sales in the year to come. They created a great story and prepared the appropriate "spin" to back their case. Even the auditors bought into the story and agreed that the increased inventory levels are justified and sound. Oh, what a year's difference it makes as you will find in our sample company that it elected to write-off $2,000,000 of worthless inventory in FYE 12/31/23 based on a change in market conditions. Thus, this is where the bullshit goes to lie.

Here is an example as to whether an asset is lying to you as on the surface, the inventory, an important asset, appears to have value but digging deeper, valuation issues may be present that indicate a significant write-off may be needed. Thus, you must always find comfort in trusting the balance sheet!

Reporting Financial Condition: The Balance Sheet for External Users

The balance sheet shown in Exhibit 7.1 follows the standardized format regarding the classification and ordering of assets, liabilities, and ownership interests in the business. Financial institutions, public utilities, railroads, and other specialized businesses use somewhat different balance sheet layouts. However, manufacturers, tech companies, wholesalers, and retailers, as well as the large majority of various types of businesses, follow the format presented in Exhibit 7.1.

The top half of the balance sheet lists *assets*. The bottom half of the balance sheet first lists the *liabilities* of the business, which have a higher-order claim on the assets. The sources of ownership (equity) capital in the business are presented below the liabilities. This is to emphasize that the owners or equity holders in a business (the stockholders of a business corporation) have a secondary and lower-order claim on the assets – after its liabilities are satisfied.

Roughly speaking, a balance sheet lists assets in their order of *nearness to cash*. Cash is listed first at the top of the assets. Next, receivables that will be collected in the short run are listed, and so on down the line. (In later chapters, I say more about the cash characteristics of different assets.) Liabilities are presented in the sequence of their nearness to payment. (I discuss this point as we go along in later chapters.)

Each separate asset, liability, and stockholders' equity reported in a balance sheet is called an *account*. Every account has a name (title) and a dollar amount, which is called its *balance*. For instance, from Exhibit 7.1 at the end of the most recent FYE 12/31/23 we can determine:

Name of Account	Amount (Balance) of Account
Accounts Receivable	$8,009,000

The other dollar amounts in the balance sheet are either subtotals or totals of account balances. For example, the $12,504,000 amount for "Current Assets" at the end of this year does not represent a single account but rather the subtotal of the four accounts making up this group of accounts. A line is drawn above a subtotal or total, indicating account balances are being added.

A double underline (such as for "Total Assets") indicates the last amount in a column. Notice also the double underline below "Net Income" in the income statement (Exhibit 6.1), indicating it is the last number in the column.

A balance sheet is prepared at the close of business on the last day of the income statement period. For example, if the income statement is for the year ending December 31, 2023, the balance sheet is prepared at midnight December 31, 2023. The amounts reported in the balance sheet are the balances of the accounts at that precise moment in time. The financial condition of the business is frozen for one split second. A business should be careful to make a precise and accurate cutoff to separate transactions between the period just ended and the next period.

EXHIBIT 7.1—AUDITED FINANCIAL STATEMENTS – BALANCE SHEET
Dollar Amounts in Thousands

Balance Sheet As of the Fiscal Year Ending	12/31/2022	12/31/2023
Assets		
Current Assets		
Cash & Equivalents	$ 775	$ 2,164
Accounts Receivable	$ 6,776	$ 8,009
Inventory	$ 3,822	$ 1,706
Prepaid Expenses	$ 600	$ 625
Total Current Assets	$11,973	$12,504
Long-Term Capital Assets		
Property, Machinery, & Equipment	$ 4,000	$ 4,500
Accumulated Depreciation	$ (1,571)	$ (2,214)
Net Property, Machinery, & Equipment	$ 2,429	$ 2,286
Other Assets		
Intangible Assets, Net	$ 2,000	$ 6,000
Other Assets	$ 100	$ 100
Total Long-Term & Other Assets	$ 4,529	$ 8,386
Total Assets	$16,502	$20,889

See Notes to Financial Statements

Cash & equivalents listed first followed by trade receivables (highly liquid). Notice the decrease in inventory from the prior year. We'll get to this later.

Capital assets are presented which include equipment, machinery, furniture, computers, etc.

Finally, other assets are presented. Large increase in intangible assets relates to intangible assets, patents, & software acquired.

EXHIBIT 7.1 — (CONTINUED)

Balance Sheet

As of the Fiscal Year Ending	12/31/2022	12/31/2023
Liabilities		
Current Liabilities		
Accounts Payable	$ 1,405	$ 1,459
Accrued Liabilities	$ 1,084	$ 1,258
Short-Term Loans Payable	$ 3,390	$ 2,400
Deferred Revenue & Other Current Liabilities	$ 1,011	$ 1,348
Total Current Liabilities	$ 6,890	$ 6,465
Long-Term Liabilities		
Loans Payable, Less Short-Term Portion	$ 750	$ 2,500
Total Liabilities	$ 7,640	$ 8,965
Stockholders' Equity		
Capital Stock	$ 7,500	$10,000
Retained Earnings (deficit)	$ 1,362	$1,924
Total Stockholders' Equity	$ 8,862	$11,924
Total Liabilities & Stockholders' Equity	$16,502	$20,889

See Notes to Financial Statements

Trade payables & accrued liabilities listed first followed by current portion of debt.

Long-term liabilities presented next. Notice increase from the prior year.

Finally, capital stock is listed by primary class followed by retained earnings. This company raised $2.5 million of capital with stock sales in 2023.

A balance sheet does not report the flows of activities in the company's assets, liabilities, and shareowners' equity accounts during the period. Only the ending balances at the moment the balance sheet is prepared are reported for the accounts. For example, the company reports an ending cash balance of $2,164,000 at the end of its most recent year (see again Exhibit 7.1). Can you tell the total cash inflows and outflows for the year? No, not from the balance sheet; you can't even get a clue from the balance sheet alone.

A balance sheet can be presented in the landscape (horizontal) layout mode or the portrait (vertical) layout as shown in Exhibit 7.1. The accounts reported in the balance sheet are not thrown together haphazardly in no particular order. According to long-standing rules, balance sheet accounts are subdivided into the following classes, or basic groups, in the following order of presentation:

Left Side (or Top Section)	**Right Side (or Bottom Section)**
Current assets	Current liabilities
Long-term operating assets	Long-term liabilities
Other assets	Owners' equity

Current assets are cash and other assets that will be converted into cash during one *operating cycle*. The operating cycle refers to the sequence of buying or manufacturing products, holding the products until sale, selling the products, waiting to collect the receivables from the sales, and finally receiving cash from customers. This sequence is the most basic rhythm of a company's operations; it is repeated over and over. The operating cycle may be short, 60 days or less, or it may be relatively long, taking 180 days or more.

Assets not directly required in the operating cycle, such as marketable securities held as temporary investments or short-term loans made to employees, are included in the current assets class if they will be converted into cash during the coming year. A business pays in advance for some costs of operations that will not be charged to expense until next period. These *prepaid* expenses are included in current assets, as you see in Exhibit 7.1.

The second group of assets is labeled "Long-Term Operating Assets" in the balance sheet. These assets are not held for sale to customers; rather, they are used in the operations of the business. Broadly speaking, these assets fall into two groups: *tangible* and *intangible* assets. Tangible assets have physical existence, such as machines, equipment, and buildings. Intangible assets do not have physical existence, but they are legally protected rights (such as patents and trademarks), or they are such things as secret processes, goodwill, and well-known favorable reputations that give businesses important competitive advantages. Generally intangible assets are recorded only when the assets are purchased from a source outside the business or internal expenditures can clearly be traced to the development of an asset that holds long-term value (e.g., internally developed software).

The tangible assets of the business are reported in the "Property, Machinery, and Equipment" account (see Exhibit 7.1 again). More informally, these assets are called *fixed assets*, although this term is generally not used in balance sheets. The word *fixed* is a little strong; these assets are not really fixed or permanent, except for the land and buildings owned by a business. More accurately, these assets are the long-term operating resources used over several years – such as buildings, machinery, equipment, trucks, forklifts, furniture, computers, and so on.

The cost of a fixed asset – with the exception of land – is gradually charged off to expense over its useful life. Each period of use thereby bears its share of the total cost of each fixed asset. This apportionment of the cost of fixed assets over their useful lives is called *depreciation*. The amount of depreciation for one year is reported as an expense in the income statement (see Exhibit 6.1). The cumulative amount that has been recorded as depreciation expense since the date of acquisition up to the balance sheet date is reported in the *accumulated depreciation* account in the balance sheet (see Exhibit 7.1). As you see, the balance in the accumulated depreciation account is deducted from the original cost of the fixed assets.

In the example, the business owns various intangible long-term operating assets. These assets report the cost of acquisition. The cost of an intangible asset remains on the books until the business determines that the asset has lost value or no longer has economic benefit. At that time, the business writes down (or writes off) the original cost of the intangible asset and charges the amount to an expense, usually *amortization expense*. At one time the general practice was to allocate the cost of intangible assets over arbitrary time periods. However, many intangible assets have indefinite and indeterminable useful lives. The conventional wisdom now is that it's better to wait until an intangible asset has lost value, at which time an expense is recorded. Businesses may elect to implement either of these methods (i.e., amortize the intangible asset over a set period or write-off 100% when determined its value is zero) or a combination of both depending on the intangible asset. For the purposes of our sample company, I elect to amortize intangible assets over a set period.

You may see an account called "Other Assets" on a balance sheet, which is a catchall title for assets that don't fit in the current assets or long-term operating assets classes. Our example company in Exhibit 7.1 has a relatively small amount of other assets.

The accounts reported in the *current liabilities* class are short-term liabilities that, for the most part, depend on the conversion of current assets into cash for their payment. Also, debts (borrowed money) that will come due within one year from the balance sheet date are put in this group. In our example, there are four accounts in current liabilities. I explain these different types of current liabilities in later chapters.

Long-term liabilities, labeled "Long-Term Notes Payable" in Exhibit 7.1, are those whose maturity dates are more than one year after the balance sheet date. There's only one such account in our example. Either in the balance sheet or in a footnote, the maturity dates, interest rates, and other relevant provisions of long-term liabilities are disclosed. To simplify, I do not include footnotes with our financial statements example in this chapter.

Liabilities are claims on the assets of a business. Cash or other assets that will be later converted into cash will be used to pay the liabilities. (Also, cash generated by future profit earned by the business will be available to pay the business's liabilities.) Clearly, all liabilities of a business should be reported in its balance sheet to give a complete picture of the financial condition of a business.

Liabilities are also sources of assets (but liabilities are also sources of expenses as well). For example, cash increases when a business borrows money. Inventory increases when a business buys products on credit and incurs a liability that will be paid later. Also, typically a business has liabilities for unpaid expenses and has not yet used cash to pay these liabilities. Another reason for reporting liabilities in the balance sheet is to account for the sources of the company's assets, to answer the question: Where did the company's total assets come from?

Some part of the total assets of a business comes not from liabilities but from its owners investing capital in the business and from retaining some or all of the profit the business earns that is not distributed to its owners. In this example the business is organized legally as a corporation. Its *stockholders' equity* accounts in the balance sheet reveal the sources of the company's total assets in excess of its total liabilities. Notice in Exhibit 7.1 the two stockholders' (owners') equity sources, which are called *capital stock* and *retained earnings*.

When owners (stockholders of a business corporation) invest capital in the business, the capital stock account is increased. Net income earned by a business less the amount distributed to owners increases the retained earnings account. The nature of retained earnings can be confusing; therefore, I explain this account in depth at the appropriate places in the book. Just a quick word of advice here: Retained earnings is *not* – I repeat, *not* – an asset. Get such a notion out of your head.

The Balance Sheet for Internal Consumers

Again, I will turn your attention to comparing a financial statement, in this case the balance sheet, between what an external user receives (Exhibit 7.1) and an internal consumer needs. Please refer to Exhibit 7.2 noting the following key presentation differences (which are basically the same at a conceptual level as with the income statement comparison presented in Chapter 6):

- First, notice the reference to audited financial statements in Exhibit 7.1 versus the reference to unaudited financial statements in Exhibit 7.2. Even though the figures are the same in each exhibit, the internally prepared balance sheet has technically not been audited by an external party, thus the reference to unaudited.

- Second, the format is much more user- and management-friendly (to drive home key points) as dictated by the company and not driven by external guidelines such as those of the IRS or SEC. A proper balance needs to be struck between providing too much information (pushing the user toward "getting lost in the forest") versus not enough, as the idea is to give the reviewing party what they ask for and need (based on their level of responsibility).

- Third, it should be obvious that far more detail is provided in the internally prepared balance sheet presented in Exhibit 7.2 compared to Exhibit 7.1. This is done to provide internal consumers with much more visibility and transparency with key financial information, figures, ratios, and trends that external users do not necessarily need or should not have access to (as the information is confidential).

- Fourth, there is now a plethora of new and valuable financial information provided, which I've decided to highlight some tidbits of key observations:

  - The company's cash is not sitting idle but displays that $1,500,000 is invested in short-term money market accounts earning interest (indicating proactive treasury management).

  - Interestingly, the company's reserve for doubtful accounts (i.e., anticipated future bad debts) has increased from .62% of total assets as of the FYE 12/31/22 to 1.53% of total assets as of the FYE 12/31/23. Does this indicate customer payment problems are surfacing, possibly?

  - Look at the huge jump in the inventory reserve for slow moving and obsolete inventory (from $191,100 as of the FYE 12/31/22 to $2,388,400 as of the FYE 12/31/23). As previously disclosed, the company incurred an other expense of $2,000,000 in the FYE 12/31/23 to account for worthless inventory. Instead of actually disposing of specific finished goods inventory, the company has estimated that a reserve for worthless inventory of $2,388,400 is needed to properly

EXHIBIT 7.2—INTERNALLY PREPARED BALANCE SHEET – COMPANY LEVEL

Unaudited – Prepared by Company Management

Balance Sheet As of the Fiscal Year Ending Assets	12/31/2022	% of Total	12/31/2023	% of Total
Current Assets				
Cash & Equivalents				
Cash in Operating Account	$ 775,161	4.70%	$ 663,747	3.18%
Cash Invested Short-Term Securities	$ 0	0.00%	$ 1,500,000	7.18%
Total Cash & Equivalents	$ 775,161	4.70%	$ 2,163,747	10.36%
Accounts Receivable				
Gross Accounts Receivable	$ 6,877,640	41.68%	$ 8,329,360	39.87%
Less: Allowance for Doubtful Accounts	$ (101,640)	-0.62%	$ (320,360)	-1.53%
Total Accounts Receivable	$ 6,776,000	41.06%	$ 8,009,000	38.34%
Inventory				
Raw Material	$ 382,200	2.32%	$ 170,600	0.82%
Work In Process	$ 191,100	1.16%	$ 85,300	0.41%
Finished Goods	$ 3,439,800	20.85%	$ 3,838,500	18.38%
Less: Reserve for slow moving & obsolete	$ (191,100)	-1.16%	$(2,388,400)	-11.43%
Total Inventory	$ 3,822,000	23.16%	$ 1,706,000	8.17%
Prepaid Expenses	$ 600,000	3.64%	$ 625,000	2.99%
Total Current Assets	$ 11,973,161	72.56%	$ 12,503,747	59.86%
Long-Term Capital Assets				
Equipment & Machinery	$ 3,200,000		$ 3,200,000	
Accumulated Depreciation - Equip. & Mach.	$ (1,257,143)		$ (1,660,714)	
Autos, Computers, & Other Fixed Assets	$ 800,000		$ 1,300,000	
Accumulated Depreciation - Other Fixed Assets	$ (314,286)		$ (553,571)	
Net Property, Machinery, & Equipment	$ 2,428,571	14.72%	$ 2,285,714	10.94%
Other Assets				
Intangible Assets - Goodwill	$ 5,000,000		$ 5,000,000	
Accumulated Amortization - Goodwill	$ (3,000,000)		$ (4,000,000)	
Intangible Assets - Acquired Software Rights & Patents	$ 0		$ 5,000,000	
Accumulated Amortization - Software & Patents	$ 0		$ 0	
Net Other Assets	$ 2,000,000	12.12%	$ 6,000,000	28.72%
Other Assets	$ 100,000	0.61%	$ 100,000	0.48%
Total Long-Term & Other Assets	$ 4,528,571	27.44%	$ 8,385,714	40.14%
Total Assets	$ 16,501,733	100.00%	$ 20,889,462	100.00%

Each asset as a percentage of total assets is now presented for quick reference. Same logic holds for liabilities and equity.

Wow, what a wealth of information is now provided related to how cash is invested, the allowance for doubtful accounts, the inventory reserve for slow-moving and obsolete products, and the distribution of long-term assets between different classes.

EXHIBIT 7.2—(CONTINUED)

Liabilities

Current Liabilities	12/31/2022	% of Total	12/31/2023	% of Total
Accounts Payable				
Credit Cards - Due in less than 30 Days	$ 70,250	0.92%	$ 72,950	0.81%
Vendors & Suppliers - Due in 30 Days	$ 1,053,750	13.79%	$ 729,500	8.14%
Vendors & Suppliers - Due in 90 Days	$ 281,000	3.68%	$ 656,550	7.32%
Total Accounts Payable	$ 1,405,000	18.39%	$ 1,459,000	16.27%
Accrued Liabilities				
Payroll Wages & Burden	$ 987,200	12.92%	$ 990,000	11.04%
Interest	$ 82,800	1.08%	$ 122,000	1.36%
Income Taxes	$ 14,000	0.18%	$ 146,000	1.63%
Total Accrued Liabilities Payable	$ 1,084,000	14.19%	$ 1,258,000	14.03%
Short Term Loans Payable				
Working Capital Line of Credit	$ 2,640,000	34.55%	$ 1,900,000	21.19%
Current Portion of Long-Term Loans	$ 750,000	9.82%	$ 500,000	5.58%
Total Short-Term Loans Payable	$ 3,390,000	44.37%	$ 2,400,000	26.77%
Deferred Revenue & Other Current Liabilities				
Deferred Revenue & Customer Deposits	$ 804,111	10.52%	$ 1,209,548	13.49%
Sales Taxes Payable & Other Current Liabilities	$ 207,000	2.71%	$ 138,600	1.55%
Total Other Current Liabilities & Deferred Revenue	$ 1,011,111	13.23%	$ 1,348,148	15.04%
Total Current Liabilities	$ 6,890,111	90.18%	$ 6,465,148	72.11%
Long-Term Liabilities				
Long-Term Loans Due in Two Years	$ 750,000	9.82%	$ 500,000	5.58%
Long-Term Loans Due after Two Years	$ 0	0.00%	$ 2,000,000	22.31%
Total Long-Term Liabilities	$ 750,000	9.82%	$ 2,500,000	27.89%
Total Liabilities	$ 7,640,111	100.00%	$ 8,965,148	100.00%
Stockholders' Equity				
Capital Stock - Par, $.01 per share	$ 10,000	0.11%	$ 10,000	0.08%
Capital Stock - APIC	$ 7,490,000	84.52%	$ 9,990,000	83.78%
Dividends & Distributions	$ 0	0.00%	$ (250,000)	-2.10%
Current Earnings	$ 77,371	0.87%	$ 812,692	6.82%
Retained Earnings - Carryforward	$ 1,284,250	14.49%	$ 1,361,621	11.42%
Total Stockholders' Equity	$ 8,861,621	100.00%	$ 11,924,314	100.00%
Total Liabilities & Stockholders' Equity	$16,501,733	n/a	$20,889,462	n/a

Confidential - Property of QW Example Tech, Inc.

> Wow, what a wealth of information is now provided related to the different age of accounts payable, the breakdown of accrued liabilities, the allocation of short-term loans payable by credit type, and what mainly comprises other current liabilities (i.e., deferred revenue).

> Added visibility is provided related to the primary equity accounts and the activity in each. Notice that the current earnings row agrees to the income statement in Exhibit 6.2.

account for worthless inventory (which may take a year or two to actually sell at bargain basement prices or actually sell for scrap to third-party recycling companies).

- Jumping to the current liabilities and more specifically, the accounts payable, notice the change in the balance due to vendors and suppliers that is not due until 90 days (from $281,000 as of the FYE 12/31/22 to $656,550 as of the FYE 12/31/23). This indicates the company is receiving extended payment terms from key suppliers and vendors, which generally results from suppliers and vendors offering better terms as they view the company as being more credit worthy (a positive development).

I could offer several additional observations related to the information presented in the internal balance sheet summarized in Exhibit 7.2, but the key concepts associated with the more robust internal balance sheet are centered on two primary areas. First, there's a wealth of additional information provided in the internal balance sheet compared to the external balance sheet that provides invaluable insight into the financial condition and operations of the company. Second, the internal balance sheet presents confidential information that is essential to the management team of our example company but which should not be provided to external parties.

8

RELYING ON THE STATEMENT OF CASH FLOWS

In Chapters 6 and 7, I made reference to the income statement and the balance sheet being the two primary financial statements that internal and external parties focus on. This may give the appearance that I'm ignoring or downplaying the importance of the statement of cash flows which is as far from the truth as possible. In fact and as a matter of professional experience, I find that I tend to start any financial analysis I complete on a business's operating results with the statement of cash flows.

One might view the statement of cash flows in the same light as the story of Cinderella. If you recall, the story of Cinderella begins with Cinderella's two stepsisters (i.e., the income statement and balance sheet) being the center of attention only to end with Cinderella blooming into a princess full of beauty, goodness, and truth. This is the essence of the statement of cash flows as once understood, it truly is beautiful, delivers a bounty of great financial information, and can be relied upon to help readers of financial statements to deliver the truth.

This is why when referring back to the titles of Chapters 6, 7, and 8 I make the following statements within the titles – Understanding the income statement, Trusting the balance sheet, and most importantly, Relying on the statement of cash flows. In actuality and in order to become proficient in reading financial statements, you must learn to understand and rely on all of the big three financial statements, but where the statement of cash flows really begins to shine, is with these three concepts:

- First, the statement of cash flows provides an invaluable source of financial information as it relates to how businesses produce and consume cash and why generating net profits and positive cash flows from internal earnings is alone often not enough to support a growing business.

- Second, the statement of cash flows can be used as a validation and/or audit tool to help affirm or verify a business's financial performance. Not only must the math in the statement of cash flows work properly but the resulting calculations must make sense.

- Third, Chapter 9 of this book focuses exclusively on the connections between the big three financial statements. What you will find is that the statement of cash flows acts as the glue, so to speak, that binds or connects the balance sheet and income statement together.

Before you dive into this chapter, I would offer one final word of advice as you consume the content presented and expand your understanding of the statement of cash flows. Don't be afraid to read this chapter multiple times and refer to it as you work through the entire book. The reason I mention this is that the statement of cash flows is often the hardest of the big three financial statements to understand. Even for accounting and financial professionals, it can often take years to master this financial statement so please don't be bashful to read, re-read, and then review this material again and again as there is no shame in being thorough.

Chapters 6 and 7 introduce the two primary financial statements that are included in the financial report of a business, the income statement (Exhibit 6.1) and the balance sheet (Exhibit 7.1). Both of these provide a comprehensive summary of the financial performance and financial condition of the business; however, this is not the end of the story. Financial reporting standards require that a *statement of cash flows* also be presented for the same time period as the income statement.

This third financial statement, as its title implies, focuses on the cash flows of the period. The cash flow statement is not more or less important than the income statement and balance sheet. Rather, it discloses additional information that supplements the income statement and balance sheet and provides invaluable insight on a business's ability to finance its on-going operations and business growth plans.

Exhibit 8.1 presents the statement of cash flows for our example company. This financial statement has three parts, or *layers*: 1) cash flows from *operating* activities, 2) cash flows from *investing* activities, and 3) cash flows from *financing* activities. Operating activities relate to the profit-making activities of the business. Of course, a business may suffer a loss instead of making profit. On a statement of cash flows, the term "operating activities" refers to revenue and expenses (as well as gains and losses) during the period that culminate in the bottom-line net income or loss for the period.

The income statement of our business example (Exhibit 6.1) divulges 14 lines of information and the related balance sheet has 23 lines (Exhibit 7.1). So, already you have 37 items of information, which take time to read. The statement of cash flows adds another 22 lines of information to read. Is this financial statement worth the additional time it takes to read it? What's the payoff?

For many financial report readers, the main value of the statement of cash flows is that it discloses the *cash flow from operating activities*. They zero in on this number, and may not read any other line of information in the financial statement. This key metric is commonly called *cash flow from profit*. In its income statement for the FYE 12/31/23 (Exhibit 6.1), the company reports that it earned $813,000 net income, or bottom-line profit. In its statement of cash flows for the year (Exhibit 8.1) the company reports that it generated $3,879,000 cash flow from operating

activities; that is, from profit-making activities. In short, profit is $813,000 in one financial statement and $3,879,000 in another statement. This can be confusing, to say the least.

How can cash flow from profit be higher than profit? Is one of the two numbers *fake* profit? Where did the *extra* cash come from? In other situations, could cash flow be less than profit? (Yes, it can be.) A short explanation for this discrepancy is that actual cash inflow from revenue is typically somewhat higher or lower than the amount of revenue recorded for the period. And actual cash outflows for expenses typically differ from the amounts of expenses recorded for the period.

In addition to understanding how net cash flow from operating activities is calculated, I would also draw your attention to two other critical components of the statement of cash flows. First is the section titled Investing Activities and second is the section titled Financing Activities. These two sections of the statement of cash flows are important to understand, especially as it relates to rapidly growing businesses and newly formed start-up businesses that require significant amounts of capital (i.e., cash) to operate. Stated different, rarely will positive cash flows generated from operating activities provide the company with enough capital to finance rapid growth plans so businesses must look elsewhere for cash to support on-going operations.

In our example company, you will notice that the business invested heavily in other assets, which in this case amounted to $5,000,000 of acquisitions of intangible assets (e.g., patents, trade secrets, customer lists, etc.). You may ask the question as to how this was achieved given that the company only generated $3,879,000 of positive cash flow from operating activities. The answer lies in the financing activities section of the statement of cash flows, as you can see that the company secured a new loan for $3,000,000 and raised $2,500,000 by selling additional stock or equity in the company. Between these two items, the

EXHIBIT 8.1—AUDITED FINANCIAL STATEMENTS – STATEMENT OF CASH FLOWS

Dollar Amounts in Thousands

Statement of Cash Flows For the Fiscal Years Ending	12/31/2022	12/31/2023
Net Income (Loss) after Income Taxes	$ 77	$ 813
Operating Activities, Cash provided (used):		
Depreciation & Amortization	$ 1,571	$ 1,643
Decrease (increase) in accounts receivables	$ (1,122)	$ (1,233)
Decrease (increase) in inventory	$ (333)	$ 2,116
Decrease (increase) in other current assets	$ (50)	$ (25)
Increase (decrease) in accounts payables	$ 155	$ 54
Increase (decrease) in accrued liabilities	$ 118	$ 42
Increase (decrease) in other liabilities	$ 217	$ 469
Net Cash Flow from Operating Activities	$ 634	$ 3,879
Investing Activities, Cash provided (used):		
Capital Expenditures	$ (250)	$ (500)
Investments in Intangible & Other Assets	$ 0	$ (5,000)
Net Cash Flow from Investing Activities	$ (250)	$ (5,500)
Financing Activities, Cash provided (used):		
Dividends or Distributions Paid	$ 0	$ (250)
Sale (repurchase) of Equity	$ 0	$ 2,500
Proceeds from Issuance of Loans (i.e., debt)	$ 0	$ 3,000
Repayments of Long-Term Loans	$ (750)	$ (1,250)
Net Borrowings (Repayments) of Short-Term Loans	$ 560	$ (990)
Other Financing Activities	$ 0	$ 0
Net Cash Flow from Financing Activities	$ (190)	$ 3,010
Net Increase (decrease) in Cash & Equivalents	$ 194	$ 1,389
Beginning Cash & Equivalents Balance	$ 581	$ 775
Ending Cash & Equivalents Balance	$ 775	$ 2,164

See Notes to Financial Statements

Statement of cash flows begins with information from the income statement including net profit or loss & depr./amort. expense.

Net cash flow from operating activities presents a company's ability to generate or consume cash from internal operations.

Net cash flow from investing activities is presented next. Note the significant investment made in other assets (acquisition of intangible assets).

Net cash flow from financing activities is presented last. The company raised money from both debt and equity sources.

Ending cash balance agrees to the balance sheet (a proper check and balance).

company secured "fresh" capital or cash of $5,500,000, more than enough to support the investment made in intangible assets of $5,000,000.

This is one of the reasons why the statement of cash flows is so critical to understand as it is imperative that a business not only is able to generate positive cash flows from operating activities but in addition, it must always maintain a proper capital structure to ensure investments in long-term assets do not impair its ability to support short-term operating activities. If the management of our example business failed to secure proper amounts of long-term capital (in the form of loans and stock sales), the business might have been left desperately short of cash, running into problems with being able to pay short-term obligations. This situation is often a fatal error and underscores just how important it is to maintain a healthy balance sheet and liquidity position to manage on-going business operations.

Cash versus Accrual Accounting

The first section of the statement of cash flows attempts to explain the differences between cash flows and revenue and expenses, line by line. But in my experience business managers, lenders, and investors generally cannot make heads or tails of this section of the cash flows statement. The main reason is that they don't have a clear picture of how revenue and expenses are recorded. Do you?

Exhibit 8.2 compares the company's revenue and expenses cash flows for the year with its revenue and expenses amounts for the year. The amounts for revenue and expenses are recorded on the *accrual basis*. This means that the transactions and other developments that affect the business are recorded when the economic event takes place, which is often before or after when cash actually changes hands. For example, this company, like many businesses, offers its customers credit. The sale is made today, but the business does not collect cash until a month or two later. The sale is recorded today but the corresponding cash is not recorded until later.

Notice in Exhibit 8.2 that the differences between cash flows and accrual amounts do not differ too much – except for those related to *depreciation & amortization* as well as other expenses. The cost of a long-term operating asset, such as a building or piece of heavy equipment, for example, is allocated over the operating life of the asset. Similarly, an intangible asset such as the cost of acquiring a patent may be amortized over its remaining legally protected life. The allocation of the cost of a tangible or intangible asset over the useful life of an asset is a prime example of the accrual basis of accounting. Depreciation and amortization expense for the year is not a cash outlay; cash was paid when the asset was acquired. Notice in the "Investing" section of the cash flows statement that the business made major cash outlays for

EXHIBIT 8.2 – UNAUDITED – REVENUE & EXPENSE COMPARISON, CASH VERSUS ACCRUAL

Dollar Amounts in Thousands

Revenue & Expenses: Cash Versus Accrual For the Fiscal Year Ending	Accrual Amounts 12/31/2023	Cash Amounts 12/31/2023
Sales Revenue, Net	$ 59,494	$ 58,261
Costs of Sales Revenue	$(21,766)	$(19,650)
Selling, General, & Administrative Expenses	$(25,289)	$(26,749)
Research & Development Expenses	$ (7,139)	$ (7,139)
Depreciation & Amortization Expenses	$ (1,643)	$ 0
Other Expenses	$ (2,000)	$ 0
Interest Expense	$ (407)	$ (407)
Income Tax Expense	$ (438)	$ (438)
Net Amounts	$ 813	$ 3,879

Confidential - Property of QW Example Tech, Inc.

long-term operating assets, in this case $5,000,000 in the acquisition of intangible assets.

A document comparing cash flows with accrual amounts, like the one shown in Exhibit 8.2, is a tool of explanation. It is not a financial statement (as such, I refer to it as financial information). It is not included in a financial report with the three required financial statements (i.e., income statement, balance sheet, and cash flows statement). Exhibit 8.2 should help you understand why cash flow from operating activities differs from bottom-line net income for the year. In reading an income statement, keep in mind that you are reading *accrual-based* amounts for revenue and expenses. Bottom-line net income is an accrual-based number. The net cash flow result of revenue and expenses is found in the statement of cash flows.

Financial Tasks of Business Managers

So far, I have introduced the three primary financial statements for a representative business example. These statements include its income statement for the year just ended, its balance sheet at the end of the year, and its statement of cash flows for the year. Suppose you're one of the *outside* stockholders of the business, meaning you're not involved in managing the business but you have a fair amount of money invested in the business. You just received the financial report from the business. What should you look for? Here are some things that you might study to get started.

I call your attention to stockholders' equity in the balance sheet. Its owners (one of whom is you) have invested $10,000,000 of capital in the business for which it issued capital stock shares to them. (See the *capital stock* account in Exhibit 7.1 for the FYE 12/31/23.) Furthermore, over the years the business has retained $1,924,000 of profit, which is called *retained earnings*. Taken together these two sources of owners' equity equal $11,924,000. One purpose of the balance sheet is to disclose such information about the ownership of the business entity and the sources of its equity capital.

The stockholders expect the managers of the business to earn a reasonable annual return on their $11,924,000 equity ownership in the business. In its most recent annual income statement the business reports $813,000 bottom-line profit, or net income. This profit equals 6.8% on the company's year-end stockholders' equity, a result that may come under scrutiny given the relatively low return. The stockholders, as well as the company's managers and its lenders, want to know more than just bottom-line profit.

They want to see the whole picture of how profit is earned. Therefore, the income statement reports totals for revenue and expenses for the period as well as bottom-line net income.

The ability of managers to make sales and to control expenses, and thereby earn profit, is summarized in the income statement. Business investors and lenders pay particular attention to the profit yield from revenue. Earning profit is essential for survival and it is the business manager's most important financial imperative. But the bottom line is not the end of the manager's job – not by a long shot!

To earn profit and stay out of trouble, managers must control the *financial condition* of the business. This means, among other things, keeping assets and liabilities within appropriate limits and proportions relative to each other and relative to the sales revenue and expenses of the business. Managers must prevent cash shortages that would cause the business to default on its liabilities when they come due, or not be able to meet its payroll on time.

Business managers really have a three-fold financial task: 1) earning enough profit, 2) controlling the company's assets and liabilities, and 3) generating cash flows. For all businesses, regardless of size, a financial statement is prepared for each financial imperative – one for profit performance (the income statement), one for financial condition (the balance sheet), and the statement of cash flows.

Earning adequate profit by itself does not guarantee survival and good cash flow. A business manager cannot fully manage profit without also managing the assets and liabilities of sales revenue and expenses. In our business example, the changes in these assets and liabilities cause cash flow to be higher than the profit for the year. In other situations, the changes can cause cash flow from profit to be lower – perhaps much lower – than profit for the period (and can cause negative cash flow in extreme situations).

Business managers use their income statements to evaluate profit performance and to ask a raft of profit-oriented questions. Did sales revenue meet the goals and objectives for the period? Why did sales revenue increase compared with last period? Which expenses increased more or less than they should have? And there are many more such questions. These profit analysis questions are absolutely essential. But the manager can't stop at the end of these questions.

Beyond profit analysis, business managers should move on to financial condition analysis and cash flows analysis. In large business corporations, the responsibility for financial condition and cash flow is separated from profit responsibility. The chief financial officer (CFO) of the company is responsible for financial condition and cash flow. The chief executive officer (CEO) and board of directors oversee the CFO. They need to see the big picture, which includes all three financial aspects of the business – profit, financial condition, and cash flow.

In smaller businesses the president or the owner/manager is directly involved in controlling financial condition and cash flow. There's no one to delegate these responsibilities to, although consultants and advisors can be hired for advice.

The Statement of Cash Flows for Internal Consumers

In Chapters 6 and 7, I presented Exhibits 6.2 and 7.2 which provided insight on how an internal income statement and balance sheet (for our example company) may be prepared for internal consumers such as executives and management. The key concepts discussed when providing internal financial statements focused on 1) offering additional levels of detail and financial analyses on which to evaluate the company's financial performance and condition and 2) clearly noting that the added level of detail was confidential in nature (suitable for internal consumers only). You might expect the same approach when preparing a statement of cash flows for internal consumers but spoiler alert, I'm going to move in the opposite direction as presented in Exhibit 8.3.

You might be taken aback by the format presented in Exhibit 8.3 as it compresses the standard statement of cash flows and simplifies the format. The reason should be relatively easy to understand. As previously explained, the statement of cash flows is often the most difficult of the big three financial statements to understand so when presenting cash flows to internal consumers (that frequently are not accounting or finance experts), it sometimes helps to remember the acronym KISS (keep it simple stupid).

In Exhibit 8.3, I've simplified the statement of cash flows into a compressed and easy to understand sources and uses of cash that focuses on the "big fish." That is, the largest financial transactions that really move the needle with cash flows. In our simplified sources and uses of cash presented in Exhibit 8.3, the big fish for the FYE 12/31/23 are as follows:

- First, our example company generated EBITDA (remember this stands for earnings before interest, taxes, depreciation, and amortization) of approximately $5,300,000.

- Second, our example company secured external financing (i.e., cash) of $5,500,000 from selling company stock of $2,500,000 and securing a new loan for $3,000,000.

- In total, our example company generated total sources of cash, from internal and external sources, of approximately $10,800,000. Not too shabby for a company this size.

- Now, how did our example company use this cash? Well to start, it purchased $5,500,000 of capital assets (both tangible and intangible assets) which represents approximately 51% of the total sources of cash generated of $10,800,000. Definitely a big chunk of change.

- Moving on, our example company remitted total debt service payments (representing total loan principal and interest payments) of $2,647,000 representing roughly 24.5% of the total sources of cash, something management needs to be aware of in terms of keeping relationships with the lenders on good terms.

- Finally, our example company used cash for other purposes including dividends, income taxes, and consumed cash in the components of networking to support continued growth

EXHIBIT 8.3—SOURCES & USES OF FUNDS

Unaudited – Prepared by Company Management

Sources & Uses of Cash Summary For the Fiscal Years Ending	12/31/2022	% of Total	12/31/2023	% of Total
Sources of Cash:				
Operating Income	$ 457,371		$ 3,657,692	
Add Back: Depreciation & Amortization Expense	$ 1,571,429		$ 1,642,857	
Adjusted EBITDA	$ 2,028,800	78.37%	$ 5,300,550	49.08%
Sale of Company Equity	$ 0	0.00%	$ 2,500,000	23.15%
Proceeds from Issuance of New Debt	$ 560,000	21.63%	$ 3,000,000	27.78%
Other	$ 0	0.00%	$ 0	0.00%
Total Sources of Cash	$ 2,588,800	100.00%	$ 10,800,550	100.00%
Uses of Cash:				
Investment in Capital Assets	$ (250,000)	-9.66%	$ (5,500,000)	-50.92%
Total Debt Service Payments (Principal & Interest)	$ (1,089,000)	-42.07%	$ (2,647,000)	-24.51%
Net Change in Working Capital (adj. for inventory)	$ (1,015,111)	-39.21%	$ (576,963)	-5.34%
Income Tax Expense & Other	$ (41,000)	-1.58%	$ (438,000)	-4.06%
Dividends & Distributions	$ 0	0.00%	$ (250,000)	-2.31%
Other	$ 0	0.00%	$ 0	0.00%
Total Uses of Cash	$ (2,395,111)	-92.52%	$ (9,411,963)	-87.14%
Net Change in Cash	$ 193,689	7.48%	$ 1,388,586	12.86%

Confidential - Property of QW Example Tech., Inc.

Notice the simplicity of the sources and uses of cash summary. This format is designed to remove the "noise" associated with changes in assets and liabilities that are smaller or immaterial and rather focus on the "big fish."

(mainly as the result of accounts receivables increasing as a result of sales revenue increasing).

- After all is said and done, the company was able to increase its cash balance by roughly $1,389,000 during the year representing approximately 13% of the total sources of cash. Is this reasonable? Well, that is up to the management team to determine. The more important question is whether the available cash is adequate to support our example company's growth plans for the coming years and if not, does our example company need to raise additional capital to "plug" its cash needs. I'll dive into this topic in Chapters 13 and 14.

The reason I've offered this presentation format for reporting sources and uses of cash is based on almost 40 years of hands-on financial and accounting consulting experience, some of which has been very painful. In a nutshell, company executives and management teams often need to have financial information broken down into easier to digest and understand bite-size pieces of data to help with their comprehension. Rather than prepare a financial report that might be deemed to be confusing, complex, and provide too much detail (enabling the internal consumer to get lost in the forest), simplicity was chosen in this situation to summarize the three key sources of cash (internal earnings, stock sales, and new loans) and three primary uses of cash (capital investments, debt service, and other). So there it is, easier to read and understand for non-accounting and financial types and a reminder of the all-important lesson I discussed in Chapter 2 of this book, know your audience!

9

CONNECTING THE FINANCIAL STATEMENT DOTS

For those of you that have been loyal customers over the years and who have read *How to Read a Financial Report* (now in its 10th edition), yes, the material presented in this chapter should look very familiar and hopefully you will find the representation of the concepts and exhibits to be a very useful refresher course. For those of you starting with this book and who have not been introduced to how the big three financial statements are connected, I would advise you to focus significant attention on the concepts and exhibits presented, as while it's one thing to understand each of the big three financial statements independently (covered in Chapters 6 through 8), seeing how the financial statements are actually connected (supported by Exhibits 9.1 and 9.2) should be enlightening.

I cannot emphasize how important it is to have a clear understanding of how financial information and financial statements are connected or for lack of a better term, intertwined, as this should greatly assist you when drafting or producing a financial report. As an example, I provide you with this simple case study to chew on.

You're a division manager tasked with producing a summary business plan, including a financial forecast model for a new division that is being spun out, and will be working with members of the finance and accounting team. Not only has senior management assigned you the responsibility of preparing a division level P&L (i.e., another term for an income statement), but they want to understand what the impact will be on the company's assets, liabilities, and how you plan on financing the new vision (i.e., how much capital will be needed and where it will come from).

This chapter summarizes how financial transactions that originate from the income statement directly connect to the balance sheet and statement of cash flows. Chapters 6, 7, and 8 introduced the income statement, the balance sheet, and the statement of cash flows independently for our business example, as you would see these three primary financial statements in a financial report. Each statement stands alone, by itself, on a separate page in the financial report. Each statement is presented like a tub standing on its own feet. The connections between the three financial statements are not made explicit. There is no clear trail of the crossover effects between the three financial statements. But, in fact, there are dual effects – specifically, what happens in one statement also happens in another financial statement.

In this chapter I explain how the financial statements interrelate at a summary level, which I then drill further into in Part Two of this book – Financial Statement Connections structured to follow a balance sheet and income statement from top to bottom as follows.

I will first focus on the primary connections between sales revenue and expenses (from the income statement) and the asset and liabilities section of the balance sheet (Exhibit 9.1). Then, I will complete our discussion on financial statement connections by reconciling cash, the income statement, and the balance sheet and tie it all together with connecting the cash flow dots (Exhibit 9.2).

EXHIBIT 9.1—CONNECTING ANNUAL INCOME STATEMENT WITH YEAR-END BALANCE SHEET
Dollar Amounts in Thousands

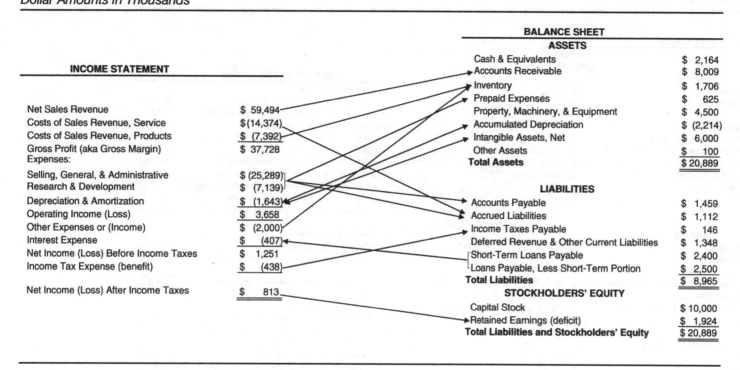

BALANCE SHEET

ASSETS

Cash & Equivalents	$ 2,164
Accounts Receivable	$ 8,009
Inventory	$ 1,706
Prepaid Expenses	$ 625
Property, Machinery, & Equipment	$ 4,500
Accumulated Depreciation	$ (2,214)
Intangible Assets, Net	$ 6,000
Other Assets	$ 100
Total Assets	**$ 20,889**

LIABILITIES

Accounts Payable	$ 1,459
Accrued Liabilities	$ 1,112
Income Taxes Payable	$ 146
Deferred Revenue & Other Current Liabilities	$ 1,348
Short-Term Loans Payable	$ 2,400
Loans Payable, Less Short-Term Portion	$ 2,500
Total Liabilities	**$ 8,965**

STOCKHOLDERS' EQUITY

Capital Stock	$ 10,000
Retained Earnings (deficit)	$ 1,924
Total Liabilities and Stockholders' Equity	**$ 20,889**

INCOME STATEMENT

Net Sales Revenue	$ 59,494
Costs of Sales Revenue, Service	$(14,374)
Costs of Sales Revenue, Products	$ (7,392)
Gross Profit (aka Gross Margin)	$ 37,728
Expenses:	
Selling, General, & Administrative	$ (25,289)
Research & Development	$ (7,139)
Depreciation & Amortization	$ (1,643)
Operating Income (Loss)	$ 3,658
Other Expenses or (Income)	$ (2,000)
Interest Expense	$ (407)
Net Income (Loss) Before Income Taxes	$ 1,251
Income Tax Expense (benefit)	$ (438)
Net Income (Loss) After Income Taxes	$ 813

EXHIBIT 9.2—CONNECTING BALANCE SHEET CHANGES WITH STATEMENT OF CASH FLOWS
Dollar Amounts in Thousands

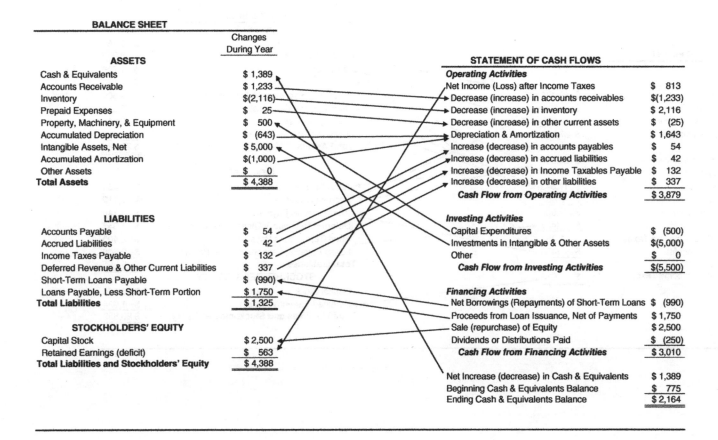

BALANCE SHEET

	Changes During Year
ASSETS	
Cash & Equivalents	$ 1,389
Accounts Receivable	$ 1,233
Inventory	$(2,116)
Prepaid Expenses	$ 25
Property, Machinery, & Equipment	$ 500
Accumulated Depreciation	$ (643)
Intangible Assets, Net	$ 5,000
Accumulated Amortization	$(1,000)
Other Assets	$ 0
Total Assets	$ 4,388
LIABILITIES	
Accounts Payable	$ 54
Accrued Liabilities	$ 42
Income Taxes Payable	$ 132
Deferred Revenue & Other Current Liabilities	$ 337
Short-Term Loans Payable	$ (990)
Loans Payable, Less Short-Term Portion	$ 1,750
Total Liabilities	$ 1,325
STOCKHOLDERS' EQUITY	
Capital Stock	$ 2,500
Retained Earnings (deficit)	$ 563
Total Liabilities and Stockholders' Equity	$ 4,388

STATEMENT OF CASH FLOWS

Operating Activities	
Net Income (Loss) after Income Taxes	$ 813
Decrease (increase) in accounts receivables	$(1,233)
Decrease (increase) in inventory	$ 2,116
Decrease (increase) in other current assets	$ (25)
Depreciation & Amortization	$ 1,643
Increase (decrease) in accounts payables	$ 54
Increase (decrease) in accrued liabilities	$ 42
Increase (decrease) in Income Taxables Payable	$ 132
Increase (decrease) in other liabilities	$ 337
Cash Flow from Operating Activities	$ 3,879
Investing Activities	
Capital Expenditures	$ (500)
Investments in Intangible & Other Assets	$(5,000)
Other	$ 0
Cash Flow from Investing Activities	$(5,500)
Financing Activities	
Net Borrowings (Repayments) of Short-Term Loans	$ (990)
Proceeds from Loan Issuance, Net of Payments	$ 1,750
Sale (repurchase) of Equity	$ 2,500
Dividends or Distributions Paid	$ (250)
Cash Flow from Financing Activities	$ 3,010
Net Increase (decrease) in Cash & Equivalents	$ 1,389
Beginning Cash & Equivalents Balance	$ 775
Ending Cash & Equivalents Balance	$ 2,164

One Problem in Financial Reporting

When preparing a financial report, accountants assume that the readers understand the interactions and mutual dependencies among the financial statements that constitute the core of the financial report. Accountants also assume that readers make use of these connections in analyzing the financial affairs of the business. Accountants assume a lot, don't they? Financial report readers can easily miss the vital interplay among the income statement, balance sheet, and statement of cash flows.

Exhibit 9.1 lays out the connections between the income statement and the balance sheet. This exhibit shows the lines of connection between sales revenue and expenses and their corresponding assets and liabilities. Exhibit 9.2 shows the connections between the changes during the year in the balance sheet accounts and the statement of cash flows. The three financial statements fit together like tongue-in-groove woodwork. The income statement, balance sheet, and cash flows statement interlock with one another.

Looking at Exhibit 9.1 closer, some connections between the income statement and balance sheet should be relatively easy to understand. For example, when a company generates sales revenue and extends credit to a customer, the direct connection that occurs is a sale recorded along with an account receivable (representing the amount the customer has agreed to pay within a set time period such as 30 days). Likewise, when products from inventory are sold, a cost of sales revenue for products is realized along with a reduction to inventory (to account for the purchase of product by a customer).

Other connections may take more of an effort to understand and conceptualize. Here, I direct you to selling, general, and administrative expenses which is connected to accounts payable and accrued liabilities payable. An example here would be for marketing expense as an advertising agency may bill the customer for advertisements run during a prior period but which has offered our example company 60 days to pay the obligation. When implementing accrual-based accounting, the expense for the advertising is recorded in the proper period (increasing an expense) but not paid for until two months later. As such, an accounts payable for the amount is recorded, which increases the balance in this account.

The connections between the income statement and balance sheet are numerous, which I explain in far more detail in our book *How to Read a Financial Report*, 10th edition. For the purposes of this book, my goal is to provide a preliminary introduction to the concept of how the big three financial statements are connected and why it is important to understand these connections when writing a financial report. The better you understand financial statement connections, the more effective you will be when writing and communicating a financial report.

Now, let us turn our attention to the connections between the balance sheet and statement of cash flows (presented in Exhibit 9.2).

To start, please note that the balance sheet information presents the changes in the assets, liabilities, and stockholders' equity

EXHIBIT 9.3—CALCULATING CHANGE IN BALANCE SHEET ACCOUNTS BETWEEN TWO YEARS

Dollar Amounts in Thousands

BALANCE SHEET

	Balance at 12/31/2022	Balance at 12/31/2023	Change
ASSETS			
Cash & Equivalents	$ 775	$ 2,164	$ 1,389
Accounts Receivable	$ 6,776	$ 8,009	$ 1,233
Inventory	$ 3,822	$ 1,706	$(2,116)
Prepaid Expenses	$ 600	$ 625	$ 25
Property, Machinery, & Equipment	$ 4,000	$ 4,500	$ 500
Accumulated Depreciation	$ (1,571)	$(2,214)	$ (643)
Intangible Assets, Net	$ 5,000	$10,000	$ 5,000
Accumulated Amortization	$ (3,000)	$ (4,000)	$(1,000)
Other Assets	$ 100	$ 100	$ 0
Total Assets	$16,502	$20,889	$ 4,388
LIABILITIES			
Accounts Payable	$ 1,405	$ 1,459	$ 54
Accrued Liabilities	$ 1,070	$ 1,112	$ 42
Income Taxes Payable	$ 14	$ 146	$ 132
Deferred Revenue & Other Current Liabilities	$ 1,011	$ 1,348	$ 337
Short-Term Loans Payable	$ 3,390	$ 2,400	$ (990)
Loans Payable, Less Short-Term Portion	$ 750	$ 2,500	$ 1,750
Total Liabilities	$ 7,640	$ 8,965	$ 1,325
STOCKHOLDERS' EQUITY			
Capital Stock	$ 7,500	$10,000	$ 2,500
Retained Earnings (deficit)	$ 1,362	$ 1,924	$ 563
Total Liabilities and Stockholders' Equity	$16,502	$20,889	$ 4,388

between the FYE 12/31/22 and the FYE 12/31/23. If you need to double check these figures, please refer to Exhibit 9.3 for ease of reference.

Here, looking at Exhibit 9.2 in more depth the connections are not quite as clear as the income statement to the balance sheet but just as important, as discussed with a couple examples. First, you will notice that accounts receivables increased by $1,233,000 between the years (per the balance sheet) but represents a negative connection on the cash flow statement. The reason for this is simple in that when accounts receivables increase, this represents cash owed from the customers that will be received at a later date (maybe 60 days down the road). Thus, when accounts receivables increase, the eventual cash received is deferred until a later date meaning that the cash was not received in the period referenced. You will also notice that an increase to cash is present for depreciation and amortization expense of $1,643,000, which is offset by a negative change in accumulated depreciation and amortization of the same amount. Remember here that depreciation and amortization expense do not represent actual cash expenses but rather an estimate of the amount of the associated assets that was consumed or used during the period. The cash used to purchase these assets happened long ago but per accounting rules, the asset values need to be expensed over a period of time as the assets are used and consumed. This creates an unusual accounting event where an expense is incurred yet no cash is involved.

Moving down a bit further, you can see where the company's capital stock increased during the year by $2,500,000 via the sale of additional stock to investors. Connecting this to the statement of cash flows, you can see the same figure as an increase or source of cash in the financing section of the statement. Finally, you will see how everything ties together as the net increase in cash during the year of $1,389,000 per the statement of cash flows equals exactly the increase in cash per the balance sheet. And this represents the beauty of the cash flow statement as it in effect acts as the glue that ties the financial statements together and answers the all-important question as to why the net income earned by our example company of $813,000 does not equal the net increase in cash during the year of $1,389,000.

Please keep in mind that Exhibits 9.1 and 9.2 are tools of explanation (and thus are reference to financial information). Financial reports do not include such exhibits with lines of connection. My purpose is to show you how the financial statements in a financial report –although shown separately – are in fact interdependent. I would encourage you to read *How to Read a Financial Report*, 10th edition if you would like to dive into more detailed discussions on the connections presented in this chapter as the entire Part Two of this book has been dedicated to this subject.

Connecting the Dots

Note that in Exhibits 9.1 and 9.2 the balance sheet is presented in the *vertical*, or portrait, format, also called the *report form* – assets on top, and liabilities and stockholders' equity below. To save space I do not include subtotals for current assets, current liabilities, and stockholders' equity in the balance sheet. (You might quickly compare the balance sheet in Exhibit 9.1 with the balance sheet example in Exhibit 7.1.) Further, please note that in Exhibit 9.1, the lines of connection are to the *ending balances* of the assets and liabilities.

Exhibit 9.2 shows the *changes* in the balance sheet accounts during the year. These changes go to or come from the statement of cash flows. The first section of the statement uses the changes in the assets and liabilities of recording revenue and expenses to reconcile net income and *cash flow from operating activities*. This important cash flow number is the net increase or decrease in cash that is attributable to the profit-making (operating) activities of the business.

The cash increase from the company's profit-making activities for the year is $3,879,000 (see Exhibit 9.2), which compared with its $813,000 net income is a fairly significant difference. In this particular example, the company's cash flow from profit is $3,066,000 higher than its profit for the year. (In Chapter 8, I explain how the changes in assets and liabilities caused by revenue and expenses determine the difference between cash flow and profit.)

The other, or *nonoperating*, cash flows of the business during the year are reported in the "Investing" and "Financing" sections of the statement of cash flows. See Exhibit 9.2 again. The business made key decisions during the year that required major outlays of cash, and it secured additional cash during the year from its lenders and stockholders. Notice that the lines of connection for these cash flow decisions go from the cash flow sources and uses to their respective assets, liabilities, and stockholders' equity.

You really can't swallow all the information in Exhibits 9.1 and 9.2 in one gulp. You have to drink one sip at a time. The exhibits serve as road maps that I refer to frequently throughout this book – so that we don't lose sight of the big picture as we travel down the particular highways of connection between the financial statements.

Before moving on, I should repeat that financial statements are not presented with lines of connection as shown in Exhibits 9.1 and 9.2. You never see tether lines like this between the financial statements. As I have already mentioned above, accountants assume that the financial statement readers mentally fill in the connections that are shown in Exhibits 9.1 and 9.2. Accountants assume too much, in my opinion. It would be helpful if a financial report included reminders of the connections between the three financial statements.

In my experience, business managers and executives, and for that matter even some certified public accountants (CPAs), do not recognize the connecting links among the financial statements that I show in Exhibit 9.1 and Exhibit 9.2. Over the years, I have corresponded with many readers who have requested the Microsoft Excel workbook file of the exhibits in this book. (See the Preface for how to request this via email.) Over and over, they mention one point – the value of seeing the connections among the financial statements.

10

THE SIGNIFICANCE
OF FINANCIAL FORECASTS

All companies, regardless of their size, ownership structure, industry in which they operate, public or private, need to undertake some form of periodic planning to effectively manage their business interests. Hopefully, this should come as absolutely no surprise to you, but I must admit I'm absolutely dumbfounded by the number of companies that either don't take the business planning process seriously or worse yet, don't plan at all (other than making the generic statement of let's improve our operating results by 10% this year, and that's it). The reason this chapter is being incorporated into the book is to not just emphasize how important the business planning process is, but that you simply cannot produce CART financial reports without having critical financial information that is generated in financial forecasts.

The Importance of Business Forecast Models

The business planning process includes numerous elements ranging from assessing current market conditions to understanding the macroeconomic environment to evaluating personnel resources to preparing budgets, forecasts, and/or projections. This chapter focuses on one of the most critical elements of the planning process – preparing a forecast. For the balance of this chapter, the term *forecasts* will be used for consistency purposes, but it should be noted that businesses often utilize other terms including *budgets* or *budgeting*, projections, and proformas (which basically all mean the same thing). I prefer to use the term forecasts as it is broader in scope and helps drive home a key concept related to building *top-down* forecast models (which I cover in this chapter).

Before I delve too deeply into the forecasting process, I make a quick attempt to properly define a forecast. Forecasts *are not* based on the concept of "How much can I spend in my division this year?" Rather, forecasts are more comprehensive in nature and are designed to capture all relevant and critical financial data, including revenue levels, costs of sales revenue, operating expenses, fixed asset expenditures, capital requirements, and the like. All too often, forecasts are associated with expense levels and management, which represent just one element of the entire forecasts.

Further, the forecasting process does not represent a chicken-and-egg riddle. From a financial perspective, the preparation of forecasts represents the end result of the entire planning process. Hence, you must first accumulate the necessary data and information on which to build a forecasting model prior to producing projected financial information (for an entire company or a specific division). There is no point in preparing a forecast that does not capture the real economic structure and viability of an entire entity or operating division.

I would also like to drive home once again the importance of preparing complete financial information within the financial forecasts (which is essential to preparing quality financial reports). All too often, companies prepare financial forecasts focused on just the income statement and downplay the importance of the balance sheet and statement of cash flows (which may get put on the back burner). The importance of preparing complete financial forecasts will be on full display in this chapter, as I include forecasts for both the balance sheet and statement of cash flows.

The bottom line with forecasting (and the entire planning process) is that without having clearly identified business financial and performance objectives, the business is operating blind. Or, put simply, it would be like flying a plane without having a destination. The need for having clearly identified benchmarks and a roadmap to reach the benchmarks is essential for every business, regardless of size, shape, or form, as often the most important question of all comes down to this: "How am I doing against the plan?"

Managing the Forecasting Process

Years ago, businesses tended to manage the forecasting process on an annual or maybe semiannual basis. The standard cycle started toward the end of each current FYE (maybe 30 to 90 days prior) as management would get the annual "budgeting" process fired up to plan for the upcoming year. I have no doubt that this annual forecasting process still occurs and is widely used but based on the economic realities of today's capitalist markets, the forecasting process must be managed as a living, breathing function that should be constantly updated as frequently as critical business information emerges, evolves, and/or changes. This does not mean that preparing updated forecasts needs to be completed weekly (which would be overkill), but trust me when I say that developing forecasting models that have the flexibility to always be rolled forward to look out 12 to 24 months from the end of any desired reporting period is now standard practice. This is not a nice-to-have, but is now a must-have.

Understanding that the forecasting process represents a living, breathing function that requires proactive management on a monthly basis, I now turn our attention to some basic concepts to assist with preparing forecasts.

◆ *Initial Forecast, New Business:* For businesses or professionals that have already prepared prior-year forecasts, this bullet point may not be all that relevant. For first-timers preparing a forecast for a new business, you will want to become familiar with three acronyms: BOTE, WAG, and SWAG. These stand for back of the envelope, wild-ass guess, and scientific wild-ass guess. You might notice a little humor when referring to these acronyms, but I am being quite serious. The forecasting process needs to start somewhere and often resides with executive management team members discussing a business idea or opportunity, jotting down some thoughts and basic numbers on the back of a napkin or envelope. This may then evolve into a wild-ass guess where an actual (albeit quite simple) preliminary forecast is prepared using a standard technology tool such as Microsoft Excel. Then, as additional information is obtained and incorporated into the forecast model, it transforms into a scientific wild-ass guess (where key data points and assumptions can be documented and defended). You would be amazed at how many businesses and forecasts get started with such a simple initial step, but you would be equally amazed at how quickly the forecast model evolves into a very sophisticated management tool.

◆ *Initial Forecast, Existing Business:* To start, you should have a solid understanding of your company's historical financial information and operating results. This history may stretch back three months, one year, five years, or longer, but the key concept is that having sound internal financial information represents an excellent place to start. However, remember that while the financial operating history of a company may provide a foundation on which to prepare a forecast, it by no means is an accurate or guaranteed predictor of future operating results. If the economic environment of a business has changed, then benchmarking off other similar businesses represents an effective means to build a reliable forecast.

- *Gather Reliable Data:* The availability of quality market, operational, and accounting/financial data represents the basis of the forecast. A good deal of this data often comes from internal sources. For example, when a sales region is preparing a budget for the upcoming year, the sales manager may survey the direct sales representatives on what they feel their customers will demand in terms of products and services in the coming year. With this information, you can determine sales volumes, personnel levels, wage rates, commission plans, and so on. While internal information is of value, it represents only half the battle because external information and data are just as critical to accumulate. Having access to quality and reliable external third-party information is essential to the overall business planning process and the production of reliable forecasts. Market forces and trends may be occurring that can impact your business over the next 24 months (that may not be reflected in the previous year's operating results).

- *Involve Key Team Members:* The forecasting process represents a critical function in most companies' accounting and financial department and rightfully so, as these are the people who understand the numbers the best. Although the financial and accounting types produce the final budget, they rely on data that comes from numerous parties such as marketing, manufacturing, and sales. You must ensure that all key management team members are involved in the forecasting process, covering all critical business functions, to produce a reliable projection. Just as you would not have a regional sales manager prepare a fixed asset schedule (tracking all asset additions, disposals, and depreciation expense), you would not have your accountant estimate sales volumes by product line during the holiday season (and what prices the products may fetch). Critical business data comes from numerous parties, all of which must be included in the forecasting process to produce the most reliable information possible.

- *Consistency and Completeness:* The financial forecasts prepared should be both complete and consistent to maximize their value. When I reference complete, I mean that all relevant financial information should be presented in the forecasts to ensure that the target audience has the proper output and data on which to base economic decisions. Consistency implies that the financial forecasts are prepared in a like format to the periodic financial information provided to the target audience (including all critical financial data points, KPIs, etc.). There is no benefit to preparing financial forecasts in a format that is different than the periodic internal financial information produced and delivered to the management team (you can imagine the confusion that would ensue). Financial forecast models should be designed to be in sync with critical reporting and utilize the same format for ease of understanding and decision-making.

- *Timing and Presentation:* As previously mentioned, the annual budgeting process is a thing of the past. While an annual forecast can be produced just prior to the beginning of a new FYE to start the process, management should be prepared, on at least a quarterly basis and for more fluid, high-paced businesses, monthly, to revise and update forecasts as business conditions change. Presentation-wise, generally the nearer the term covered by the forecasts the more detailed the information and frequency of reporting periods being prepared. If you are preparing a forecast for the coming fiscal year, the monthly financial information should be provided, but if you are looking out three to five years, then providing quarterly financial information should suffice (for years three through five).

If you did not notice, the concept of CART is alive and well and fully embedded in best-in-class business planning and forecasting functions. Companies need to develop and utilize financial forecasting models that are highly flexible and easily adaptable, to adjust to rapidly changing business conditions. In the following section, I provide additional insight on how you can develop more powerful forecasts.

Increasing the Power and Value of Your Forecast

I start this section noting that the list of concepts, strategies, and tools overviewed here are not meant to be all-inclusive but rather have been selected to assist with helping make financial forecasts even more useful and powerful, starting with *SWOT*. This acronym stands for strengths, weaknesses, opportunities, and threats and is a business management assessment tool designed to assist the company's management team with preparing a qualitative assessment of the business, helping to keep all parties focused on key issues. The SWOT analysis is often incorporated into a company's planning function (a topic touched on in Chapter 13) but can also be extremely helpful with preparing financial forecasts.

A SWOT analysis is usually broken down into a matrix of four segments. Two of the segments are geared toward positive attributes – strengths and opportunities – and two are geared toward negative attributes – weaknesses and threats. In addition, the analysis differentiates between internal company source attributes and external, or outside of the company, source attributes. Generally, the SWOT analysis is prepared by senior management team members to ensure that critical conditions are communicated to management for inclusion in the budget. If used correctly, a SWOT analysis not only can provide invaluable information to support the forecasting process but, more importantly, can help identify what type of management you have in place. The responses you receive provide invaluable information as to whether the party completing the SWOT analysis is nothing more than a front-line manager (a captain needing direction) or a bona fide businessperson (the colonel leading the charge).

Next up, I discuss two different forecasting strategies or approaches used by most businesses: *top-down* versus *bottom-up*. *Top-down* forecasting is exactly how it sounds (i.e., the top line for a company, which is sales), as it starts with projecting critical sales revenue data, including sales unit volumes (by all significant product lines or SKUs), pricing by product, any potential sales discounts, seasonality in sales, customer contact to sales timing relationships, and similar data. Once this information is incorporated into the forecast model, the balance of the forecast model, including cost of sales, direct operating expenses, business overhead expenses, and other expenses or income (for the income statement), as well as all critical balance sheet assumptions, are incorporated by utilizing relationships or correlations rather than inputting hard data and information. For example, using a top-down forecasting model, the number of sales representatives required and any commissions earned would be determined based on X number of product sales at Y price. A relationship for the business might be established that states for every 250,000 units of products sold, one senior sales rep is required and would earn a commission of 5% on the sales.

Using a bottom-up approach is quite different as, although certain key correlations or relationships may be incorporated into the forecast model, this approach tends to be much more detailed and includes a large number of hard or firm data points and assumptions being built into the forecast model. For example, in a top-down approach, an expense estimate of $1,000 per month per sales rep may be input to capture all travel, lodging, meals, and entertainment-related costs. In other words, estimated sales revenue drives the number of sales reps, which drives the monthly TLM&E expense. In a bottom-up approach, an estimate of each type of expense is prepared on a line-by-line basis that then rolls up into a subtotal. Further, sales revenue may be driven by how many sales reps are working or employed, so if 10 sales reps are working any given month and, on average, each sales rep should be able to generate $250,000 of sales, total sales for the month would be forecast at $2.5 million.

Quite often, companies use a hybrid of these two approaches, as almost all financial forecast models utilize some type of correlation and relationship assumptions as well as incorporate hard data for various overhead or fixed costs. The bottom-up approach tends to be better suited for well-established, predictable business models that have a large amount of historical data and operational stability. It also tends to be detailed and static but definitely has value within the right business framework, such as when detailed or specific management reporting is required for cost analysis of a bill of material or expense control is a high priority (to track all expenses at a line-item level).

The top-down approach tends to be better suited for newer businesses or companies operating in rapidly changing environments where you need to understand important financial results quickly under different or "what-if" operating scenarios (see the next topic). Top-down forecasting approaches are focused on understanding financial correlations and relationships at a macro level to assist the management team in evaluating multiple operating scenarios with potentially vastly different outcomes. To be quite honest, most properly structured top-down forecasting models end up relying on a select few key business drivers or assumptions that really are "make or break" for the company

in terms of producing profitable results. Senior-level management members are usually so well versed in understanding their businesses that once as few as a half dozen assumptions and data inputs that drive sales are known, the senior management team members can usually accurately and quickly calculate what the net profit or loss will be. This is why top-down forecasting models are utilized more frequently at the strategic business planning level (i.e., the macro level of big picture) whereas bottom-up forecasting models are utilized actively at the business tactical and implementation level. Under either approach, the goal is to make it easy for team members to participate in the forecasting process and utilize the financial information to assist with improving operating results.

One concept that is strongly associated with the top-down forecasting approach is the *what-if* analysis. It should be obvious that the purpose of the what-if analysis is just like it sounds – that is, what will the results or impact be if this situation or set of events occurs? For example, if a company has to implement a significant product price reduction to match the competition, a what-if analysis will help it quickly calculate and decipher the potential impact on its operating results and associated cash flows. The reason the what-if analysis is easier to use with a top-down forecast approach is that the goal of this analysis tool is to focus on the macro-level impact (to a business) from a potential material change in key business operating metrics. Thus, by being able to change 6 to 12 key variables or forecast assumptions, a management team can quickly assess the impact on the business (which is one of the key strengths of the top-down forecasting approach). This is not to say that what-if analyses cannot be generated using a bottom-up forecasting approach, but when focusing on macro-level company operating results, starting at the top with sales revenue and watching the waterfall impact on overall operations is a particularly useful and powerful analysis for senior management.

I would also like to mention that what-if analyses are extremely helpful when preparing multiple versions of the financial forecasts, which almost all companies do (or should do). It is common practice for companies to produce high, medium, and low versions of the financial forecasts to assist with business planning and evaluate different operating scenarios. Having this information available well in advance will allow a business to build different plans to ensure that financial performance targets are achieved. For example, if sales revenue is trending down, management can develop a plan that identifies expenses to cut and by how much and when. Conversely, if the company is having a strong year, this may dictate that additional capital may be needed to support the unanticipated growth (again, allowing management to identify when, what, and how much will be needed).

As you will see in Exhibits 10.1 through 10.3, the forecast operating results from our high, medium, and low scenarios are vastly different and indicate that management will need to have proactive plans in place to address potential underperformance issues. By the way, another version of the forecast model that companies have incorporated into their planning process is the "Arm" (which stands for Armageddon) version – or when all hell breaks loose. Companies generally keep a tight lid on this version, as whether you are dealing with internal or external parties, nobody wants to entice unwarranted panic.

Finally, I close this section by discussing the value and benefits of employing *rolling forecasts* (e.g., 12 months, 18 months, or longer). The purpose of utilizing rolling forecasts is to always have at least one year's visibility (and preferably longer) on your business's operating performance at any point in time. For example, if a business uses a standard FYE of 12/31/23, a 12-month rolling forecast model updated at, let me say, the third quarter ending 9/30/23 would provide visibility for the 12-month period of 10/1/23 through 9/30/24. After each month, the forecast model is "rolled" forward as part of the company's ongoing planning process to provide executive management with the proper business management visibility.

Companies often utilize rolling forecasts to assist with managing their business interests as summarized in the following two examples:

1. *Recast Operating Results:* In our example above, a company could combine the actual operating results for the nine months of operations ending 9/30/23 with the updated three months of forecast operating results for the period of 10/1/23 through 12/31/23 to produce recast operating results for the FYE 12/31/23. I use the term *recast* in the context of combining actual operating results with updated forecast operating results to produce revised or recast operating results for a specific time period. Companies often need to provide both internal and external parties with updated outlooks on a periodic basis and will utilize recast operating results to achieve this objective.

2. *Operational Pivots:* Companies that may experience an unexpected shock to their operations (e.g., COVID-19 shutdowns in March of 2020) can utilize rolling forecasts to reset operating targets and objectives for internal management planning purposes. For example, employee commission or bonus plans can be adjusted (based on a revised 12-month outlook) to reflect a new operating norm that was not anticipated. This allows the company to proactively manage difficult environments as well as effectively communicate with the employee base.

Other examples and benefits of utilizing rolling forecasts could be presented but the primary purpose remains the same: to provide forward-looking visibility, over the appropriate time period, that is clear, concise, and complete. This forecasting strategy can prove to be invaluable for companies operating in dynamic, rapidly changing, or unstable business environments, which today is now more important than ever before.

Forecast Examples

Thus far in this chapter I have covered the topic of forecasts from a conceptual perspective, so now I will offer examples of financial forecasts for our example company. Each exhibit will present high, medium, and low case forecasts, with Exhibit 10.1 presenting the income statement, Exhibit 10.2 presenting the balance sheet, and Exhibit 10.3 presenting the statement of cash flows. I call out a couple of key issues in each exhibit to help you understand the importance of preparing multiple forecast versions.

Exhibit 10.1 presents the income statement. Overall, the operating results in the high and medium versions of the forecast model appear reasonable. Solid sales growth, strong profitability, and key financial ratios, including the current ratio and the debt service coverage ratio, are more than adequate. Turning our attention to the low version, significant concerns start to emerge or, in the words of Scooby Doo, "Ruh-roh." On top of the company performing poorly with negative YOY sales growth and basically operating at a breakeven level, two important ratios need further attention.

First, the company's current ratio has fallen below 2.0 (to 1.98, refer to Exhibit 10.1). This may appear to still be relatively strong but if the debt facility has a covenant that requires the company to maintain a current ratio above 2.0, then the company may be technically in default. The same goes for the debt service coverage ratio; if the debt facility has a covenant that requires this ratio be

1.5 or above (not at all unreasonable for lenders), then again, the company may be in technical default. Obviously, the company is not in default of these covenants today and does not expect to be in default, as even under the medium case forecast the company has more than enough breathing room. But for management purposes, having a clear understanding of at what operating performance level does the company begin to operate under financial stress is extremely helpful so that if the business does head south, the executive management team can plan for and implement necessary adjustments (e.g., expense reductions) to avoid a rather messy situation with the lender.

I now turn our attention to the balance sheet presented in Exhibit 10.2. Here again I provide high, medium, and low forecast scenarios for evaluation and draw your attention to a couple of items. First, you will notice that the ending inventory balance in the low version is actually higher than the high version. This may make sense on the surface, as FYE 12/31/24 product sales in the low version are forecast to reach only $7.6 million versus $11.4 million in the high version (so lower sales equals more inventory on hand and a higher value). However, it may also mean that the company's inventory is rapidly becoming obsolete and it is becoming harder and harder to sell, raising an all-important question as to whether the remaining inventory balance of $1.52 million is worth this much or should management incur another write-off of the inventory as worthless (which means the company would have to incur an additional expense and most likely push it from profitability under the low version to a loss – Ouch!). If you recall, our example company already wrote off $2 million of inventory in the FYE 12/31/23 so having to take another "hit" may be painful.

Second, you may ask why the company would pay a dividend when at best it is operating at a breakeven level. An excellent question and no doubt something that our example company's board of directors will discuss and be sensitive to as issuing a dividend during a breakeven year would generally be frowned upon.

EXHIBIT 10.1—HIGH, MEDIUM, & LOW CASE FORECASTS – INCOME STATEMENT
Unaudited – Prepared by Company Management

Income Statement - Forecast for the Fiscal Year Ending	High 12/31/2024	% of Net Rev.	Medium 12/31/2024	% of Net Rev.	Low 12/31/2024	% of Net Rev.
Key Performance Indicators:						
Revenue Per Full Time Employee	$ 530,400		$ 453,000		$ 389,567	
Product Sales, Avg. Order Value (net)	$ 13,680		$ 11,400		$ 8,613	
Software Platform & SAAS Sales:						
SAAS Sales, Total Customer Accounts	700		700		700	
SAAS Sales, Total Earned Avg. Per Account	$ 99,000		$ 84,857		$ 74,250	
Macro Level Analysis:						
Year Over Year Sales Growth	33.73%		14.21%		-1.78%	
Gross Margin	65.41%		63.33%		61.17%	
Operating Income Margin	17.58%		9.44%		1.59%	
Debt Service Coverage Ratio	10.48		5.41		1.67	
Current Ratio	3.12		2.77		1.98	
Sales Revenue:						
Software Platform & SAAS Sales	$ 69,300,000	87.10%	$ 59,400,000	87.42%	$ 51,975,000	88.94%
Product Sales	$ 11,400,000	14.33%	$ 9,500,000	13.98%	$ 7,600,000	13.01%
Other Sales, Discounts, & Allowances	$ (1,140,000)	-1.43%	$ (950,000)	-1.40%	$ (1,140,000)	-1.95%
Net Sales Revenue	$ 79,560,000	100.00%	$ 67,950,000	100.00%	$ 58,435,000	100.00%
Costs of Sales Revenue:						
Direct Product Costs	$ 6,270,000	7.88%	$ 5,225,000	7.69%	$ 4,560,000	7.80%
Wages & Burden	$ 20,247,500	25.45%	$ 18,690,000	27.51%	$ 17,132,500	29.32%
Direct Overhead	$ 750,000	0.94%	$ 750,000	1.10%	$ 750,000	1.28%
Other Costs of Sales Revenue	$ 250,000	0.31%	$ 250,000	0.37%	$ 250,000	0.43%
Total Costs of Sales Revenue	$ 27,517,500	34.59%	$ 24,915,000	36.67%	$ 22,692,500	38.83%
Gross Profit	$ 52,042,500	65.41%	$ 43,035,000	63.33%	$ 35,742,500	61.17%
Gross Margin	65.41%		63.33%		61.17%	

Issues are present w/performance and debt covenants.

EXHIBIT 10.1—(CONTINUED)

Direct Operating Expenses:							
Advertising, Promotional, & Selling	$ 6,930,000	8.71%	$ 6,534,000	9.62%	$ 6,237,000	10.67%	
Personnel Wages, Burden, & Compensation	$ 5,171,400	6.50%	$ 5,096,250	7.50%	$ 4,966,975	8.50%	
Facility Operating Expenses	$ 1,500,000	1.89%	$ 1,375,000	2.02%	$ 1,250,000	2.14%	
Other Operating Expenses	$ 517,140	0.65%	$ 509,625	0.75%	$ 496,698	0.85%	
Total Direct Operating Expenses	$ 14,118,540	17.75%	$ 13,514,875	19.89%	$ 12,950,673	22.16%	
Contribution Profit	$ 37,923,960	47.67%	$ 29,520,125	43.44%	$ 22,791,828	39.00%	
Contribution Margin	47.67%		43.44%		39.00%		
Corporate Expenses & Overhead:							
Corporate Marketing, Branding, & Promotional	$ 4,000,000	5.03%	$ 3,250,000	4.78%	$ 2,750,000	4.71%	
Research, Development, & Design	$ 11,934,000	15.00%	$ 11,891,250	17.50%	$ 11,687,000	20.00%	
Corporate Overhead & Support	$ 6,250,000	7.86%	$ 6,250,000	9.20%	$ 5,750,000	9.84%	
Depreciation & Amortization Expense	$ 1,750,000	2.20%	$ 1,714,286	2.52%	$ 1,678,571	2.87%	
Total Corporate Operating Expenses	$ 23,934,000	30.08%	$ 23,105,536	34.00%	$ 21,865,571	37.42%	
Operating Income (EBIT)	$ 13,989,960	17.58%	$ 6,414,589	9.44%	$ 926,256	1.59%	
Operating Margin (EBIT Margin)	17.58%		9.44%		1.59%		
Other Expenses (Income):							
Other Expenses, Income, & Discontinued Ops.	$ 500,000	0.63%	$ 500,000	0.74%	$ 500,000	0.86%	
Interest Expense	$ 277,500	0.35%	$ 277,500	0.41%	$ 333,750	0.57%	
Total Other Expenses (Income)	$ 777,500	0.98%	$ 777,500	1.14%	$ 833,750	1.43%	
Net Income (Loss) Before Income Taxes	$ 13,212,460	16.61%	$ 5,637,089	8.30%	$ 92,506	0.16%	
Income Tax Expense (Benefit)	$ 4,624,361	5.81%	$ 1,972,981	2.90%	$ 32,377	0.06%	
Net Income (Loss) After Income Taxes	$ 8,588,099	10.79%	$ 3,664,108	5.39%	$ 60,129	0.10%	

Further expense cuts may be needed in these areas.

Confidential - Property of QW Example Tech, Inc.

Finally, I reach the statement of cash flows as presented in Exhibit 10.3, which also sheds additional valuable information in the low version of the forecast model. Reviewing the statement of cash flows in more detail, you will notice that the low version of the forecast model produces approximately $2.4 million of positive cash flow from operations, which is 70% consumed by the financing related payments (for the company) of roughly $1.65 million, which is comprised of common equity dividend payment and debt repayments. Okay, so the good news is that the company can generate enough internal positive cash flow to cover these committed payments, but looking closer, this really could become a problem as in effect the company is using short-term working capital to repay long-term financial commitments (an imbalance that should be avoided).

I could highlight additional issues and findings with the financial information presented in the forecast versions but the points I would like to emphasize here are as follows. First, having complete financial forecasts including the income statement, balance sheet, and statement of cash flows is critical for management planning purposes and financial reporting. Second, the power and importance of utilizing the what-if forecasting tool is on full display. And third, even in a forecast, the all-important concept of realizing that accounting (and finance) is more of an art than a science holds true.

EXHIBIT 10.2—HIGH, MEDIUM, & LOW CASE FORECASTS – BALANCE SHEET
Unaudited – Prepared by Company Management

Balance Sheet - Forecast as of the Fiscal Year Ending	High 12/31/2024	Medium 12/31/2024	Low 12/31/2024
Assets			
Current Assets			
Cash & Equivalents	$ 9,456,751	$ 5,048,417	$ 2,575,673
Accounts Receivable	$ 9,945,000	$ 8,493,750	$ 8,034,813
Inventory	$ 1,045,000	$ 979,688	$ 1,520,000
Prepaid Expenses	$ 626,846	$ 535,371	$ 460,404
Total Current Assets	$21,073,597	$15,057,226	$12,590,889
Long-Term Capital Assets			
Property, Machinery, & Equipment	$ 5,250,000	$ 5,000,000	$ 4,750,000
Accumulated Depreciation	$ (2,964,286)	$ (2,928,571)	$ (2,892,857)
Net Property, Machinery, & Equipment	$ 2,285,714	$ 2,071,429	$ 1,857,143
Other Assets			
Intangible Assets, Net	$ 5,000,000	$ 5,000,000	$ 5,000,000
Other Assets	$ 150,000	$ 150,000	$ 150,000
Total Long-Term & Other Assets	$ 7,435,714	$ 7,221,429	$ 7,007,143
Total Assets	$28,509,311	$22,278,655	$19,598,032

Company pivoting away from product sales yet inventory balance remains high. Valuation problem may be present.

EXHIBIT 10.2—(CONTINUED)

Liabilities

Current Liabilities			
Accounts Payable	$ 2,486,250	$ 2,123,438	$ 1,807,833
Accrued Liabilities	$ 872,058	$ 838,550	$ 988,412
Short-Term Loans Payable	$ 500,000	$ 500,000	$ 2,000,000
Income Taxes Payable	$ 1,156,090	$ 493,245	$ 8,094
Deferred Revenue & Other Current Liabilities	$ 1,732,500	$ 1,485,000	$ 1,559,250
Total Current Liabilities	$ 6,746,898	$ 5,440,233	$ 6,363,589
Long-Term Liabilities			
Loans Payable, Less Short-Term Portion	$ 2,000,000	$ 2,000,000	$ 2,000,000
Other Long-Term Liabilities	$ 0	$ 0	$ 0
Total Long-Term Liabilities	$ 2,000,000	$ 2,000,000	$ 2,000,000
Total Liabilities	$ 8,746,898	$ 7,440,233	$ 8,363,589
Stockholders' Equity			
Capital Stock	$10,000,000	$10,000,000	$10,000,000
Dividends	$ (750,000)	$ (750,000)	$ (750,000)
Retained Earnings	$ 1,924,314	$ 1,924,314	$ 1,924,314
Current Earnings (Loss)	$ 8,588,099	$ 3,664,108	$ 60,129
Total Stockholders' Equity	$19,762,413	$14,838,422	$11,234,443
Total Liabilities & Stockholders' Equity	$28,509,311	$22,278,655	$19,598,032

(circle annotation near Short-Term Loans Payable:) Notice added short-term borrowings are required in low case as cash flows are poor.

(circle annotation near Stockholders' Equity:) Can the company afford to issue a dividend in low cash scenario, probably not.

Confidential - Property of QW Example Tech, Inc.

EXHIBIT 10.3—HIGH, MEDIUM, & LOW CASE FORECASTS – STATEMENT OF CASH FLOWS

Unaudited – Prepared by Company Management

Statement of Cash Flows - Forecast for the Fiscal Year Ending	High 12/31/2024	Medium 12/31/2024	Low 12/31/2024
Net Income (Loss) after Income Taxes	$ 8,588,099	$ 3,664,108	$ 60,129
Operating Activities, Cash provided (used):			
Depreciation & Amortization	$ 1,750,000	$ 1,714,286	$ 1,678,571
Decrease (increase) in accounts receivables	$ (1,936,000)	$ (484,750)	$ (25,812)
Decrease (increase) in inventory	$ 661,000	$ 726,313	$ 186,000
Decrease (increase) in other current assets	$ (1,846)	$ 89,629	$ 164,596
Increase (decrease) in accounts payables	$ 1,027,250	$ 664,438	$ 348,833
Increase (decrease) in accrued liabilities	$ (239,942)	$ (273,450)	$ (123,588)
Increase (decrease) in other liabilities	$ 1,394,442	$ 484,098	$ 73,196
Net Cash Flow from Operating Activities	$11,243,004	$ 6,584,670	$ 2,361,925
Investing Activities, Cash provided (used):			
Capital Expenditures	$ (750,000)	$ (500,000)	$ (250,000)
Investments in Intangible & Other Assets	$ (50,000)	$ (50,000)	$ (50,000)
Net Cash Flow from Investing Activities	$ (800,000)	$ (550,000)	$ (300,000)
Financing Activities, Cash provided (used):			
Dividends or Distributions Paid	$ (750,000)	$ (750,000)	$ (750,000)
Sale (repurchase) of Equity	$ 0	$ 0	$ 0
Proceeds from Issuance of Loans (i.e., debt)	$ 0	$ 0	$ 0
Repayments of Long-Term Loans	$ (500,000)	$ (500,000)	$ (500,000)
Net Borrowings (Repayments) of Short-Term Loans	$ (1,900,000)	$ (1,900,000)	$ (400,000)
Net Cash Flow from Financing Activities	$ (3,150,000)	$ (3,150,000)	$ (1,650,000)
Net Increase (decrease) in Cash & Equivalents	$ 7,293,004	$ 2,884,670	$ 411,925
Beginning Cash & Equivalents Balance	$ 2,163,747	$ 2,163,747	$ 2,163,747
Ending Cash & Equivalents Balance	$ 9,456,751	$ 5,048,417	$ 2,575,673

Breakeven year yet produces $2.4 million in net cash flow. However, almost all committed to debt and dividend payments. So cash will not increase during the year compared to the medium and high case scenarios.

Confidential - Property of QW Example Tech, Inc.

Financial Forecasts and the Big Picture

Chapters 6 through 8 of this book introduced you to the big three financial statements and the purpose and importance of each one. Those chapters covered a large amount of information, as does this chapter on financial forecasting. My goal is not to bury you with too much information (i.e., burying you in the BS) but rather to help you understand just how important CART financial information really is and how top management teams utilize the accounting and finance departments as a competitive weapon.

With this said, I would like to summarize this chapter by rehashing some invaluable gems related to financial forecasting and why the financial forecasting process is so important and integral to the financial reporting function.

♦ Graduate: Bottom-up forecast models are valuable tools for businesses but for you to move up in the executive management hierarchy, you will need to graduate and become comfortable using top-down forecasts. Top executives (remember, know your target audience) usually have such a solid understanding of the economic structure of their business that they can simply change a select number of critical operating assumptions and will almost immediately know what the end result will be (e.g., a change to top-line sales revenue will lead to a bottom-line result). To be an effective executive-level manager, you need to efficiently understand the macro-level impact on your business from changing economic conditions. That is, you "can't see the forest for the trees."

♦ The P&L focus: There is no question that too many businesses focus first and only on the P&L when preparing forecasts. It should be clear from this chapter just how important the balance sheet and cash flow statement are, especially as they relate to cash flow and third-party capital source management. Remember the acronym CART.

♦ External/internal: Internal financial forecasts include significant amounts of detail and confidential information that should not be distributed to external parties. Not only is the level of detail on a line-item basis excessive but the high and low versions of the forecast model should not be distributed externally (as these are for internal management use). Again, what a business distributes to external parties is vastly different than for internal consumption.

Part Three

THE TYPES AND TARGETS OF FINANCIAL REPORTS

11

THE ROLE OF ACCOUNTING

At this point in the book, I'm going to take a small break from "number crunching" (which was covered extensively in Chapters 6 through 10 and which I will dive into again in Chapters 12 through 15) and turn our attention to the "Where" part of the financial reporting process. That is, where does the financial information come from that will be the basis of your financial report?

In a nutshell, the majority of all financial information originates from the accounting and financial information system. Here, I'm not talking about or limiting our discussion to automated accounting systems such as QuickBooks or an ERP system (which stands for enterprise resource planning) such as NetSuite. Nobody would argue that accounting technology systems and platforms are an invaluable tool to assist with producing CART financial information. However, you must understand that accounting and financial information systems extend well beyond just the technological tools used by companies to produce financial information as there are significant influences (from outside the technological systems) that will shape the accounting and financial information system and the resulting financial reports and statements that is generated. To this point I offer three examples to illustrate this concept:

◆ Accounting is a profession that is governed by multiple parties, groups, and pronouncements that originate from different sources, the majority of which are external to the company. As an example, accounting rules have been established by professional groups that assist companies by providing guidelines on how sales revenue should be recognized as "earned" in the income statement (and the proper period). These guidelines are not automatically built into the technology system but rather are directed by the company's accounting management team (which establishes the company's sales revenue recognition policy) which rely on both the accounting technology system and proper independent controls (external to the system) to ensure the accuracy of reporting sales revenue.

◆ Properly functioning accounting and financial information systems must incorporate proper policies, procedures, controls, checks, and balances to ensure CART financial information is generated. While a portion of these processes can be completed within an accounting technology system, almost all accounting and financial information systems rely on external processes to ensure proper checks, balances, and segregation of duties are established to validate the financial information being produced.

◆ And I would be remiss in not disclosing and referencing one of the most important concepts you must understand about accounting. That is, accounting is just as much of an art form as a science. To this point, let's just say that more than a few companies receive "input" (for lack of a better term) from the executive management team or the board of directors that help direct if not outright influence accounting policies that may be construed as somewhat aggressive (e.g., accelerate sales revenue recognition and defer expenses). In the accounting world, sometimes economic politics and accounting policies are very closely connected.

I could offer countless other examples but the point I'm highlighting and the reason for this chapter is simple. The accounting and financial system represents the source of basically all financial information so the better you understand the source of the information, and the role accounting and finance plays in an organization, the more credible you will be when preparing and communicating a financial report.

Finally, in helping you connect the dots with financial reporting, you should remember this thought.

The best communicators are those that can bridge the gap between understanding the source of financial data (accounting), the meaning of financial results (finance), how to prepare the financial results in a financial report, presenting clear and concise economic decisions that need to be made, and how best to communicate the financial information, in the most efficient manner possible. This can take years of experience and hard knocks to develop, refine, and master, as it is no easy task. Hence, enter the role of a true CFO (chief financial officer) – their job comes down to managing people, concepts, risks, and capital, which all require excellent communication skills.

A Crash Course in Accounting

I know, it's hard to believe that a bunch of accountants would want to spend some of your valuable time talking about accounting concepts and theories. Yes, I agree that this topic is generally best left to a bunch of bean counters who live and breathe debits and credits. In fact, most readers of this book might take this opportunity to peruse through this portion of the chapter when they are having trouble falling asleep at night (as reading this material will certainly do the trick). However, before you doze off and if you elect to remember anything about our brief, albeit extremely important, conversation on accounting, it would be these two thoughts:

1. Accounting is the function responsible for producing basically all financial information, data, reports, statements, and so on (herein and throughout the book referred to as financial information). Or, put differently, the accounting system is the primary source of generating critical business financial data.

2. Finance is the function responsible for analyzing, evaluating, and assessing the accounting data on which business and economic decisions are based. The finance function is often referred to as FP&A, which stands for financial planning and analysis. To break down this thought further, remember the acronym GIGO (garbage in, garbage out) or actually in today's world, DIGO may be more appropriate

(data in, garbage out). It should be readily apparent now just how important the accounting function is, as if the accounting system is producing garbage data, there is no way sound business and economic decisions can be made and reliable financial analyses can be completed.

Most everyone would agree that both accounting and finance represent critical business functions and often overlap and/or are "joined at the hip," but they differ from an input/output perspective, as accounting is, for lack of a better term, the start of the food chain (as it relates to generating financial information) and finance tends to be the end of the food chain (as it relates to analyzing financial information).

So now that I have your attention, I'll attempt to provide a crash course in accounting principles and theory in less than a chapter. My goal is not to provide a detailed overview of accounting rules or guidelines such as the theory behind accounting for capital asset leases or applying Black-Scholes to account for stock option expense, but rather to offer a 10,000-foot overview of accounting and key concepts every business must address, starting with this fundamental statement:

To produce accurate financial information, every business must develop, implement, maintain, and manage a properly functioning accounting system that at its foundation relies on establishing, implementing, and adhering to agreed-upon accounting policies, procedures, and controls applied on a consistent basis and in accordance with GAAP.

And what does GAAP stand for? Generally Accepted Accounting Principles, whose simplest definition is "a set of rules that encompass the details, complexities, and legalities of business and corporate accounting." These rules are established by various accounting organizations, boards, and groups, with the primary group being the Financial Accounting Standards Board (FASB), which uses GAAP as the foundation for its comprehensive set of approved accounting methods and practices.

There you have it – when producing financial information, which represents the base for preparing financial reports, businesses should adhere to GAAP as established by FASB. Seems simple enough, but as you work through this chapter it should become abundantly clear that GAAP is more or less a series of guidelines businesses can use that provide a certain amount of leeway when actual financial information is produced. Or maybe the best way to think of it is referring to this quote from Captain Barbosa from the *Pirates of the Caribbean* franchise: "And thirdly, the code (translation to accounting – GAAP) is more what you'd call *guidelines* than actual *rules*." With this said, let us expand on your understanding of GAAP by providing a summary of various macro-level accounting concepts that help provide certain guardrails for businesses when producing financial information.

Key Accounting Theories, Concepts, and Trends

One thing that I'm not going to do is get into a detailed discussion on understanding accounting concepts, rules, and principles (from a technical perspective). If you genuinely want to understand accounting in more depth, please refer to a book my late father and I wrote, *Accounting for Dummies*, 7th edition, which provides an excellent introduction into the basics of accounting. Further, it would be pointless in the span of one chapter (or for that matter, in one book) to try and explain the concepts that dance around in an accountant's head each day. Even myself, being an accountant, would simply rather be put out of my misery than spend hours upon hours deciphering all the technical concepts and guidelines accountants follow when producing financial statements, reports, and information.

Rather, what I have elected to do is summarize macro-level accounting theories, concepts, and current trends to help you gain a better understanding of how financial information is prepared and what overlying broad governances and yes, politics, come into play when preparing financial information.

◆ Art versus science: Probably the single most important concept to understand with accounting is that it really is more of an art than a science. Accounting rules and guidelines are not set in stone or laid out in black-and-white terms. Rather, accounting includes a fair amount of subjectivity when it comes to producing financial information (as you will see shortly) and relies just as much on qualitative factors as quantitative analyses.

◆ Internal pressure and politics: It must be noted that accounting is a profession that is not immune from politics and internal reporting pressures. You can be assured that there have been many lively internal discussions between the executive management team members or C-suite (i.e., chief level positions including the CEO, COO, CFO, etc.), the board of directors, and the finance and accounting groups as to finalizing periodic financial statements and reports to ensure that the company "hit the numbers." Please note that I'm not saying that companies are committing fraud to achieve certain financial operating results but rather a more subtle approach may be used to change an estimate here or adjust an analysis there to squeeze a few more dollars out of the financial results.

◆ Accrual versus cash (or other basis): Simply put, accrual-based accounting measures a company's performance, position, or results by recognizing economic events regardless of when cash transactions occur. This is the essence of GAAP. For example, in the income statement, revenue is recognized when it is earned (as opposed to collecting cash) and expenses are realized when they are incurred (as opposed to when cash is disbursed).

Almost every business professional, at one time or another, has heard reference made to financial statements being prepared on an accrual versus a cash basis. While cash basis reporting is allowed in certain circumstances (e.g., for reporting taxable income to the IRS), it should be noted that no serious business utilizes the cash basis of reporting for external reporting to capital sources or to make important business and economic decisions. For almost all businesses (and to be taken seriously), GAAP must be adhered to and implemented. Period!

- The matching principle: This concept is relatively straightforward and best understood by referring to an example from the income statement. Under the matching principle, earned revenues should be matched against appropriate expenses during a given period. For example, if a company recognizes earned revenue of $1 million over a monthly reporting period, any sales commissions that are owed to a sales representative should be expensed in the same period, regardless of when the commissions are paid. Another perfect example relates to Tesla. When Tesla records sales of vehicles, it must also estimate and record an appropriate expense for future warranty claims (as Tesla provides a multiyear warranty for product defects on new auto sales), even though it may be years before the warranty claims are presented and paid by the company.

- Conservative by nature: By being conservative I mean that accounting principles tend to be structured to realize expenses earlier and not recognize revenue/sales until the entire earnings process is complete (see below). Maybe being conservative is not all that fair but maybe it is just smart planning, as the accounting governance organizations realize that companies tend to be more aggressive with presenting results (so building in a conservative bias helps provide some balance). Of course, there are always exceptions to this rule, as anyone familiar with the epic failures at Enron will attest.

- Policies, procedures, and controls: The foundation of accuracy is centered in properly functioning accounting policies,

procedures, and controls, administered by qualified professionals, adhering to GAAP, and applied on a consistent basis. This represents the bedrock of any sound accounting system and incorporates these critical components:

- Qualified staff: An experienced, qualified, committed, ethical, and diverse accounting staff that is respected by management and supported by the board of directors is a necessity. In addition, two essential traits are best summarized by Duke, played by Jack Palance in the movie *City Slicker's 2* when explaining that "one thing is" honesty, integrity – two traits of upmost importance.

- Segregation of duties: Accounting and financial functions are intentionally segregated between different staff to protect company assets and produce CART financial information. I'm sure everyone has heard the story of the reliable nice old lady who has been the company's bookkeeper for 20+ years only to realize she has bilked the company out of hundreds of thousands of dollars over the years. What better parties are there at committing and hiding fraud than the top accounting and financial staff, as they know exactly how to hide the dirt and conceal the truth? Therefore, it is always recommended that while it's fine to have the accounting or finance department review, account for, and authorize payments, the movement of cash and final approval of the payments should come from a segregated department.

- Materiality: All businesses must evaluate and manage the tradeoff between accounting for every dollar (flowing in and out of a company) and the cost of implementing this effort. This represents the heart of the materiality concept, as it is literally impossible for companies like Amazon or McDonald's to assure 100% accuracy with all financial transactions.

Companies will establish accounting policies, procedures, and controls to ensure that no material misstatements are present in the financial information produced (but are willing to accept a small tolerance for errors if they are not significant). But remember, different parties have different perspectives on what exactly is "material," so be aware of this concept.

- Use of estimates: Basically, every operating business of size, in one fashion or another, will use estimates when preparing financial information. Businesses can range from a large, mature retailer that must record estimated returns and refunds after holiday selling season to a newer company such as Tesla that must estimate potential future warranty claims as a cost today against the sale. But similar to the concept of materiality, the use of estimates can be a sign or flag of potential accounting issues or misstatements. As a rule of thumb, the more a company must rely on the use of estimates to prepare financial statements or the newer or greener a company is (without having years of data available to properly analyze), the higher the chance an error may occur in the financial information prepared.

- Disclosing accounting changes: Speaking of estimates, companies will often update or revise estimates as additional data becomes available. This represents a perfectly normal process (if it is kept within reason). In addition, companies may also change an accounting policy to improve the accuracy of their financial reporting. Again, this happens from time to time and is not out of the ordinary. What does become a problem is when companies change estimates or accounting policies on a suspiciously frequent basis and, worse yet, do not properly disclose or communicate these changes (i.e., they bury the decision deep in the financial report

somewhere). Lack of timely and clear disclosure of accounting changes is definitely a red flag.

- Current trends: Accounting and GAAP represent constantly evolving principles or functions that must adapt to changing economic and market conditions. This has been the case for the past 100 years and will undoubtedly be the case moving forward. Today is no different, as highlighted by the following three examples of current trends or hot topics:

  - The earnings process: Revenue recognition is an extremely important and hot issue in today's economic environment – and rightfully so, as companies are always looking to drive top-line sales and display high rates of growth to justify nosebleed valuations. This issue really boils down to one key question that is much easier asked than answered: When is the earnings process complete? Or stated differently, when can a customer sale be recorded as earned revenue based on the company's operating model? Ask five different accountants and five different executives and you may get 10 different interpretations; that is how divisive this topic can be.

    For example, a technology company that sells an annual software subscription may take a position that 50% of the annual subscription should be recognized as earned revenue in the first three months, as this is when the customers need the most support (from internal staff to implement) and tend to use the software more frequently. An accountant, seeing that the term of the subscription is for one year, may say that only 25% of the subscription can be recognized as earned revenue in the first three months. Let the discussions and debates begin as in reality, it may be somewhere between (to ensure that expenses are matched against revenue). GAAP has provided guidelines to help determine when revenue can be recognized but remember, accounting is just as much an art form as a science. I am not going to get into the details on GAAP revenue recognition but if you remember one thing it should be this – revenue recognition is often an area that is abused by companies (looking to improve operating results) and is almost always a heavy area of focus by CPA firms when conducting audits.

- Balance sheet comparability: For years, external parties have struggled with comparing balance sheets of two like companies operating in similar markets or industries. The reason for this is differences in how debt is disclosed and how companies may utilize "off-balance-sheet" debt to finance operations. A perfect example of this is the use of leases (or perceived rental agreements) compared to loans. A lease for equipment or real property, if properly structured, will generally not appear as debt on a company's balance sheet; rather, the periodic payment is recorded as rent or lease expense in the income statement. A similar company that secured a loan to buy the equipment (rather than lease it) will record the equipment as an asset, recognize the loan as debt, and then depreciate the equipment and realize interest expense on the loan. Same equipment, similar businesses, yet the balance sheets of the two companies will look different (and not be comparable).

Off-balance-sheet transactions such as leases, special-purpose entities, and other clever financing vehicles have been used and abused for years, so the various accounting authoritative groups, including FASB, have sharpened their focus on this topic and are requiring companies to tighten up financial statement reporting to ensure that all debt and equivalents are properly presented and disclosed. There is no question that the trend is now squarely in the court of complete and full disclosure of all debt instruments.

- Company equity transactions: Companies will often use equity incentive plans to reward employees with additional compensation that is tied to the improved performance of a company's stock (or similar equity). This is a common practice with technology companies, as lucrative employee stock option grants are often made to key employees that can turn out being worth hundreds of thousands, if not millions, of dollars. The accounting industry recognized this issue and after much debate, evaluation, and discussion, now requires companies to report employee stock option expense in their financial statements (based on approved models and formulas that calculate the expense).

Additional examples could be provided that explain how companies leverage their own equity to support their business plan and finance operations, but the key trend to remember is that if a company's equity is going to be used in a financially meaningful manner, then the transaction(s) will need to be properly reported and disclosed in the financial statements and reports prepared. The concepts of comparability, matching, and disclosure all hold here as, again, two companies may utilize different strategies to finance operations and incentivize employees but need to be evaluated on a level playing field.

By now I'm guessing that you have had more than your fill of accounting, so I will end our discussion at this point. But please remember that the very foundation of preparing best-in-class financial information and financial reports starts with accuracy, all of which originate in a properly and efficiently functioning accounting system.

Rounding Out Our Discussion

I would be remiss in our discussion on accuracy and accounting without providing some final thoughts, tips, and tidbits on the always-relevant topic of accounting and financial reporting fraud. Names such as Enron, Madoff, and, more recently, Wirecard, FTX, and the Trump Organization, should quickly come to mind as these represent high-profile frauds that resulted in millions and in some cases, billions of dollars of losses. But fraud is certainly not limited to billion-dollar companies, as it occurs at every level of business in almost every type of operating environment. So here are some thoughts on fraud that you may want to remember along the way.

First, it is important to understand the difference between financial errors and irregularities. Errors basically equate to an unintentional mistake that might be centered in a poor analysis, inexperienced staff, lack of proper reviews being completed, and so on. Irregularities represent an intentional effort to mislead or make a material misstatement with the willful intent to deceive or defraud.

Second, errors are more prone to occur in companies that are understaffed, lack proper segregations of duties, do not utilize external parties (e.g., a CPA firm completing an audit) to validate financial information, have poorly functioning accounting systems, and so on. It should be noted that the financial damage inflicted from errors may be as great as from irregularities, as businesses that do not take the accounting function seriously can quickly experience significant pain.

Third, when management collusion is present, it is almost impossible for external parties to detect fraud over the short term. By management collusion I mean when the senior or executive management team is conspiring or colluding to mislead external parties or misstate financial information – good luck figuring this out before the company implodes.

Fourth, periods of irrational exuberance (coined by former chairman of the Federal Reserve Board Alan Greenspan) tend to lead to more wild business claims, success stories, growth trajectories, and valuations, which can feed the fraud beast. When money's flowing freely, it seems that accounting is not a priority or is placed on the back burner. However, when business and market conditions turn, fraud starts to emerge and flow to the top of the pond (and stinks). Remember, the cash flow statement can help ferret out fraud, as it reports how a company generates and consumes cash and just how reliant a company may be on external financial sources (which tend to evaporate during financial crises).

Fifth and finally, the smartest and most cunning fraudsters seem to always be one step ahead of GAAP and the accounting industry. Eventually, fraud catches up with most everyone, but the crafty and clever parties seem to be able to get in front of it and push accounting to the limits (and seem to exit before all hell breaks loose, leaving someone else holding the bag). If you would like to expand your knowledge on fraud, I would direct you to our book *How to Read a Financial Report*, 10th edition as

I dedicate an entire chapter to the subject of fraud and summarize certain qualitative and quantitative flags that may indicate fraud is present.

In closing, I would like to emphasize that fraudulent financial information is the exception rather than the rule, as most companies make a concerted effort to produce CART financial information. However, in cases or situations where there are enough red flags to pause and take a step back, ask yourself these two questions: "Does it sound too good to be true?" and "Am I being sold or educated with the financial information?" If the answer is yes and sold, then you want to abide by the advice provided by one of the greatest investors of all time, Warren Buffett, who so diligently noted about expectations, "Honesty is a very expensive gift. Do not expect it from cheap people." What you will generally find when fraud is involved is that cheap people (i.e., without morals and ethics) are also present.

12

PREPARING FINANCIAL REPORTS FROM COMPANY FINANCIAL STATEMENTS – EXTERNAL USERS

In this chapter, I'm going to turn our attention back toward analyzing and preparing financial information (for distribution to third parties) as we dive into preparing sample financial reports for our example company, for external users. Chapter 12 will be dedicated toward preparing financial reports centered on the big three financial statements for external users and Chapter 13 will then be dedicated to preparing financial reports centered on the big three financial statements for internal consumers. Then, in Chapter 14, I will shift our focus to preparing financial reports that are based on a portion of the big three financial statements (with a concentration on the income statement).

More specifically, this chapter will be dedicated toward preparing a financial report for the big three financial statements that will target external users with a focus on external capital sources such as investors and lenders. Then, in Chapter 13, we will dedicate our discussion to preparing a financial report for the big three financial statements that will target internal consumers or more specifically, our example company's Board of Directors and "C" level executive management suite. In both cases it is important to remember that you must know your audience first before you prepare the financial reports.

Also, I would like to note that comparison financial reports (both directed toward external users) will also be presented, one representing a base case, for lack of a better term, and the other representing a preferred case. The base case will mirror what I've seen used time and time again in the business world as it relates to providing a basic or minimal level of financial information and reports to third parties to evaluate and draw a conclusion on. I'm not saying this is necessarily right or wrong, as the financial reports presented are correct and reasonable. Rather, the challenge with the base case is that if a full financial report is not presented, you often allow the external parties to potentially drift and draw incorrect or incomplete conclusions from the financial information presented.

In the preferred case, you will see an expanded financial report that offers additional information that will include KPIs (key performance indicators), trend analysis, and a management discussion of operating results ("MDOR") to help not only relay the company's story but more importantly, help focus the external users on key concepts, operating results, and financial data points. I should note that there is no perfect financial report format or structure that I can offer as a reference for future use as it is extremely important to understand that for each industry, company, and business operating environment, financial reports must be constantly adapted and updated to reflect the current "state of the union." Financial reports represent a living and breathing document that will need to evolve as the business progresses through its life, which for most companies includes resounding successes and heartbreaking losses. This is the life of a business and entrepreneurs; as the old saying goes, "if it was easy, everybody would be doing it." So with this said, let's dig into our sample financial reports for our example business.

Financial Reports from Financial Statements – External Users

To being, let's dive into our base case scenario by providing some background on our example company. Our example company has recently retained a CFO that had an impressive background working for a large private technology company generating more than $1 billion in annual sales revenue. In addition, our example company recently evaluated their financial and accounting executive management needs and elected to create the CFO position in the business for the first time in its history (in the past, our example company managed its financial and accounting function via a VP of Finance and Accounting, a party that recently retired).

This individual rose through the ranks of the technology company reaching the title of director of corporate accounting and risk compliance. Pretty impressive, as there is no doubt that this individual (now with the company a little more than nine months) is experienced, of high quality, and knowledgeable in the field of accounting and finance. What excited this individual about joining our example company is a chance to elevate to the CFO status, as their future career path at the large private technology company appeared to be limited. Thus, the reason they jumped ship and took on the role of CFO, as not only was the title of CFO exciting, but the ability to help lead our example company through an aggressive growth phase (often referred to as "scaling the business") fit well within their experience wheelhouse.

For the most recent FYE 12/31/23, our qualified but inexperienced CFO took on the responsibility of preparing an annual financial report for the company's financial statements that will be delivered to both independent investors and key lenders. And here is what was produced and forwarded to the target audience in late March of 2024.

First, an overview letter was prepared as follows (which should come from the company's CEO and President):

To Whom It May Concern:

Attached are the annual audited financial statements and audit report for QW Example Tech., Inc. (the "Company") for the fiscal years ending 12/31/23 and 12/31/22 as completed by the CPA firm of Dewey, Fixum, & Howe, LLC. We are providing this financial information to you as part of our annual financial reporting compliance requirements to all Company capital sources, including both equity investors and lenders.

We are pleased to report that the Company grew its top-line sales revenue by approximately $5.3 million or roughly 10% during the most recent fiscal year ending 12/31/23 as compared to the prior fiscal year ending 12/31/22. Further, net profit after tax increased from approximately $77,000 for the fiscal year-end 12/31/22 to roughly $813,000 (a 10.5x increase) for the fiscal year-end 12/31/23. The Company's executive management team and board of directors are both pleased with the improved operating results and look for these trends to continue in 2024 and beyond.

Please feel free to reach out to me with any questions, feedback, and/or additional information needs as it relates to your assessment of the Company's operating results and financial condition. We appreciate your continued support and look forward to working with each and every one of you in the years to come.

Sincerely,
_____ (signed)
CEO/President

Next, our example company's audited financial statements were provided, which encompassed the entire audited financial statements and reports received from the company's external auditors. For ease of presentation and to save space, I have elected to not include the actual audit report and financial statement footnotes, which I covered in Chapter 2 (so please refer to this discussion as needed). However, I have included our example company's audited financial statements in Exhibits 12.1 through 12.3.

Please note that the financial statements provided are basically the same as those provided in Exhibits 6.1, 7.1, and 8.1 with the exception of some formatting changes. Ok, so here we have a nice cover letter written by the company's CEO providing a brief summary of the operating results and thanking various partners for

their support. There's nothing wrong with providing the financial report as presented but it lacks real substance as follows:

• Lack of Story: There's no discussion of how the company achieved its growth and the strategic initiatives undertaken to improve the operating results. Just a simple statement that references X growth and Y improvement.

• Lack of Analysis: No detailed analysis has been provided related to gross margins, trend analysis, KPIs, and similar items. While nothing overly detailed or confidential needs to be provided, offering some basic analysis would help two key objectives. First, a simple analysis would indicate the company is undertaking critical financial analyses (building credibility with the external parties). Second, an analysis would help direct the external party toward key operating results keeping them focused on the task at hand.

EXHIBIT 12.1—AUDITED FINANCIAL STATEMENTS – BALANCE SHEET

Dollar Amounts in Thousands

Balance Sheet As of the Fiscal Year Ending	12/31/2022	12/31/2023
Assets		
Current Assets		
Cash & Equivalents	$ 775	$ 2,164
Accounts Receivable	$ 6,776	$ 8,009
Inventory	$ 3,822	$ 1,706
Prepaid Expenses	$ 600	$ 625
Total Current Assets	$11,973	$12,504
Long-Term Capital Assets		
Property, Machinery, & Equipment	$ 4,000	$ 4,500
Accumulated Depreciation	$ (1,571)	$ (2,214)
Net Property, Machinery, & Equipment	$ 2,429	$ 2,286
Other Assets		
Intangible Assets, Net	$ 2,000	$ 6,000
Other Assets	$ 100	$ 100
Total Long-Term & Other Assets	$ 4,529	$ 8,386
Total Assets	$16,502	$20,889

See Notes to Financial Statements

EXHIBIT 12.1—(CONTINUED)

Balance Sheet As of the Fiscal Year Ending	12/31/2022	12/31/2023
Liabilities		
Current Liabilities		
Accounts Payable	$ 1,405	$ 1,459
Accrued Liabilities	$ 1,084	$ 1,258
Short-Term Loans Payable	$ 3,390	$ 2,400
Deferred Revenue & Other Current Liabilities	$ 1,011	$ 1,348
Total Current Liabilities	$ 6,890	$ 6,465
Long-Term Liabilities		
Loans Payable, Less Short Term Portion	$ 750	$ 2,500
Total Liabilities	$ 7,640	$ 8,965
Stockholders' Equity		
Capital Stock	$ 7,500	$10,000
Retained Earnings (deficit)	$ 1,362	$ 1,924
Total Stockholders' Equity	$ 8,862	$11,924
Total Liabilities & Stockholders' Equity	$16,502	$20,889

See Notes to Financial Statements

♦ Periodic Presentation: Finally, the sample financial report is being provided only once a year, after the company's annual financial audit is completed. This represents the bare minimum in reporting as most external capital sources, especially lenders, would prefer more frequent financial reporting such as quarterly as it allows the lenders to keep much closer tabs on the company's operations (and identify any potential problems, concerns, or issues as early as possible).

EXHIBIT 12.2—AUDITED FINANCIAL STATEMENTS – INCOME STATEMENT

Dollar Amounts in Thousands

Income Statement For the Fiscal Years Ending	12/31/2022	12/31/2023
Net Sales Revenue	$ 54,210	$ 59,494
Costs of Sales Revenue	$(23,922)	$(21,766)
Gross Profit (aka Gross Margin)	$ 30,288	$ 37,728
Operating Expenses:		
Selling, General, & Administrative	$ 22,567	$ 25,289
Research & Development	$ 5,692	$ 7,139
Depreciation & Amortization	$ 1,571	$ 1,643
Total Operating Expenses	$ 29,831	$ 34,071
Operating Income (Loss)	$ 457	$ 3,658
Other Expenses (Income):		
Other Expenses or (Income)	$ 0	$ 2,000
Interest Expense	$ 339	$ 407
Total Other Expenses (Income)	$ 339	$ 2,407
Net Income (Loss) Before Income Taxes	$ 118	$ 1,251
Income Tax Expense (benefit)	$ 41	$ 438
Net Income (Loss) After Income Taxes	$ 77	$ 813

See Notes to Financial Statements

EXHIBIT 12.3—AUDITED FINANCIAL STATEMENTS – STATEMENT OF CASH FLOWS

Dollar Amounts in Thousands

Statement of Cash Flows For the Fiscal Years Ending	12/31/2022	12/31/2023
Net Income (Loss) after Income Taxes	$ 77	$ 813
Operating Activities, Cash provided (used):		
Depreciation & Amortization	$ 1,571	$ 1,643
Decrease (increase) in accounts receivables	$ (1,122)	$ (1,233)
Decrease (increase) in inventory	$ (333)	$ 2,116
Decrease (increase) in other current assets	$ (50)	$ (25)
Increase (decrease) in accounts payables	$ 155	$ 54
Increase (decrease) in accrued liabilities	$ 118	$ 42
Increase (decrease) in other liabilities	$ 217	$ 469
Net Cash Flow from Operating Activities	$ 634	$ 3,879
Investing Activities, Cash provided (used):		
Capital Expenditures	$ (250)	$ (500)
Investments in Intangible & Other Assets	$ 0	$ (5,000)
Net Cash Flow from Investing Activities	$ (250)	$ (5,500)
Financing Activities, Cash provided (used):		
Dividends or Distributions Paid	$ 0	$ (250)
Sale (repurchase) of Equity	$ 0	$ 2,500
Proceeds from Issuance of Loans (i.e., debt)	$ 0	$ 3,000
Repayments of Long-Term Loans	$ (750)	$ (1,250)
Net Borrowings (Repayments) of Short-Term Loans	$ 560	$ (990)
Other Financing Activities	$ 0	$ 0
Net Cash Flow from Financing Activities	$ (190)	$ 3,010
Net Increase (decrease) in Cash & Equivalents	$ 194	$ 1,389
Beginning Cash & Equivalents Balance	$ 581	$ 775
Ending Cash & Equivalents Balance	$ 775	$ 2,164

See Notes to Financial Statements

Now, let's move on to the preferred case and provide a financial report that has more substance and value to our target audience. Here I would direct you to Exhibit 12.4, which presents the company's income statement with additional information and analyses provided. With the preferred case, I'm going to focus first on the income statement and then the balance sheet (presented in Exhibit 12.5) but begin by providing the following MDOR:

To Our Investors, Lenders, and Critical Business Partners:

Attached are QW Example Tech, Inc.'s (the "Company") unaudited quarterly financial statements and associated financial analyses for the fiscal years ending 12/31/23 and 12/31/22 as prepared by our internal executive management team. We are providing this financial information to you as part of our quarterly financial reporting compliance requirements to all Company investors, lenders, and critical business partners.

We, as a management team, are very proud of the Company's financial results for the fiscal year ending 12/31/23 and improvement compared to the prior fiscal year ending 12/31/22 as highlighted by the following key operating achievements and financial trends:

- *Net sales revenue increased by $5.3 million year over year representing a 9.75% increase in total net sales revenue. More importantly, the Company achieved sales revenue growth of roughly $12.2 million or 34.2% in its software and services division, which substantiates the Company's strategic business pivot shift into new markets that offer higher growth potential and gross margins. Net product sales revenue decreased by approximately $6.9 million year over year which is in line with management's expectations and directly the result of the Company eliminating selling and supporting certain technology products that were becoming obsolete and offered little opportunity to generate profits.*

- *The Company's gross profit increased on a year over year basis by approximately $7.4 million (a 24.6% increase), generating a gross margin of 63.4% compared to a gross margin of 55.9% for the prior year. The improvement in the Company's gross margin is the direct result of a.) a sales revenue mix change toward higher profit software and services sales (increasing from 65.9% in 2022 to 80.5% in 2023) and b.) improving gross margins being realized in the software and services segment of the business as a result of economies of scale (from 63.9% in 2022 to 72.3% in 2023). While the gross margin in the products segment of the business decreased from 40.3% in 2022 to 26.1% in 2023, this was largely expected and a direct result of more aggressive sales discounting strategies used to move older products.*

- *Selling, general, and direct operating expenses increased from roughly $29.8 million in 2022, representing 55% of total sales revenue to approximately $34.1 million in 2023, representing 57.3% of total sales revenue. Increases in selling and research & development expenses were incurred as a result of implementing a more aggressive selling and support program associated with the launch of new software products, again within management's expectations.*

- *The result of the Company's efforts, including increased sales revenue and improved gross margins, provided for an increase in its annual EBIT from less than $500,000 in 2022 representing less than 1% of total sales revenue to approximately $3.66 million in 2023, representing 6.2% of total sales revenue. Even taking into consideration the Company absorbing a $2 million charge (non-cash) related to discontinued operations and to reserve for obsolete inventory, the Company was able to increase profits before tax from just $118,000 in 2022 to $1.25 million in 2023, a 10.6x increase.*

- *The Company's financial strength continues to improve as measured by an increase of almost $1 million in net working capital, an improvement in the Company's current ration from 1.74 as of the fiscal year ending 12/31/22 to 1.93 as of the fiscal year ending 12/31/23, and a reduction in the Company's financial leverage as measured by a reduction in its debt to equity ratio from .86 as of the fiscal year ending 12/31/22 to .75 as of the fiscal year ending 12/31/23.*

All in all, the Company's executive management team and board of directors are pleased with the fiscal year ending 12/31/23 operating results but also understand that the Company's pivot into pursuing new opportunities with the software and services division is just getting started. As such, we anticipate that the operating results for future years will continue to strengthen as we execute our business plan.

As always, feel free to reach out to me with any questions, feedback, and/or additional information needs as it relates to your assessment of the Company's operating results and financial condition. We appreciate your continued support and look forward to working with each and every one of you in the years to come.

Sincerely,
_____ (signed)
CEO/President

Note: I elected to not include the statement of cash flows again (to save space) as for the most part, it would be the same as presented in Exhibit 12.3. However, if the management team of our example company wanted to highlight specific operating results and trends that originate from the statement of cash flows, it could easily be included.

Well, now we have something to work with in our preferred case as follows:

- The Story Is Now Clearer: The MDOR clearly helps the external user connect the Company's improved financial performance with the vision established by the management team in the business plan. Specific financial performance achievements, supported by additional analyses, have been incorporated into the financial report to help the external user understand the operating results.

- Proper Level of Analysis: A reasonable level of financial analysis has been provided related to gross margins, trend analysis, and similar items. The level of financial analysis provided is not overly detailed or confidential in nature as in reality, our example company is simply doing the work that would normally be completed by analysts within the external user organizations. As noted previously, we've now addressed two key concerns related to our base case. First, the company is completing financial analyses and understands the operating results (building credibility). Second and more importantly, the MDOR is steering the external user toward critical financial data and operating results to keep them focused and on track (rather than letting their minds wander).

- Periodic Presentation: Finally, the sample financial report is being provided on a quarterly basis which is much more preferrable than annually (as previously covered in this chapter). In our sample financial report, we have based on the fiscal year-end operating results, but this is the type of financial report that can easily be produced on a quarterly basis and distributed to the external users.

In closing, the differences between our financial reporting base and preferred cases should be very clear. The format changes, ratios and operating trends offered (such as the sales revenue growth rate, gross margins, etc.), additional disclosures provided, and a robust MDOR have all been prepared with more clarity and confidence to assist external users, but at the same time, has not provided any significant confidential information that may place the company at risk. It is important when preparing financial reports for external users to stick to the facts as much as possible, remain at a summary level, offer only a limited amount of future visibility (i.e., forward looking statements), design the financial report with ease of understanding in mind, and above all, remember to remain very conservative with the terminology used. Instead of stating that future operating results will strengthen considerably, just use the term strengthen as this provides much more leeway in future years if results are less than robust.

EXHIBIT 12.4—COMPANY EXPANDED INCOME STATEMENT

Unaudited - Prepared by Company Management

Income Statement for the Fiscal Years Ending	12/31/2022	% of Net Rev.	12/31/2023	% of Net Rev.	Annual Change $	Annual Change %
Sales Revenue:						
Software Platform & SAAS Sales, Net	$35,705,000	65.86%	$48,037,521	80.74%	$ 12,332,521	34.54%
Product Sales, Net	$18,505,000	34.14%	$11,456,800	19.26%	$ (7,048,200)	-38.09%
Net Sales Revenue	$54,210,000	100.00%	$59,494,321	100.00%	$ 5,284,321	9.75%
Costs of Sales Revenue:						
Direct Product Costs	$11,040,000	20.37%	$ 7,392,000	12.42%	$ (3,648,000)	-33.04%
Wages, Burden, & Other Direct Costs of Sales	$12,882,000	23.76%	$14,374,000	24.16%	$ 1,492,000	11.58%
Total Costs of Sales Revenue	$23,922,000	44.13%	$21,766,000	36.59%	$ (2,156,000)	-9.01%
Gross Profit	$30,288,000	55.87%	$37,728,321	63.41%	$ 7,440,321	24.57%
Gross Margin Analysis by Sales Revenue Type:						
Software Platform & SAAS Sales, Net	63.92%		72.32%			8.40%
Product Sales, Net	40.34%		26.07%			-14.27%
Operating Expenses:						
Corporate Marketing, Branding, & Promotional	$16,093,575	29.69%	$18,517,500	31.12%	$ 2,423,925	15.06%
Research, Development, & Design	$ 5,692,000	10.50%	$ 7,139,000	12.00%	$ 1,447,000	25.42%
Corporate Overhead & Support	$ 6,473,625	11.94%	$ 6,771,272	11.38%	$ 297,647	4.60%
Depreciation & Amortization Expense	$ 1,571,429	2.90%	$ 1,642,857	2.76%	$ 71,429	4.55%
Total Operating Expenses	$29,830,629	55.03%	$34,070,629	57.27%	$ 4,240,000	14.21%
Operating Income (EBIT)	$ 457,371	0.84%	$ 3,657,692	6.15%	$ 3,200,321	699.72%
Operating Margin (EBIT Margin)	0.84%		6.15%			5.30%
Other Expenses (Income):						
Other Expenses, Income, & Discontinued Ops.	$ 0	0.00%	$ 2,000,000	3.36%		
Interest Expense	$ 339,000	0.63%	$ 407,000	0.68%		
Total Other Expenses (Income)	$ 339,000	0.63%	$ 2,407,000	4.05%		
Net Income (Loss) Before Income Taxes	$ 118,371	0.22%	$ 1,250,692	2.10%		
Income Tax Expense (Benefit)	$ 41,000	0.08%	$ 438,000	0.74%		
Net Income (Loss) After Income Taxes	$ 77,371	0.14%	$ 812,692	1.37%		

Confidential - Property of QW Example Tech, Inc.

EXHIBIT 12.5—COMPANY EXPANDED BALANCE SHEET

Unaudited - Prepared by Company Management

Balance Sheet as of the Fiscal Year Ending	12/31/2022	12/31/2023	Financial Strength	Amount
Assets				
Current Assets				
Cash & Equivalents	$ 775,161	$ 2,163,747	Net Working Capital	
Accounts Receivable	$ 6,776,000	$ 8,009,000	FYE 12/31/22	$5,083,050
Inventory	$ 3,822,000	$ 1,706,000	FYE 12/31/23	$6,038,600
Prepaid Expenses	$ 600,000	$ 625,000	Change	$ 955,550
Total Current Assets	$11,973,161	$12,503,747	Current Ratio:	
			FYE 12/31/22	1.74
Long-Term Capital Assets			FYE 12/31/23	1.93
Property, Machinery, & Equipment	$ 4,000,000	$ 4,500,000	Debt to Equity Ratio:	
Accumulated Depreciation	$ (1,571,429)	$ (2,214,286)	FYE 12/31/22	0.86
Net Property, Machinery, & Equipment	$ 2,428,571	$ 2,285,714	FYE 12/31/23	0.75
Other Assets				
Intangible Assets, Net	$ 2,000,000	$ 6,000,000		
Other Assets	$ 100,000	$ 100,000		
Total Long-Term & Other Assets	$ 4,528,571	$ 8,385,714		
Total Assets	$16,501,733	$20,889,462		

Confidential - Property of QW Example Tech, Inc.

EXHIBIT 12.5—(CONTINUED)

Balance Sheet

As of the Fiscal Year Ending	12/31/2022	12/31/2023
Liabilities		
Current Liabilities		
Accounts Payable	$ 1,405,000	$ 1,459,000
Accrued Liabilities	$ 1,084,000	$ 1,258,000
Short Term Loans Payable	$ 3,390,000	$ 2,400,000
Deferred Revenue & Other Current Liabilities	$ 1,011,111	$ 1,348,148
Total Current Liabilities	$ 6,890,111	$ 6,465,148
Long-Term Liabilities		
Loans Payable, Less Short-Term Portion	$ 750,000	$ 2,500,000
Total Liabilities	$ 7,640,111	$ 8,965,148
Stockholders' Equity		
Capital Stock	$ 7,500,000	$ 10,000,000
Retained Earnings (deficit)	$ 1,361,621	$ 1,924,314
Total Stockholders' Equity	$ 8,861,621	$ 11,924,314
Total Liabilities & Stockholders' Equity	$ 16,501,733	$ 20,889,462

Confidential - Property of QW Example Tech, Inc.

A Final Thought

If I haven't emphasized this enough, I'm going to one more time. Always know and understand your target audience before a financial report is structured, produced, and distributed. Keep a clear focus on the objective of the financial report related to telling the financial story by highlighting key economic drivers and operating results and avoid creating and including unnecessary noise and clutter. And whatever you do, never, ever hang yourself out to dry by using overly creative and aggressive terminology that may mislead the external user. Or as the old saying goes, it usually is very prudent to remember to not over-promise and under-deliver. This is a place you should really try and avoid.

13

PREPARING FINANCIAL REPORTS FROM COMPANY FINANCIAL STATEMENTS – INTERNAL CONSUMERS

Chapter 12 was dedicated to preparing and presenting sample financial reports from our example company's financial statements for delivery to external users such as lenders, investors, analysts, and similar parties. In revisiting the sample financial reports prepared in Chapter 12 (especially for our preferred case), I would like to highlight the following key concepts related to presenting financial information to external users:

- Formality: The financial reports were prepared in a more formal manner or format, one which external users are comfortable receiving and analyzing. This would include receiving clear and well-written MDORs, full audited financial statements (with footnotes), and similar supporting information.

- Story Clarity: In our preferred case, we took the opportunity to provide a much more informative MDOR, which was supported by expanded and more robust financial statements. The idea behind this was to communicate a very clear and concise story on how the business is performing and successes (or failures) with implementing its business plan.

- Confidentiality: External users should not receive highly confidential and/or privileged financial information that may divulge too much detail or operating trade secrets. This is not to say that external users are not trustworthy as by and large, they are. Rather, the risk you need to manage and understand is that externally prepared financial reports and information can often inadvertently be distributed or slip through to parties that should not be in the financial information chain. Keeping tight control of the financial reports and information distributed to external parties can help lessen the risk of a financial "accident" (for lack of a better term) down the road that can occur from the handling of financial reports and information

by inexperienced, overworked, or unqualified parties (that don't know what they're doing).

- Consistency: Finally, externally prepared and distributed financial reports and information should be done in the most consistent manner possible. That is, most external users or parties receiving financial reports and information should really receive the same reports, information, documents, etc. This helps keep the financial information flow controlled and helps avoid potentially embarrassing situations where six different external parties all received different financial reports and information, which not only makes your job more challenging (i.e., remembering which external party received what financial information) but also having to try and explain why one external party received X documents and another Y. You would be amazed how small the financial world is and how often different external parties (such as lenders or investors) end up evaluating and analyzing the same business.

In contrast with Chapter 12, Chapter 13 has been structured with our internal audience and consumers being kept at the forefront when preparing financial reports based on our example company's financial statements. Here, I discuss the same key concepts previously presented at the start of this chapter but from a different perspective.

- Formality: Formal financial reports will still be present for our internal consumers but the formality of communicating the operating results will shift toward being more direct (i.e., let's just cut to the chase) as in theory, our internal audience should have far more knowledge and a much deeper understanding of the company's operating results and financial condition. Rather than preparing formal letters, MDORS, and similar financial overviews, we're going to shift our communication strategy to being direct and to the point via using summary bullet points. Remember, our target internal audience is generally extremely busy business executives that need to review and understand the "financial facts" in the most efficient manner possible.

- Key Performance Indicators ("KPIs"): Internal financial reports and financial information tend to rely heavily on presenting critical company-based KPIs to help the target internal audience with assessing whether the company's business plan and story are being achieved. Unlike external users that often require being educated as to the company's business plan and economic viability, internal consumers should already have a clear understanding of the business plan and story. What they need is a snapshot of critical financial and operating KPIs to use as a tool to understand what is going well (and expand on this) and what has missed the mark (and take corrective action).

- Confidentiality: You might have already anticipated the change in my tone on confidentiality as for internal consumers, far more confidential financial and operating information is going to be prepared, presented, shared, and assessed. By the way, I would like to mention that as we move our financial reporting discussion to Chapter 14, you will notice that the concept of confidentiality arises again, specifically as it relates to providing financial reports and information to internal company employees that are within their "pay grade." Translation, employees should only be provided financial reports and information that is most relevant and valuable to them in order to perform their job duties.

- Consistency: Here again, I'm going to pivot similar to how I did with confidentiality where I explained the difference between the level of financial and operating information external users

and internal consumers of financial reports and information receive. Large businesses can often develop and utilize hundreds of different financial reports within one organization, with each financial report tailored for the specific needs of the target internal consumer. For example, senior sales representatives need periodic financial flash reports that keep them focused on understanding their sales performance by product, service, and software lines (i.e., what sales were booked during the period for each item and what sales were earned during the period for each item). The senior sales representatives don't need to understand the expense budget of the corporate general and administrative team that manages the legal, accounting, and human resource functions. Similarly, the general and administrative team doesn't need access to sales flash financial reports the senior sales representatives receive. Rather, each target audience needs financial reports and information that are specifically structured to support them with completing their job duties.

Before we move forward with presenting our base and preferred case financial reports for our example company, I would like to comment on a key concept related to employees having access to financial reports and information. That is, the further you move up the food chain (in a business) the more financial reports and information you'll need to access and understand. Needless to say, a company president or CEO needs to understand the "big" and complete financial picture of the business and should have access to all financial reports and information (required to complete their job responsibilities). On the other hand, an operations manager that is responsible for managing the technology, hardware, software, and security functions of a business does not and should not have access to the same level of financial reports and information as the president or CEO.

Financial Reports from Financial Statements – Internal Consumers

To start, please refer to Exhibit 13.1, which presents our base case internally prepared financial report (based on the company's financial statements) for our example company. In this situation, only the income statement has been presented as our rather inexperienced accounting Controller hasn't developed their financial reporting skills to the level of a CFO (at least not yet).

Ok, not bad as the format of the income statement is far more informative (and something that was introduced to you in Exhibit 6.2) in terms of presenting a much more complete picture of our example company's income statement. However, where this financial report falls short is as follows:

- The target audience is the internal executive management team; that is the "C" suite (including the chief executive officer, CEO, chief financial officer, CFO, chief operating officer, COO, chief marketing officer, CMO, and chief technology officer, CTO) as well as the board of directors. They absolutely need more insight into the company's complete financial performance and condition so including the balance sheet and statement of cash flows is essential.

- The historical comparison of year over year operating results between the fiscal year ending 12/31/22 and the fiscal year ending 12/31/23 is helpful but fails to incorporate a critical analysis. That is, how did the company's financial operating results compare to projections for the year as well as against

industry standards or benchmarks? This financial information and analysis is nowhere to be found.

- Also, take notice of the notes and comments provided by our inexperienced accounting Controller. The notes and comments highlight certain financial achievements but only from the perspective of "what" happened as opposed to "why" something happened. For example, the note and comment indicates total company sales revenue increased by approximately 10% YOY. Great, what does this mean against projected sales revenue for the year and why did it exceed or fail to meet expectations?

Again, Exhibit 13.1 as a financial report isn't all that bad as it does provide some useful financial information. To be quite honest, it's better than most of the internally prepared financial reports I see on a day-to-day basis when working with small- to medium-sized privately held businesses. However, as you will see in Exhibits 13.2 and 13.3, there's so much more vital information that can be provided to our internal target audience that will assist them with truly understanding our example company's financial performance and condition.

Pivoting from our base case, now I present our preferred case for review. Please note that our preferred case financial report includes an income statement, a balance sheet, and a supplemental summary (prepared by management) of key operating trends, which is provided at the end of this chapter. Taken individually,

EXHIBIT 13.1—INTERNALLY PREPARED INCOME STATEMENT – BASE CASE

Unaudited - Prepared by Company Management

Income Statement for the Fiscal Years Ending	12/31/2022	% of Net Rev.	12/31/2023	% of Net Rev.	Notes/Comments
Sales Revenue:					
Software Platform & SAAS Sales	$36,400,000	67.15%	$48,533,321	81.58%	Sales increase, 33%.
Product Sales	$19,200,000	35.42%	$13,440,000	22.59%	Sales decrease, 30%.
Other Sales, Discounts, & Allowances	$ (1,390,000)	-2.56%	$ (2,479,000)	-4.17%	Discounting increased.
Net Sales Revenue	$54,210,000	100.00%	$59,494,321	100.00%	Total sales increase, approximately 10%.
Costs of Sales Revenue:					
Direct Product Costs	$11,040,000	20.37%	$ 7,392,000	12.42%	Function of lower sales.
Wages & Burden	$12,012,000	22.16%	$13,589,000	22.84%	Function of increased software sales.
Direct Overhead	$ 800,000	1.48%	$ 700,000	1.18%	n/a.
Other Costs of Sales Revenue	$ 70,000	0.13%	$ 85,000	0.14%	n/a.
Total Costs of Sales Revenue	$23,922,000	44.13%	$21,766,000	36.59%	
Gross Profit	$30,288,000	55.87%	$37,728,321	63.41%	
Gross Margin	55.87%		63.41%		GM improved 7.5%.
Direct Operating Expenses:					
Advertising, Promotional, & Selling	$ 3,659,000	6.75%	$ 3,867,000	6.50%	Increased sales.
Personnel Wages, Burden, & Compensation	$10,300,000	19.00%	$11,899,000	20.00%	Increased sales.
Facility Operating Expenses	$ 1,219,725	2.25%	$ 1,264,254	2.13%	n/a.
Other Operating Expenses	$ 375,000	0.69%	$ 450,000	0.76%	n/a.
Total Direct Operating Expenses	$15,553,725	28.69%	$17,480,254	29.38%	
Contribution Profit	$14,734,275	27.18%	$20,248,067	34.03%	
Contribution Margin	27.18%		34.03%		CM improved 6.8%.
Corporate Expenses & Overhead:					
Corporate Marketing, Branding, & Promotional	$ 2,134,575	3.94%	$ 2,751,500	4.62%	Within reason/support business expansion.
Research, Development, & Design	$ 5,692,000	10.50%	$ 7,139,000	12.00%	Added investments made.
Corporate Overhead & Support	$ 4,878,900	9.00%	$ 5,057,017	8.50%	Consistent.
Depreciation & Amortization Expense	$ 1,571,429	2.90%	$ 1,642,857	2.76%	Consistent.
Total Corporate Operating Expenses	$14,276,904	26.34%	$16,590,374	27.89%	
Operating Income (EBIT)	$ 457,371	0.84%	$ 3,657,692	6.15%	
Operating Margin (EBIT Margin)	0.84%		6.15%		
Other Expenses (Income):					
Other Expenses, Income, & Discontinued Ops.	$ 0	0.00%	$ 2,000,000	3.36%	Reserve/write-off of obsolete inventory.
Interest Expense	$ 339,000	0.63%	$ 407,000	0.68%	n/a.
Total Other Expenses (Income)	$ 339,000	0.63%	$ 2,407,000	4.05%	
Net Income (Loss) Before Income Taxes	$ 118,371	0.22%	$ 1,250,692	2.10%	
Income Tax Expense (Benefit)	$ 41,000	0.08%	$ 438,000	0.74%	Increased as a result of higher profits.
Net Income (Loss) After Income Taxes	$ 77,371	0.14%	$ 812,692	1.37%	

Confidential - Property of QW Example Tech, Inc.

the financial report would be incomplete as all three components of the financial report are essential to understanding the company's entire financial results and financial position.

To start, please refer to Exhibit 13.2, which presents a financial report for our example company starting with the income statement and note the differences (both exclusions and inclusions).

- The FYE 12/31/22 financial information has been eliminated. Why? Well, the answer is simple. If our target internal audience was only to fixate on the YOY operating results improvement between the FYE 12/31/22 and 12/31/23, they may be patting themselves on the back for a job well done and break out the champagne as sales revenue, gross profits, and net profits all increased, and in some cases, quite handsomely (refer to Exhibit 13.1).

- Instead, I've elected to present the actual FYE 12/31/23 financial information and more specifically, the income statement comparing it with the forecast FYE 12/31/23 income statement (refer to chapter 10 for further information on financial forecasts). And now, we have a different story as sales revenue, gross profits, operating income, and net profit have all "missed" (i.e., came in below projected levels) and in some cases, significantly (e.g., actual net profit of approximately $813,000 compared to a forecast net profit of roughly $2,917,000, representing a shortfall of $2,104,000). This is supported by the variance analysis that has been included along with internal note references that act as a mini-MDOR if you will, but in bullet point fashion. Please refer to *Summary of Key Operating Trends, etc.* presented later that provides a summary level narrative explaining our example company's financial operating results and challenges for the FYE 12/31/23.

- Also, note the inclusion of some critical KPIs including net sales revenue per full time employee, average product sales

order, total software sales number of accounts and average sales per account (all located at the top of the report), and an expanded view of the company's gross margin by primary sales revenue source (product versus software). Almost all the variances associated with these KPIs are trending negative, an issue that should raise eyebrows with the C suite and board of directors in terms of gaining a better understanding of the underlying challenges facing the company. Curiously, however, the number of new customer accounts actual realized a 25-unit positive variance which as explained below, resides in the fact that the entry level software SaaS product is performing above expectations (at the expense of the advanced and expert level SaaS software products).

Moving on, Exhibit 13.3 now presents our preferred case financial report for our example company's balance sheet. For ease of review and formatting, I split the balance sheet into two halves but again, certain key inclusions should be noted as it relates to presenting critical financial information pertaining to the company's financial condition as of the FYE 12/31/23:

- First up, it should be noted a balance sheet has actually been included, which is in contrast to our base case scenario where only the income statement was presented. This point emphasizes an issue addressed earlier in the book which is centered in the fact that most companies are overly income statement focused and tend to ignore the balance sheet and statement of cash flows (which they don't understand or don't think are important). As you will subsequently see, significant financial condition issues have been called out and need to be addressed by the executive management team.

- Again, the information for the prior FYE 12/31/22 has been eliminated as our target audience needs to focus on the

EXHIBIT 13.2—INTERNALLY PREPARED INCOME STATEMENT – PREFERRED CASE

Unaudited - Prepared by Company Management

Income Statement for the Fiscal Year Ending	Ref.	Actual 12/31/2023	% of Net Rev.	Projected 12/31/2023	% of Net Rev.	Variance
Key Performance Indicators:						
Net Sales Revenue Per Full Time Employee	(a)	$ 487,658		$ 505,440		$ (17,782)
Product Sales, Avg. Order Value (net)	(b)	$ 15,659		$ 19,543		$ (3,884)
Software Platform & SAAS Sales:						
SAAS Sales, Total Customer Accounts	(a)	525		500		25
SAAS Sales, Total Earned Avg. Per Account	(a)	$ 74,667		$ 81,180		$ (6,513)
Sales Revenue:						
Software Platform & SAAS Sales	(a)	$48,533,321	81.58%	$49,500,000	78.35%	$ (966,679)
Product Sales	(b)	$13,440,000	22.59%	$15,200,000	24.06%	$(1,760,000)
Other Sales, Discounts, & Allowances	(b)	$ (2,479,000)	-4.17%	$ (1,520,000)	-2.41%	$ (959,000)
Net Sales Revenue		$59,494,321	100.00%	$63,180,000	100.00%	$(3,685,679)
Costs of Sales Revenue:						
Direct Product Costs	(b)	$ 7,392,000	12.42%	$ 7,600,000	12.03%	$ 208,000
Wages & Burden	(a)	$13,589,000	22.84%	$15,575,000	24.65%	$ 1,986,000
Direct Overhead	n/a	$ 700,000	1.18%	$ 750,000	1.19%	$ 50,000
Other Costs of Sales Revenue	n/a	$ 85,000	0.14%	$ 100,000	0.16%	$ 15,000
Total Costs of Sales Revenue		$21,766,000	36.59%	$24,025,000	38.03%	$ 2,259,000
Gross Profit		$37,728,321	63.41%	$39,155,000	61.97%	$(1,426,679)
Gross Margin Analysis by Sales Revenue Type:						
Software Platform & SAAS Sales	(a)	72.32%		70.37%		1.95%
Product Sales	(b)	26.07%		33.64%		-7.57%

EXHIBIT 13.2—(CONTINUED)

Income Statement for the Fiscal Year Ending	Ref.	Actual 12/31/2023	% of Net Rev.	Projected 12/31/2023	% of Net Rev.	Variance
Direct Operating Expenses:						
Advertising, Promotional, & Selling	(c)	$ 3,867,000	6.50%	$ 4,000,000	6.33%	$ 133,000
Personnel Wages, Burden, & Compensation	(c)	$11,899,000	20.00%	$12,500,000	19.78%	$ 601,000
Facility Operating Expenses	n/a	$ 1,264,254	2.13%	$ 1,250,000	1.98%	$ (14,254)
Other Operating Expenses	n/a	$ 450,000	0.76%	$ 500,000	0.79%	$ 50,000
Total Direct Operating Expenses		$17,480,254	29.38%	$18,250,000	28.89%	$ 769,746
Contribution Profit		$20,248,067	34.03%	$20,905,000	33.09%	$ (656,933)
Contribution Margin		34.03%		33.09%		0.95%
Corporate Expenses & Overhead:						
Corporate Marketing, Branding, & Promotional	(c)	$ 2,751,500	4.62%	$ 2,500,000	3.96%	$ (251,500)
Research, Development, & Design	(c)	$ 7,139,000	12.00%	$ 6,318,000	10.00%	$ (821,000)
Corporate Overhead & Support	n/a	$ 5,057,017	8.50%	$ 5,000,000	7.91%	$ (57,017)
Depreciation & Amortization Expense	n/a	$ 1,642,857	2.76%	$ 1,750,000	2.77%	$ 107,143
Total Corporate Operating Expenses		$16,590,374	27.89%	$15,568,000	24.64%	$(1,022,374)
Operating Income (EBIT)		$ 3,657,692	6.15%	$ 5,337,000	8.45%	$(1,679,308)
Operating Margin (EBIT Margin)		6.15%		8.45%		45.56%
Other Expenses (Income):						
Other Expenses, Income, & Discontinued Ops.	(b)	$ 2,000,000	3.36%	$ 500,000	0.79%	$(1,500,000)
Interest Expense	n/a	$ 407,000	0.68%	$ 350,000	0.55%	$ (57,000)
Total Other Expenses (Income)		$ 2,407,000	4.05%	$ 850,000	1.35%	$(1,557,000)
Net Income (Loss) Before Income Taxes		$ 1,250,692	2.10%	$ 4,487,000	7.10%	$(3,236,308)
Income Tax Expense (Benefit)		$ 438,000	0.74%	$ 1,570,450	2.49%	$ 1,132,450
Net Income (Loss) After Income Taxes	(d)	$ 812,692	1.37%	$ 2,916,550	4.62%	$(2,103,858)

Confidential - Property of QW Example Tech, Inc.

EXHIBIT 13.3(A)—INTERNALLY PREPARED BALANCE SHEET – PREFERRED CASE (TOP HALF)

Unaudited - Prepared by Company Management

Balance Sheet as of the Fiscal Year Ending	Ref.	Actual 12/31/2023	% of Total	Projected 12/31/2023	% of Total	Variance
Assets						
Current Assets						
Cash & Equivalents						
Cash in Operating Account		$ 663,747	3.18%	$ 1,054,643	4.52%	
Cash Invested Short-Term Securities		$ 1,500,000	7.18%	$ 4,218,570	18.09%	
Total Cash & Equivalents	(d)	$ 2,163,747	10.36%	$ 5,273,213	22.61%	$(3,109,465)
Accounts Receivable						
Gross Accounts Receivable	(d)	$ 8,329,360	39.87%	$ 7,521,429	32.26%	$ 807,931
Less: Allowance for Doubtful Accounts	(d)	$ (320,360)	-1.53%	$ (150,429)	-0.65%	$ (169,931)
Total Accounts Receivable		$ 8,009,000	38.34%	$ 7,371,000	31.61%	$ 638,000
Inventory						
Raw Material	n/a	$ 170,600	0.82%	$ 175,000	0.75%	$ (4,400)
Work In Process	n/a	$ 85,300	0.41%	$ 87,500	0.38%	$ (2,200)
Finished Goods	(b)	$ 3,838,500	18.38%	$ 2,058,824	8.83%	$ 1,779,676
Less: Reserve for slow moving & obsolete	(b)	$ (2,388,400)	-11.43%	$ (571,324)	-2.45%	$(1,817,076)
Total Inventory		$ 1,706,000	8.17%	$ 1,750,000	7.51%	$ (44,000)
Prepaid Expenses		$ 625,000	2.99%	$ 645,000	2.77%	$ (20,000)
Total Current Assets	(d)	$12,503,747	59.86%	$15,039,213	64.50%	$(2,535,465)
Current Ratio	(d)	*1.93*		*2.22*		*-0.28*
Quick Ratio	(d)	*1.57*		*1.86*		*-0.29*
Long-Term Capital Assets						
Equipment & Machinery		$ 3,200,000		$ 3,150,000		
Accumulated Depreciation - Equip. & Mach.		$ (1,660,714)		$(1,625,000)		
Autos, Computers, & Other Fixed Assets		$ 1,300,000		$ 1,350,000		
Accumulated Depreciation - Other Fixed Assets		$ (553,571)		$ (696,429)		
Net Property, Machinery, & Equipment	n/a	$ 2,285,714	10.94%	$ 2,178,571	9.34%	$ 107,143
Other Assets						
Intangible Assets - Goodwill		$ 5,000,000		$ 5,000,000		
Accumulated Amortization - Goodwill		$ (4,000,000)		$(4,000,000)		
Intangible Assets - Acquired Software Rights & Patents		$ 5,000,000		$ 5,000,000		
Accumulated Amortization - Software & Patents		$ 0		$ 0		
Net Other Assets	n/a	$ 6,000,000	28.72%	$ 6,000,000	25.73%	$ 0
Other Assets	n/a	$ 100,000	0.48%	$ 100,000	0.43%	$ 0
Total Long-Term & Other Assets	n/a	$ 8,385,714	40.14%	$ 8,278,571	35.50%	$ 107,143
Total Assets	(d)	$20,889,462	100.00%	$23,317,784	100.00%	$(2,428,322)

Confidential - Property of QW Example Tech, Inc.

financial condition of our example company comparing actual FYE 12/31/23 balance sheet amounts against projected balance sheet amounts. As will be summarized in the supplemental narrative included in the full financial report, the impact on the company's balance sheet and more specifically, available liquidity, from the negative net income variance of approximately $2,104,000 will be on full display.

- I took the opportunity to slip in some basic balance sheet KPIs including calculating certain key financial strength ratios as well as to present an analysis of actual versus projected asset, liability, and stockholders' equity balances as a percentage of their respective totals. For further information on financial ratio analysis, please refer to our sister book titled *How to Read a Financial Report*, 10th edition as we cover this topic at length. Certain key financial strength ratios have been called out and highlighted in Exhibit 13.3 and include the current and quick ratios (measurements of a company's short-term liquidity strength) and two debt to equity ratios (measurements of a company's use of debt and financial leverage). For the financial strength ratios presented, the trending is negative, indicating the company's liquidity is not as strong as forecast, and the company's use of debt and financial leverage is above projected levels as well. These financial strength ratios are important for management to understand and proactively address as if the company's financial strength is weaker than anticipated, it may impair its ability to support rapid growth in the future.

- Finally, please note that two dollar-based variances have been highlighted and called out in Exhibit 13.3 – the negative cash balance variance of roughly $3,100,000 in the Current Assets section of the balance sheet and the negative current earnings variance of approximately $2,100,000 in the Stockholders'

Equity section of the balance sheet. The reason these two items are important is due to their significance. In the case of cash, the company projected a year-end balance of roughly $5,300,000 and ended up finishing the year with just under $2,200,000, a $3,100,000 negative dollar variance and even more profound, a 58% negative percentage variance. Wow, that's not chump change and something the executive management team needs to understand, as while the negative current earnings variance of $2,100,000 helps explain a large portion of the cash shortfall of $3,100,000 (roughly 68%), other factors have also contributed to the cash shortfall including the accounts receivable balance that finished the year $638,000 higher than forecast, as well as changes to other assets and liability accounts. But from a big picture perspective (which is what we're having our target audience focus on), the negative cash balance of roughly $3,100,000 is mainly comprised of two items, negative net income variance of $2,100,000 and the increase in accounts receivables of $638,000 as combined, these two items account for approximately 88% of the total cash shortfall.

Note: I elected to not include a preferred case statement of cash flows as the last bullet point basically explains the cash flow difference for the FYE 12/31/23 (so including a statement of cash flows would have been overkill at this point). However, if a company does have significant variances present in its periodic cash flows that are not easily identified or isolated to a couple of key variances, inclusion of an internally prepared statement of cash flows would be appropriate, similar to the format presented in Exhibit 8.3.

For both the preferred case income statement presented in Exhibit 13.2 and the preferred case balance sheet presented in Exhibit 13.3 (both the top half and bottom half of the balance

EXHIBIT 13.3(B)—INTERNALLY PREPARED BALANCE SHEET - PREFERRED CASE (BOTTOM HALF)

Unaudited - Prepared by Company Management

Balance Sheet as of the Fiscal Year Ending	Ref.	12/31/2023	% of Total	12/31/2023	% of Total	Variance
Liabilities						
Current Liabilities						
Accounts Payable						
Credit Cards - Due in less than 30 Days		$ 72,950	0.81%	$ 168,500	1.81%	
Vendors & Suppliers - Due in 30 Days		$ 729,500	8.14%	$ 842,500	9.07%	
Vendors & Suppliers - Due in 90 Days		$ 656,550	7.32%	$ 674,000	7.26%	
Total Accounts Payable	n/a	$ 1,459,000	16.27%	$ 1,685,000	18.14%	$ (226,000)
Accrued Liabilities						
Payroll Wages & Burden		$ 990,000	11.04%	$ 962,000	10.36%	
Interest		$ 122,000	1.36%	$ 100,000	1.08%	
Income Taxes		$ 146,000	1.63%	$ 392,613	4.23%	
Total Accrued Liabilities Payable	n/a	$ 1,258,000	14.03%	$ 1,454,613	15.66%	$ (196,613)
Short-Term Loans Payable						
Working Capital Line of Credit		$ 1,900,000	21.19%	$ 1,500,000	16.15%	
Current Portion of Long-Term Loans		$ 500,000	5.58%	$ 500,000	5.38%	
Total Short Term Loans Payable	(d)	$ 2,400,000	26.77%	$ 2,000,000	21.53%	$ 400,000
Deferred Revenue & Other Current Liabilities						
Deferred Revenue & Customer Deposits		$ 1,209,548	13.49%	$ 1,500,000	16.15%	
Sales Taxes Payable & Other Current Liabilities		$ 138,600	1.55%	$ 150,000	1.61%	
Total Other Current Liabilities & Deferred Revenue	(a)	$ 1,348,148	15.04%	$ 1,650,000	17.76%	$ (301,852)
Total Current Liabilities		$ 6,465,148		$ 6,789,613		
Long-Term Liabilities						
Long-Term Loans Due in Two Years		$ 500,000	5.58%	$ 2,500,000	26.91%	
Long-Term Loans Due after Two Years		$ 2,000,000	22.31%	$ 0	0.00%	
Total Long-term Liabilities	n/a	$ 2,500,000	27.89%	$ 2,500,000	26.91%	$ 0
Total Liabilities		$ 8,965,148	100.00%	$ 9,289,613	100.00%	$ (324,465)
Stockholders' Equity						
Capital Stock - Par, $.01 per share		$ 10,000	0.08%	$ 10,000	0.07%	
Capital Stock - APIC		$ 9,990,000	83.78%	$ 9,990,000	71.21%	
Dividends & Distributions		$ (250,000)	-2.10%	$ (250,000)	-1.78%	
Current Earnings	(d)	$ 812,692	6.82%	$ 2,916,550	20.79%	$(2,103,858)
Retained Earnings - Carryforward		$ 1,361,621	11.42%	$ 1,361,621	9.71%	
Total Stockholders' Equity		$11,924,314	100.00%	$14,028,171	100.00%	$(2,103,858)
Debt to Equity (net worth) Ratio		0.75		0.66		(0.09)
Debt to Tangible Equity (net worth) Ratio		1.51		1.16		(0.36)
Total Liabilities & Stockholders' Equity		$20,889,462	n/a	$23,317,784	n/a	$(2,428,322)

Confidential - Property of QW Example Tech, Inc.

sheet), other important trends, KPIs, financial information, etc. could have been presented and discussed in addition to the bullet points summarized above. In fact, and depending on the company and industry in which it operates, the income statement presented in Exhibit 13.2 and balance sheet presented in Exhibit 13.3 could have been formatted and structured differently based on the critical financial information needs of the executive management team and board of directors. What I provided was a sample preferred case income statement and balance sheet for a technology-based company focused on software and SaaS sales.

My goal with summarizing the critical financial results was to again emphasize the importance of knowing the target audience (in this case, the executive management team and board of directors),

avoid burying them in too much BS, and rather, have them focus on the key financial results. That is, why did top line sales revenue miss by approximately 10%, how severe are the problems in the product division of the company given the $2,000,000 expense "hit" taken related to inventory values (refer to Chapter 14 for more information on this topic), and could short-term liquidity issues be present as it relates to the cash balance finishing the year far below the forecast levels? These are critical issues the company needs to address as it develops and implements its business plan for the coming years, including building projection models of value.

As noted previously, here is the final component of the financial report, the Summary of Key Operating Trends that should be digested along with the income statement and balance sheet.

Summary of Key Operating Trends, Narratives, and Financial Results for the FYE 12/31/23

Four significant operating performance issues impacted the Company's operating results and financial condition for the FYE 12/31/23 as follows:

(a) *Net sales revenue missed in both the product and software/SaaS divisions for different reasons. Software/SaaS sales, as measured by the number of customers, actually exceeded projections but the mix of the software/SaaS sales was skewed toward the basic version of the software, which is cheaper and easier to implement than the expert and advanced versions of the software. This resulted in total software/ SaaS sales falling short of projections by roughly 2% and average software/SaaS sales revenue per customer falling short of projected levels by approximately 8%. Overall, the company's software/SaaS offerings have been well received by the market but customer preference indicates a slower adoption rate of the advanced and expert versions of the software. This also negatively impacted deferred revenue as lower average sales per software/SaaS customer resulted in reduced advance payments for future software/SaaS sales.*

(b) *Product sales were challenging during the year as the company's products have become obsolete quicker than forecast and competition in the market is fierce. Price cuts and aggressive sales discounting strategies were used to move older products (negatively impacting product sales). These events had a significant drag on the product division's gross margin which finished the year at approximately 26% compared to a forecast gross margin of roughly 33.6%. It should further be noted that the company absorbed an other expense of $2,000,000 (which was reviewed and approved by the BOD) during the year as a result of writing down the value of old, obsolete* *inventory. Looking forward, the company needs to undertake a detailed review and analysis of the financial viability of the product's division as excess levels of obsolete finished goods are still present that may not have a viable market in 2024.*

(c) *Direct operating and corporate expenses generally performed in line with management's expectations and trended as anticipated with lower sales. Direct advertising and promotional expenses along with personnel wages, burden, and compensation finished the year slightly below projected levels for three reasons. First, sales commissions were lower than forecast as a result of reduced sales. Second, staffing challenges were present in the software/SaaS division as recruitment of qualified sales reps proved to be challenging during the year. Third, direct advertising expense in the product division was controlled as the company utilized more aggressive sales discounting strategies. Corporate marketing and research & development expenses both finished the year slightly above forecast levels as a result of investing additional resources in improving a.) the brand recognition of the company's new software/SaaS products (with additional marketing initiatives undertaken during the year) and b.) investing in additional software development efforts to improve the ease of use of implementation of the advanced and expert versions of the company's software/SaaS product lines. These additional investments were made during the second half of the FYE 12/31/23 which should produce financial returns starting in 2024 and extending through 2026.*

(d) *The company's liquidity and financial condition as of the FYE 12/31/23 underperformed compared to projected levels for two primary reasons. First, the negative variance realized in net income amounted to approximately $2,100,000 which had a direct effect of reducing the cash balance at the end of the year by approximately the same amount. Second, the year-end balance in customer accounts receivable amounted to $638,000 above the forecast level as customer payments slowed during the fourth quarter. The combination of these two items contributed to $2,738,000 of the total cash shortfall of roughly $3,100,000 for the year (accounting for 88% of the shortfall).*

Further, I would direct your attention to the company's current ratio which finished the year below 2.00x at 1.93x and the company's quick ratio which finished the year at 1.57x compared to a projected ratio of 1.86x. Both of these ratios are still relatively solid but may be focal points of the company's lenders which were anticipating more financial strength to be present at the end of the year (when new loans were extended to the company). Similar negative trending is present with the company's debt to equity ratios as these indicate the company is using more debt and financial leverage (to support business operations) compared to the original projections.

In summary and based on the company's FYE 12/31/23 financial statements, I would anticipate mild to moderate inquiries and feedback from both the company's external lenders and newly added investors (during the year). In effect, the external parties will be focused on just how the company anticipates it will "right the slightly listing ship" in 2024 and beyond. The company should proactively prepare a financial report for the external parties that clearly addresses its successes, challenges, and future opportunities moving forward. Combining this with coordinating direct meetings to discuss the company's financial performance and condition should help build additional credibility and restore confidence after experiencing a somewhat turbulent and bumpy FYE 12/31/23.

Signed by the appropriate party/CFO or CEO.

Some Additional Perspective

I covered a lot of ground in this chapter, including providing three exhibits that all expanded the level of financial information and analyses that is being presented to the executive management team and BOD of the company. This is the type of chapter that you may want to revisit and digest again given the volume of content covered and the breadth of the issues presented. You may ask yourself if this level of financial reporting is required for the target audience and the response from me would be a resounding and adamant YES!

First, if you are ever going to elevate to an executive management position, the "C" suite, or occupy a seat on a board of directors, the financial information presented in the financial report is not a "nice" to have (and understand) but represents an actual "must" have (and understand). You simply cannot reach the highest rungs in a business without having a basic knowledge of financial reports, financial statements, and financial information.

Second, as an executive or BOD member, while it's important to understand the company's most recent financial operating results and financial condition (historically speaking), it's even more important to clearly understand the financial outlook of the company including how its story should be packaged and pitched (for lack of better terms) to external parties such as lenders and investors, what, if any, additional capital (in the form of debt or equity) will be required to support the execution of the company's business plan, and most importantly, what challenges and opportunities are coming down the road that need to be managed and understood today, so that financial reports and what is communicated to external users and internal consumers is as effective and efficient as possible.

Learning how to set the expectations of external and internal parties is an invaluable talent that can take years to develop. If you notice in the Summary of Key Operating Trends presented above, the CFO and CEO are setting expectations as it relates to socializing the problems and challenges with the company's product division and that active management of external parties will be required. By doing this, they have set the table for everyone to be on the same page with delivering some news that may appear unpleasant but at the same time, also highlighting that new opportunities are present in the software/SaaS business division (e.g., recent investments made in marketing and research & development expenses that should yield future positive results). Mastering the art of the financial report, which includes adding the appropriate amount of spin to the story that helps offset what might be viewed as bad news (the product business unit) with good news (the software/SaaS business unit), is a topic I'll close the book on in Chapter 15.

14

PREPARING FINANCIAL REPORTS FROM COMPANY FINANCIAL INFORMATION

"I feel the need for speed" was a quote made famous by the character Maverick, played by Tom Cruise, in the movie *Top Gun*. Today, this quote no doubt rings close to home for business executives and senior management across the board as given the digital transformation of the global economy, speed in financial information reporting is no longer an option but a necessity. In today's hyperconnected world that analyzes millions of pieces of data in a split second, the ability to decipher key operating and financial data quickly and efficiently (at a senior management level) is critical.

Unlike Chapters 12 and 13, where our discussions were centered on using our example company's financial statements as the basis to prepare financial reports for both external users and internal consumers, Chapter 14 will focus on preparing financial reports for internal consumers that sources financial information from the accounting and financial information system (and not necessarily directly from the financial statements). While hundreds of financial report examples could be provided, I'm going to focus on two simple (and often used) financial report types including first, preparing a sales flash financial report and second, structuring a truncated divisional operating performance financial report.

One word of caution to start this chapter is to clarify that speed in producing a financial flash report should not be confused with an ultra-short time period, as some flash reports are in fact speed and time period centric whereas other financial flash reports may be delivered quickly (e.g., one day after the month end) but cover a longer period of time (e.g., one month of data). For example, an e-commerce company that is highly sensitive to the holiday selling season from Thanksgiving through Christmas may produce hourly sales flash reports to gauge the effectiveness of an aggressive Black Friday sales promotion. Here, the sales flash report is both speed and time period sensitive as the sales flash report delivers updates each hour that cover just one hour of sales during the day. While this type of financial reporting may seem like overkill, trust me when I say that for retailers, monitoring customer purchase activities over very short time periods is an absolute must in today's ultra-competitive economy.

Finally, it's important to remember that the range of the target audience within a business is generally far wider and more dynamic than that associated with external users. As previously covered in Chapter 2, external users of financial reports usually come in one of two forms – capital sources (investors or lenders) and compliance sources (taxing authorities and governments). Preparing financial reports for these audiences is generally more controlled, formal, consistent, structured, and protects confidential information.

Inside a business, the internal consumers are generally very diverse and can range from the senior-most parties and employees in an organization (such as the board of directors and C suite) to front line managers and staff. From a financial reporting strategy perspective, the following summary level guidelines have been provided as to what each management level in the organization will most likely need and should have access to on a periodic basis:

- Board of Directors ("BOD"): Access to all financial statements, lending agreements, equity capitalization tables, and critical financial information and analyses. The BOD operates in a very strategic manner and as such, should really have access to any and all financial information, statements, and reports. Further, the BOD should be provided financial and economic data, reports, and other relevant information that may originate outside the company, especially if it has a direct impact on the company's operations. When preparing a financial report for this group, you need to think at a very high level with a strategic message or story offered. That is, don't just relay what has happened, as while this is important, the why it happened and how can the company adjust are even more important. The BOD always needs to be looking forward!

- ◆ C Suite & Senior Executives: Again, this group should be focused on the "big" picture but will need additional levels of detail as not only is this group managing the company from a strategic perspective, but a tactical one as well. Generally, another layer of detail (or ability to drill down into the detail) will be needed, such as having access to financial reports that summarize sales revenue by source or type, by region, and by quarter along with the associated gross profit and gross margins. If you are preparing a financial report for this group, make sure you focus on the key message and critical issues, and deliver a story that supports it. If sales are lagging, this should be highlighted and if expenses are too high, hit it hard. There's no point in being bashful, as delivering bad news is just as important as good news!

- ◆ Middle Management: The key here is to target their level of responsibility. For a corporate cost center, budget management and adherence should be emphasized, which may be accomplished by providing a detailed variance analysis in your financial report. As presented in Exhibit 14.1 later in this chapter, a detailed example of a sales flash financial report has been presented that has been directed at the director of sales for the company's Western territory. The key with preparing financial reports for this group is to provide just enough information to keep them focused on their direct management responsibility; avoid including too much "noise" in the financial report that will only distract them, and above all else, limit access to confidential information they don't need to have access to.

- ◆ Rank and File: Finally, it's not uncommon for companies to prepare simple financial reports for the base staff or rank and file. For example, a manufacturing productivity report could be prepared for the manufacturing team to help everyone understand productivity cost or product quality trends and how they can possibly be improved to a point of hitting a bonus target (where everyone shares in a financial goal if certain targets are met). Remember, however, that this target audience is probably not going to understand many accounting and financial concepts so it's important to deliver the financial report and message with KISS in mind. That is, keep it simple stupid.

With this summary in mind, we can now turn our attention to the two sample internally focused financial reports prepared for our specific target audiences in our example company.

The Flash Report

To start, it is important to remember that the most effective financial reports are designed to provide the right financial information at the right time and in the right format for management to assess critically sensitive operating data. Financial flash reports (or just flash reports) represent nothing more than a timely snapshot of critical company operating and financial data, which is then used to support the ongoing operations of the business. All types of flash reports are used in business, ranging from a printed circuit board manufacturing company evaluating its book-to-bill ratio on a weekly basis to Walmart reporting hourly sales by selling department by SKU during the holiday season to an auto manufacturer evaluating weekly finished goods inventory levels.

The goal with all flash reports remains the same in that critical business information is delivered to management for review much more frequently. As such, flash reports tend to have the following key attributes present:

- *Simplicity of Report:* Flash financial reports are generally more simplistic than traditional financial statements and annual financial reports. As has been discussed throughout this book, the amount of financial information presented in financial statements and financial reports can be extensive (as the goal is to report on the entire operations of a company). Flash reports are much more focused and designed to capture 5 to 10 key operating data points or KPIs that represent critical information to the target audience.

- *Frequency of Report:* Flash reports tend to be produced much more frequently. Unlike the production of more formal financial reports and financial statements (which generally occurs monthly), flash reports are often produced weekly and, in numerous cases, daily or even hourly. In today's competitive marketplace, management is demanding that information be provided more frequently than ever to stay on top of rapidly changing markets.

- *Critical Data:* Flash reports are designed to capture critical operating and financial performance data of your business or the real information that can make or break your business. As a result, sales activities and/or volumes are almost always a part of a business's flash reporting effort. Once management has a good handle on the top line, the bottom line should be relatively easy to calculate.

- *Range of Data:* Flash reports are not limited to presenting financial data. Flash reports can be designed to capture all kinds of data, including retail store foot volume (or customer traffic levels), labor utilization rates, and the like. While the president of a division may want to know how sales are tracking this month, the manufacturing manager will want to keep a close eye on labor hours incurred in the production process.

- *Source of Data:* Financial flash reports should obtain their base information from the same accounting and financial information system that produces periodic financial statements, forecasts, and other reports. While the presentation of the information may be different, the source of the information should come from the same transactional basis (of your company).

- *Internal Focus:* Flash reports are almost exclusively used for internal management needs and are rarely delivered to external parties. Flash reports are usually more detailed in nature and tend to contain far more confidential data than, say, audited financial statements, and are almost never audited.

- *Close Friends with Forecasts:* Flash reports are closely related to the forecasting process. For example, if a company is experiencing a short-term cash flow squeeze, management will need to have access to a rolling 13-week cash flow projection to properly evaluate cash inflows and outflows on a weekly basis. Each week, the rolling 13-week cash flow projection is provided to management for review in the form of a flash report, which is always being updated to look out 13 weeks.

A critical concept to understand with flash reports is that these reports should act more as a confirmation of your company's performance than a report that offers original information. By this I mean that once the key data in a flash report is evaluated and understood, the resulting impact on other financial and operating results should be relatively straightforward. For example, if a flash report that presents sales volumes for the first two weeks of February compared to the similar two-week period for the prior year is reporting new sales information, the format of the report and the presentation of the information in the report should be consistent. Thus, management should be able to quickly decipher the results and determine whether the company is performing within expectations and what to expect on the bottom line for the entire month.

Key Performance Indicators

If it is not evident yet, it will be after you read this section: flash reports and KPIs are almost always the absolute best and closest of friends. Flash reports are most beneficial when they effectively combine and report key financial information alongside pivotal KPIs (e.g., a crucial ratio or relationship). For example, when a sales flash report is prepared, it should not only include gross sales dollars but also report net sales dollars (taking into account any discounts), total unit sales, average unit selling price, average order value, and the like. Taking this flash report one step further, it may also report gross profit dollars, gross margin, and other critical information related to how much advertising expense was incurred to generate the sales.

Exhibit 14.1 provides an example of a financial flash report prepared for our example business that is focused on customer sales data for the previous week. This sales flash report is prepared weekly and delivered to the sales team each Monday morning for the following week's sales activity (running from Monday through Sunday of each week).

The sample flash report presented in Exhibit 14.1 has been prepared for the company's Western operating division that is responsible for 25% of our example company's annual budgeted sales revenue. Further and to keep the analysis relatively simple, I assume that sales are generated in equal amounts over the year so for one week, 1/52nd of the company's sales are used as the baseline. I should note that dividing a company's annual sales over 52 equal weeks is not the norm as most companies experience peaks and valleys during the year via having to manage seasonal factors, the timing of new product releases, etc. but for ease of presentation, I simply divided 25% of the company's total annual forecast by 52.

The length of time covered in a flash report and the level of detail are determined by the needs of the management team. In this situation, the management team felt it was important to communicate the results on a weekly basis to identify any trends, performance issues, and/or other concerns that require additional attention. Some items of particular interest in the sales flash report are the following:

- From a formatting perspective, you will notice that both weekly and YTD operating and financial information has been presented. The reason for this is to assist with obtaining a better understanding of the financial results by not just focusing on the weekly data (which can be volatile) but more importantly, the YTD data (which helps smooth out the data over a longer period of time).

- Critical data points have been incorporated into the sales flash report that originate from other information sources including the number of sales reps and customer levels (both new and in total). This data most likely originated from the company's

EXHIBIT 14.1—SALES FLASH FINANCIAL REPORT

Unaudited - Prepared by Company Management

Software Sales by Type For the Week & YTD Period Ending	Ref.	Projected One Week End 10/28/2023	% of Net Rev.	Actual One Week End 10/28/2023	% of Net Rev.	Variance	Projected YTD 43 Week End 10/28/2023	% of Net Rev.	Actual YTD 43 Week End 10/28/2023	% of Net Rev.	Variance
KPIs:											
Number of Active Sales Reps	(a)	6.00		5.00		-1.00	6.00		5.50		-0.50
Average Sales per Active Sales Rep	(a)	$ 39,667		$ 39,250		$ (417)	$ 1,705,667		$1,812,727		$ 107,061
New Customer Leads Generated	(b)	6.00		7.00		1.00	258.00		245.00		-13.00
New Customer Conversion Ratio	(b)	2.00		1.00		-1.00	86.00		78.00		-8.00
Conversion Ratio	(b)	33.33%		14.29%		-19.05%	33.33%		31.84%		-1.50%
Total Active Customers, Period End	(c)	125.00		135.00		10.00	125.00		135.00		10.00
Average Period Revenue per Customer, Total	(c)	$ 1,904		$ 1,454		$ (450)	$ 81,872		$ 73,852		$ (8,020)
Average Period Revenue per Customer, SaaS	(c)	$ 1,560		$ 1,163		$ (397)	$ 67,080		$ 61,259		$ (5,821)
Sales Revenue, Gross:											
Software Installation Platform		$ 36,000	15.13%	$ 34,250	17.45%	$ (1,750)	$ 1,548,000	15.13%	$1,425,000	14.29%	$(123,000)
SaaS Platform Basic		$ 48,000	20.17%	$ 65,000	33.12%	$ 17,000	$ 2,064,000	20.17%	$2,100,000	21.06%	$ 36,000
SaaS Platform Advanced		$ 83,000	34.87%	$ 60,000	30.57%	$(23,000)	$ 3,569,000	34.87%	$3,525,000	35.36%	$ (44,000)
SaaS Platform Expert		$ 64,000	26.89%	$ 32,000	16.31%	$(32,000)	$ 2,752,000	26.89%	$2,645,000	26.53%	$(107,000)
Other Software Sales		$ 7,000	2.94%	$ 5,000	2.55%	$ (2,000)	$ 301,000	2.94%	$ 275,000	2.76%	$ (26,000)
Total Sales Revenue, Gross		$238,000	100.00%	$196,250	100.00%	$(41,750)	$10,234,000	100.00%	$9,970,000	100.00%	$(264,000)
Percentage of Goal						82.46%					97.42%
Direct Advertising, Promotional, & Selling Expenses	(d)	$ 18,000		$25,000		$ (7,000)	$ 7,74,000		$ 815,000		$ (41,000)
Average Cost to Acquire a New Customer, $	(d)	$ 9,000		$25,000		$(16,000)	$ 9,000		$ 10,400		$ (1,400)
Average Direct Acquisition Cost, % of Total Revenue	(d)	9.09%		33.07%		-23.98%	10.99%		14.08%		-3.09%

KPIs & Sales Report Notes:

(a) - Average sales revenue per sales rep continues to overperform YTD with a positive variance of $107k. Challenge has been recruiting, training, and retaining sales reps as quality of labor pool is weak and competition fierce (for quality sales reps). Weekly sales figures beginning to reflect being short one sales rep.

(b) - New customer leads trending slightly below forecast as a result of not being fully staffed with sales reps. New customer conversion ratio within reason.

(c) - Average sales revenue in total (for all software sales) and for SaaS products only below targets by roughly 10%. Customers are finding the advanced and expert SaaS products have functions and features that are not needed and do not want to spend the extra money. The basic product has more interest due to simplicity of use and lower price point. Upselling opportunities may be present next year to move customers up the food chain into higher priced products but pricing and functionality adjustments will be required.

(d) - Direct advertising, promotional, and related discretionary expenses have been running above projected levels as a result of front loading advertising spends prior to the holidays. These ratios should normalize by the end of the year as forecast advertising spends for the last 9 weeks of the year should be lower.

Confidential - Property of QW Example Tech, Inc.

CRM system, which has been integrated with financial information to produce KPIs.

- Three interesting financial trends have been identified in both the financial information presented and in the financial flash report notes included.

  - First, sales revenue per active sales representative is trending higher, indicating solid performance from the selling team. This may seem counterintuitive related to the underperformance of total sales but as clearly noted, the problem lies in having too few active sales reps.

  - Second, average revenue per customer is trending below projected levels, which has been clearly communicated in the report notes as customers are purchasing the simpler and lower-priced SaaS product for ease of use and lower cost.

  - Third, the cost to acquire customers from direct advertising, promotional, and selling expenses is running above forecast levels through the YTD 10/28/23. However, the footnote indicates that this should normalize by the end of the year due to the fact that advertising spends were front loaded through October (with lower spends expected in November and December).

The level of detail that can be presented in these types of flash reports is extensive and really, almost endless. The idea with presenting the financial report in Exhibit 14.1 is not to make you an expert in understanding KPIs associated with the sales function in our example business, but rather to highlight these two key concepts:

- First, Exhibit 14.1 does represent a financial report, but maybe not in the format you would expect (such as the financial reports presented in Chapters 13 and 14). You should notice a much more focused and summarized format that has been prepared in a manner that allows the internal consumer to quickly decipher and interpret the outputs and conclusions from the financial report. Needless to say, this financial report has been prepared for internal consumers only and should not be distributed to external parties. Further, I might add that the report notes provided have been structured in a summarized format using text (i.e., internal business language) that the internal consumers clearly understand.

- Second, the party producing this financial report clearly understands their target audience (in this case, the divisional sales manager for the Western business region of our example company) and what KPIs are critical for them to understand and act on to improve financial operating results. Enough critical information is provided and highlighted to keep the party on track (but at the same time, excessive financial "noise" is excluded so as to not confuse the target audience).

You might notice that I'm touching on the concept of completeness again, as if a party were only focused on the negative top-line sales trend and did not understand the importance of the causes of these sales trends (i.e., having fewer sales reps and preferences from customers to purchase the simpler and lower cost version of the product), they might draw an incorrect conclusion on the outlook for the business for the remainder of 2023 and how to plan effectively in 2024.

Closing out this section of the chapter, I would like to remind our readers to keep these two thoughts in mind. First, flash reports are not solely reserved for just financial data or dollar amounts, as invaluable information needs to be reported and understood that involves qualitative data. For example, the sales flash report presented in Exhibit 14.1 could have been expanded to include several other data points such as the number of outbound calls a sales rep makes per week, the number of live demos presented to customers every month, an active listing of the current sales pipeline by customer, and so on and so forth. I do not explain each of these information points as my goal is to emphasize the importance of generating qualitatively based flash reports that fit the needs of each business.

Second, the sales flash report example provided has been isolated to a specific industry, the software technology industry, which is sensitive to this type of reporting. Given the importance technology plays in everyone's life, not to mention just about every aspect of everyone's life, the goal was to include an example company of relevance in today's economic environment. However, please note that all industries ranging from auto manufacturing to public utilities to banking to you name it will aggressively implement the use of flash reporting to improve the overall effectiveness of management's performance. The key is to design, implement, and analyze flash reports and KPIs that offer the most value to the business.

A Second Internal Financial Report Example

The last financial report example I'm going to present has been prepared for the divisional general manager for our example company's product business unit. Here, we have an individual (who hopefully has thick skin and plenty of experience) who's been assigned the unenviable task of somehow managing the "dying" product segment of the business as our example company transitions to becoming a full software/SaaS and service organization (which it hopes to achieve by the FYE 12/31/26, just three years away) and terminate basically all product business activity as the company can simply not compete in this market. With this strategy in mind, please refer to Exhibit 14.2, which presents a divisional P&L financial analysis for the FYE 12/31/23, that includes a variance analysis, as well as offers a preliminary projection or budget for the FYE 12/31/24 (which you will learn why this has been included in this chapter as well as in Chapter 15) along with performance report notes for reference.

Man, what a year and as mentioned above, I hope this individual has thick skin and can explain the poor performance as the results are rather ugly, but not completely unanticipated (given the state of the market). And to assist with communicating the P&L performance for the products division, the financial report prepared includes the following three disclosures that should support a more comprehensive review by the executive management team of not just the current year financial performance but more importantly, what the hell to do with the product division moving forward.

+ First, informative performance report notes were included to provide a summary level management assessment of the poor financial performance. Rather than digging into every sales, costs of sales revenue, and direct operating expense line item, the macro level message was delivered loud and clear. Products are becoming obsolete, competition is fierce, and aggressive sales discounting strategies have been implemented to move the old inventory.

+ Second, a financial variance analysis was included to clearly highlight the problem performance areas including large negative variances in total net sales revenue, gross profit, gross margin, contribution profit, and contribution margin. In this situation, there's no point in beating around the bush as the company needs to clearly understand this division's poor financial operating performance as a base to assist with making future economic business decisions (see next bullet point).

+ Third, you will notice that a preliminary "medium" version (refer to Chapter 10 on preparing forecasts for further information) of the company's projections for the FYE 12/31/24 has been included. Why would this financial information be included in this financial report? Well, the answer is simple. In the words of Gordon Gekko from the movie *Wall Street*, he makes a reference to a poorly run company that is a "dog with a different set of fleas." This same simple but powerful statement holds true for our example company's product division as a frank and honest discussion of the FYE 12/31/24 preliminary projections needs to be held as to whether or not they are even remotely achievable (given the state of the market). Does keeping this division alive make sense or would a better solution be to shut it down, write-off the remaining assets associated with this division, record a liability reserve for potential termination related expenses, and basically "clean house" during the FYE 12/31/23 to bury the product's division once and for all?

Ultimately, our example company's executive management team needs to make the final call on the product division's operating status in relation to supporting continued operations (and bleed red ink over the years to come) or bite the bullet and clean house in the current FYE 12/31/23. As a spoiler alert, I'll offer an alternative financial reporting scenario for the FYE 12/31/23 in Chapter 15, but before you dive into the alternative scenario, you should keep in mind three key concepts I have harped on throughout this book. Know your audience, effectively communicate the story, and remember, accounting is just as much of an art form as a science.

EXHIBIT 14.2 — PRODUCT DIVISION P&L FINANCIAL REPORT & ANALYSIS

Unaudited - Prepared by Company Management

Divisional P&L for the Fiscal Year Ending	Ref.	Actual FYE 12/31/2023	% of Net Rev.	Projected FYE 12/31/2023	% of Net Rev.	Variance FYE 12/31/2023	Projected Med - FYE Net Rev.	% of Net Rev.
Sales Revenue:								
Software Platform & SAAS Sales		$ 970,666	7.81%	$ 0	0.00%	$ 970,666	$ 0	0.00%
Product Sales	(a)	$13,440,000	108.15%	$15,200,000	105.26%	$(1,760,000)	$7,600,000	108.11%
Other Sales, Discounts, & Allowances	(a)	$ (1,983,200)	-15.96%	$ (760,000)	-5.26%	$(1,223,200)	$ (570,000)	-8.11%
Net Sales Revenue		$12,427,466	100.00%	$14,440,000	100.00%	$(2,012,534)	$7,030,000	100.00%
Costs of Sales Revenue:								
Direct Product Costs		$ 7,392,000	59.48%	$ 7,600,000	52.63%	$ 208,000	$4,560,000	64.86%
Wages & Burden		$ 1,358,900	10.93%	$ 1,557,500	10.79%	$ 198,600	$ 856,625	12.19%
Direct Overhead		$ 350,000	2.82%	$ 375,000	2.60%	$ 25,000	$ 375,000	5.33%
Other Costs of Sales Revenue		$ 42,500	0.34%	$ 50,000	0.35%	$ 7,500	$ 125,000	1.78%
Total Costs of Sales Revenue	(b)	$ 9,143,400	73.57%	$ 9,582,500	66.36%	$ 439,100	$5,916,625	84.16%
Gross Profit	(b)	$ 3,284,066	26.43%	$ 4,857,500	33.64%	$(1,573,434)	$1,113,375	15.84%
Gross Margin	(b)	26.43%		33.64%		-7.21%	15.84%	
Direct Operating Expenses:								
Advertising, Promotional, & Selling		$ 580,050	4.67%	$ 600,000	4.16%	$ 19,950	$ 311,850	4.44%
Personnel Wages, Burden, & Compensation		$ 1,784,850	14.36%	$ 1,875,000	12.98%	$ 90,150	$ 993,395	14.13%
Facility Operating Expenses		$ 632,127	5.09%	$ 625,000	4.33%	$ (7,127)	$ 250,000	3.56%
Other Operating Expenses		$ 225,000	1.81%	$ 250,000	1.73%	$ 25,000	$ 49,670	0.71%
Total Direct Operating Expenses	(c)	$ 3,222,027	25.93%	$ 3,350,000	23.20%	$ 127,973	$1,604,915	22.83%
Contribution Profit	(d)	$ 62,039	0.50%	$ 1,507,500	10.44%	$(1,445,461)	$ (491,540)	-6.99%
Contribution Margin		0.50%		10.44%		-9.94%	-6.99%	

Performance Report Notes:

(a) - Sales volumes for all product SKUs/types carried by the company were below forecast as the rate of technology change created a more rapid deterioration in the value of the products than forecast at the beginning of the year. Further, more aggressive sales discounting efforts were required to move products.

(b) - Total costs of sales revenue were below forecast levels due to decreased product unit sales and average selling prices. When possible, our division implemented accelerated expense reductions, staff layoffs, and other cost-cutting measures to match lower sales levels with expenses but cost cutting alone could not protect the significant underperformance in the company's gross profit (negative variance of $1.445 million) and gross margin (negative variance of 7.2%).

(c) - Operating expenses were in line with expectations with a slight positive variance realized as a result of late in the year cost-cutting efforts.

(d) - Large negative variances were realized at both the contribution profit and contribution margin levels which were the direct result of lower sales and more aggressive sales discounting strategies being implemented. Looking forward, the company's ability to compete in the market will most likely come under significant pressure as the current products are now obsolete from a technical functional perspective and grossly overpriced. 2024's preliminary projections looks unattainable.

Confidential - Property of QW Example Tech, Inc.

A Few Parting Thoughts

The economic reality for most businesses is usually quite simple. That is, a business or a specific operating unit's financial performance (of the business) generally comes down to three to four key performance metrics or economic drivers that are "make or break" in terms of realizing positive or negative results. These include understanding top-line sales (volume and net price), direct costs of sales revenue (know your gross margin), and operating expenses (keep in check). Master your knowledge of this financial information and you should be able to predict your income statement results in advance, as once you know your sales figures, you should have a clear/reliable understanding of profits.

But, as stressed throughout this book with the concept of completeness, it is one thing to be able to efficiently understand the income statement from a top-down perspective but something else to understand the impact on the company's entire financial picture. That is, I know my sales, gross margin, and operating expenses and I am confident with the net profit or loss that will be generated. Okay, this is great, but what if the conversation moves one step further to understand the impact on cash resources and liquidity?

And this is what really separates the financial adults (experts) from the children (novices). Being able to translate the results of the income statement to their corresponding influence on the balance sheet and statement of cash flows, to know in advance and with confidence what type of impact may transpire on a company's cash resources, liquidity, and capital needs, is essential in gaining the trust of the executive management team, board of directors, and external capital sources.

REVISITING OUR EXAMPLE COMPANY WITH A SLIGHT TWIST

Throughout this book, I referenced our example company numerous times, QW Example Tech, Inc. As a refresher, our example company operates in the technology industry and is pivoting its business plan from focusing on selling both hardware technology products and software (different SaaS products) to becoming more of a standalone software and services business. Numerous financial exhibits and supplemental information have been presented, which have acted as the basis for preparing different types of financial reports, for both internal and external parties.

In this closing chapter, we're going to revisit our example company from three different perspectives, two of which have been covered extensively in the book. The first will look at our example company and the financial reports prepared from a base case perspective. The second will look at our example company and the financial reports prepared from a preferred case perspective. And the third and most intriguing view of our example company will be completed by presenting an "alternative ending." The alternative ending will look at our example company from the perspective of taking a different approach to the product business unit during the FYE 12/31/23, which includes both significant risks and potential rewards, one that the executive management team and board of directors have given significant consideration to as it relates to both external users and internal consumers.

Base Case Financial Reports and Story

First up, I'll quickly summarize our base case presentation of our example company. If you refer back to Chapters 12 and 13, the base case financial reports prepared for the company were rather straightforward, did not provide much added depth (for the external users and internal consumers), and focused heavily on reporting and analyzing historical operating results for the past two years. To refresh your memory, here is the external presented short management overview provided by the company's CFO:

To Whom It May Concern:

    Attached are the annual audited financial statements and audit report for QW Example Tech., Inc. (the "Company") for the fiscal years ending 12/31/23 and 12/31/22 as completed by the CPA firm of Dewey, Fixum, & Howe, LLC. We are providing this financial information to you as part of our annual financial reporting compliance requirements to all Company capital sources, including both equity investors and lenders.

    We are pleased to report that the Company grew its top-line sales revenue by approximately $5.3 million or roughly 10% during the most recent fiscal year ending 12/31/23 as compared to the prior fiscal year ending 12/31/22. Further, net profit after tax increased from approximately $77,000 for the fiscal year-end 12/31/22 to roughly $813,000 (a 10.5x increase) for the fiscal year-end 12/31/23. The Company's executive management team and board of directors are both pleased with the improved operating results and look for these trends to continue in 2024 and beyond.

    Please feel free to reach out to me with any questions, feedback, and/or additional information needs as it relates to your assessment of the Company's operating results and financial condition. We appreciate your continued support and look forward to working with each and every one of you in the years to come.

Sincerely,
_____ (signed)
CEO/President

I'm also going to re-present Exhibit 12.2 which presents the audited income statement (one of the big three financial statements) of our example company. For the sake of space and avoiding too much duplication, the balance sheet and statement of cash flows have not been re-presented.

To the untrained and underinformed party, the base case financial report doesn't look too bad at all as sales revenue and gross profits have both increased, as well as the net income (which increased substantially over the two-year period from $77,000 to $813,000). Yes, not too bad at all as the company appears to have had a successful year.

EXHIBIT 12.2—AUDITED FINANCIAL STATEMENTS – INCOME STATEMENT

Dollar Amounts in Thousands

Income Statement For the Fiscal Years Ending	12/31/2022	12/31/2023
Net Sales Revenue	$ 54,210	$ 59,494
Costs of Sales Revenue	$(23,922)	$(21,766)
Gross Profit (aka Gross Margin)	$ 30,288	$ 37,728
Operating Expenses:		
Selling, General, & Administrative	$ 22,567	$ 25,289
Research & Development	$ 5,692	$ 7,139
Depreciation & Amortization	$ 1,571	$ 1,643
Total Operating Expenses	$ 29,831	$ 34,071
Operating Income (Loss)	$ 457	$ 3,658
Other Expenses (Income):		
Other Expenses or (Income)	$ 0	$ 2,000
Interest Expense	$ 339	$ 407
Total Other Expenses (Income)	$ 339	$ 2,407
Net Income (Loss) Before Income Taxes	$ 118	$ 1,251
Income Tax Expense (benefit)	$ 41	$ 438
Net Income (Loss) After Income Taxes	$ 77	$ 813
See Notes to Financial Statements		

Preferred Case Financial Reports and Story

Now, let's refresh our example company by presenting the preferred case financial report, but not what has been forwarded to external users but rather what has been provided to internal consumers. If you recall, here is the summary of key operating trends, an internally structured MDOR (from Chapter 13) prepared by the company's CFO and CEO and presented for review and discussion with the entire executive management team and BOD.

Summary of Key Operating Trends, Narratives, and Financial Results for the FYE 12/31/23

Four significant operating performance issues impacted the Company's operating results and financial condition for the FYE 12/31/23 as follows:

(a) Net sales revenue missed in both the product and software/SaaS divisions for distinct reasons. Software/SaaS sales, as measured by the number of customers, actually exceeded projections but the mix of the software/SaaS sales was skewed toward the basic version of the software, which is cheaper and easier to implement than the expert and advanced versions of the software. This resulted in total software/SaaS sales falling short of projections by roughly 2% and average software/SaaS sales revenue per customer falling short of projected levels by approximately 8%. Overall, the company's software/SaaS offerings have been well received by the market but customer preference indicates a slower adoption rate of the advanced and expert versions of the software. This also negatively impacted deferred revenue as lower average sales per software/SaaS customer resulted in reduced advance payments for future software/SaaS sales.

(b) Product sales were challenging during the year as the company's products have become obsolete quicker than forecast and competition in the market is fierce. Price cuts and aggressive sales discounting strategies were used to move older products (negatively impacting product sales). These events had a significant drag on the product division's gross margin which finished the year at approximately 26% compared to a forecast gross margin of roughly 33.6%. It should further be noted that the company absorbed an other expense of $2,000,000 (which was reviewed and approved by the BOD) during the year as a result of writing down the value of old, obsolete inventory. Looking forward, the company needs to undertake a detailed review and analysis of the financial viability of the product's division as excess levels of obsolete finished goods are still present that may not have a viable market in 2024.

(c) *Direct operating and corporate expenses generally performed in line with management's expectations and trended as anticipated with lower sales. Direct advertising and promotional expenses along with personnel wages, burden, and compensation finished the year slightly below projected levels for three reasons. First, sales commissions were lower than forecast as a result of reduced sales. Second, staffing challenges were present in the software/SaaS division as recruitment of qualified sales reps proved to be challenging during the year. Third, direct advertising expense in the product division was controlled as the company utilized more aggressive sales discounting strategies. Corporate marketing and research & development expenses both finished the year slightly above forecast levels as a result of investing additional resources in improving a.) the brand recognition of the company's new software/SaaS products (with additional marketing initiatives undertaken during the year) and b.) investing in additional software development efforts to improve the ease of use of implementation of the advanced and expert versions of the company's software/SaaS product lines. These additional investments were made during the second half of the FYE 12/31/23 which should produce financial returns starting in 2024 and extending through 2026.*

(d) *The company's liquidity and financial condition as of the FYE 12/31/23 underperformed compared to projected levels for two primary reasons. First, the negative variance realized in net income amounted to approximately $2,100,000 which had a direct effect of reducing the cash balance at the end of the year by approximately the same amount. Second, the year-end balance in customer accounts receivable amounted to $638,000 above the forecast level as customer payments slowed during the fourth quarter. The combination of these two items contributed to $2,738,000 of the total cash shortfall of roughly $3,100,000 for the year (accounting for 88% of the shortfall).*

Further, I would direct your attention to the company's current ratio which finished the year below 2.00x at 1.93x and the company's quick ratio which finished the year at 1.57x compared to a projected ratio of 1.86x. Both of these ratios are still relatively solid but may be focal points of the company's lenders which were anticipating more financial strength to be present at the end of the year (when new loans were extended to the company). Similar negative trending is present with the company's debt to equity ratios as these indicate the company is using more debt and financial leverage (to support business operations) compared to the original projections.

In summary and based on the company's FYE 12/31/23 financial statements, I would anticipate mild to moderate inquiries and feedback from both the company's external lenders and newly added investors (during the year). In effect, the external parties will be focused on just how the company anticipates it will "right the slightly listing ship" in 2024 and beyond. The company should proactively prepare a financial report for the external parties that clearly addresses its successes, challenges, and future opportunities moving forward. Combining this with coordinating direct meetings to discuss the company's financial performance and condition should help build additional credibility and restore confidence after experiencing a somewhat turbulent and bumpy FYE 12/31/23.

Signed by the appropriate party/CFO or CEO.

_____

To support this summary, I've included Exhibit 13.2 again which presents the company's income statement. For the sake of space and avoiding too much duplication, the balance sheet and statement of cash flows have not been re-presented.

EXHIBIT 13.2—INTERNALLY PREPARED INCOME STATEMENT – PREFERRED CASE

Unaudited - Prepared by Company Management

Income Statement for the Fiscal Year Ending	Ref.	Actual 12/31/2023	% of Net Rev.	Projected 12/31/2023	% of Net Rev.	Variance
Key Performance Indicators:						
Net Sales Revenue Per Full Time Employee	(a)	$ 487,658		$ 505,440		$ (17,782)
Product Sales, Avg. Order Value (net)	(b)	$ 15,659		$ 19,543		$ (3,884)
Software Platform & SAAS Sales:						
SAAS Sales, Total Customer Accounts	(a)	525		500		25
SAAS Sales, Total Earned Avg. Per Account	(a)	$ 74,667		$ 81,180		$ (6,513)
Sales Revenue:						
Software Platform & SAAS Sales	(a)	$48,533,321	81.58%	$49,500,000	78.35%	$ (966,679)
Product Sales	(b)	$13,440,000	22.59%	$15,200,000	24.06%	$(1,760,000)
Other Sales, Discounts, & Allowances	(b)	$ (2,479,000)	-4.17%	$ (1,520,000)	-2.41%	$ (959,000)
Net Sales Revenue		$59,494,321	100.00%	$63,180,000	100.00%	$(3,685,679)
Costs of Sales Revenue:						
Direct Product Costs	(b)	$ 7,392,000	12.42%	$ 7,600,000	12.03%	$ 208,000
Wages & Burden	(a)	$13,589,000	22.84%	$15,575,000	24.65%	$ 1,986,000
Direct Overhead	n/a	$ 700,000	1.18%	$ 750,000	1.19%	$ 50,000
Other Costs of Sales Revenue	n/a	$ 85,000	0.14%	$ 100,000	0.16%	$ 15,000
Total Costs of Sales Revenue		$21,766,000	36.59%	$24,025,000	38.03%	$ 2,259,000
Gross Profit		$37,728,321	63.41%	$39,155,000	61.97%	$(1,426,679)
Gross Margin Analysis by Sales Revenue Type:						
Software Platform & SAAS Sales	(a)	72.32%		70.37%		1.95%
Product Sales	(b)	26.07%		33.64%		-7.57%

EXHIBIT 13.2—(CONTINUED)

Income Statement for the Fiscal Year Ending	Ref.	Actual 12/31/2023	% of Net Rev.	Projected 12/31/2023	% of Net Rev.	Variance
Direct Operating Expenses:						
Advertising, Promotional, & Selling	(c)	$ 3,867,000	6.50%	$ 4,000,000	6.33%	$ 133,000
Personnel Wages, Burden, & Compensation	(c)	$11,899,000	20.00%	$12,500,000	19.78%	$ 601,000
Facility Operating Expenses	n/a	$ 1,264,254	2.13%	$ 1,250,000	1.98%	$ (14,254)
Other Operating Expenses	n/a	$ 450,000	0.76%	$ 500,000	0.79%	$ 50,000
Total Direct Operating Expenses		$17,480,254	29.38%	$18,250,000	28.89%	$ 769,746
Contribution Profit		$20,248,067	34.03%	$20,905,000	33.09%	$ (656,933)
Contribution Margin		34.03%		33.09%		0.95%
Corporate Expenses & Overhead:						
Corporate Marketing, Branding, & Promotional	(c)	$ 2,751,500	4.62%	$ 2,500,000	3.96%	$ (251,500)
Research, Development, & Design	(c)	$ 7,139,000	12.00%	$ 6,318,000	10.00%	$ (821,000)
Corporate Overhead & Support	n/a	$ 5,057,017	8.50%	$ 5,000,000	7.91%	$ (57,017)
Depreciation & Amortization Expense	n/a	$ 1,642,857	2.76%	$ 1,750,000	2.77%	$ 107,143
Total Corporate Operating Expenses		$16,590,374	27.89%	$15,568,000	24.64%	$(1,022,374)
Operating Income (EBIT)		$ 3,657,692	6.15%	$ 5,337,000	8.45%	$(1,679,308)
Operating Margin (EBIT Margin)		6.15%		8.45%		45.56%
Other Expenses (Income):						
Other Expenses, Income, & Discontinued Ops.	(b)	$ 2,000,000	3.36%	$ 500,000	0.79%	$(1,500,000)
Interest Expense	n/a	$ 407,000	0.68%	$ 350,000	0.55%	$ (57,000)
Total Other Expenses (Income)		$ 2,407,000	4.05%	$ 850,000	1.35%	$(1,557,000)
Net Income (Loss) Before Income Taxes		$ 1,250,692	2.10%	$ 4,487,000	7.10%	$(3,236,308)
Income Tax Expense (Benefit)		$ 438,000	0.74%	$ 1,570,450	2.49%	$ 1,132,450
Net Income (Loss) After Income Taxes	(d)	$ 812,692	1.37%	$ 2,916,550	4.62%	$(2,103,858)

Confidential - Property of QW Example Tech, Inc.

Now, the company's story is not as rosy as it seems, as while historical financial operating trends appear positive, the company's current year performance, when measured against the forecast operating results, significantly underperformed. This doesn't mean the company is failing or about to go bankrupt as clearly it has made financial progress, improved operating results, and strengthened its financial condition. The more important concept that I'm driving home is the importance of providing CART financial reports and information to the appropriate audience on which they can base sound economic business decisions (even if it means taking one step back to move two forward).

In our base case, I'm not sure (and actually doubt) the financial reports as presented by themselves would provide enough information on which to base a critical business decision. There's just not enough financial information. However, in our preferred case, we now have a significant amount of financial information within the financial report on which to make more confident and informed business decisions. As you will see in our alternative ending (presented next), the executive management team and BOD need to make a major/critical decision related to the product's business unit from both the perspective of presenting historical operating results and more importantly, from positioning the company to improve its business value moving forward.

An Alternative Ending

Let's travel back in time into late 2023 at which time the executive management team and BOD of our example company was making a decision on how much of a reserve to build to account for slow moving, obsolete, and worthless inventory. Up to this point, all the financial exhibits presented in this book have referenced an other expense of $2,000,000 incurred to account for worthless inventory. Now, let's assume our executive management team and BOD (in late 2023), working closely with the external CPA firm completing the audit, realized that the company had far bigger problems with worthless inventory and the entire product division and elected to increase the one-time expense to $5,000,000 during the FYE 12/31/23 (refer to Exhibit 15.1). The increase from $2,000,000 to $5,000,000 was based in the following items:

- An additional $1,500,000 of finished goods inventory was determined to be worthless and written-off.

- A $500,000 increase to accrued liabilities was realized to account for employee termination and severance packages that would be needed to close the product division over the next 90 days.

- An additional $1,000,000 of anticipated other short-term liabilities was recorded to account for potential legal settlements, termination of a facility lease from abandoning a portion of their product assembly space, and to account for other division termination expenses anticipated to be incurred in early 2024.

Wow, just like that, our example company increased other expenses from $2,000,000 to $5,000,000 and turned a small profit of $813,000 into a loss of $1,749,000 but somehow, miraculously, actually increased its cash position from $2,164,000 as of the FYE 12/31/23 (refer to Exhibit 12.1) to approximately $2,852,000 (Exhibit 15.2), an increase of $688,000. How could this possibly happen? The answer is relatively straightforward through the magic of accounting.

First, the $3,000,000 of added other expenses did not involve any cash transactions, at least not during the FYE 12/31/23. What transpired was a decrease to the inventory asset of $1,500,000 and increases to current liability accounts of $1,500,000. These additional "adjustments" did not involve processing any cash payments but rather represent accounting estimates made to reflect that the product division was better off being closed down at the end of the FYE 12/31/23 (than continue to operate).

Second, our example company elected not to make a dividend payment of $250,000 as declaring a dividend during a year of significant losses would send the wrong message to external capital partners.

Third, given the loss incurred, our example company did not realize an income tax expense, which was reduced from $438,000 to $0 for the FYE 12/31/23 (as there should be no income tax expense when pre-tax net income is less than zero).

And just like that, $688,000 of additional cash was generated from not paying a dividend of $250,000 and not paying income tax

EXHIBIT 15.1 — ALTERNATIVE ENDING – INCOME STATEMENT COMPARISON

Unaudited - Prepared by Company Management

Income Statement for the Fiscal Years Ending	Actual 12/31/2022	% of Net Rev.	Actual 12/31/2023	% of Net Rev.	Annual Change $	Annual Change %	Forecast 12/31/2024	% of Net Rev.
Sales Revenue:								
Software Platform & SAAS Sales, Net	$35,705,000	65.86%	$48,037,521	80.74%	$12,332,521	34.54%	$68,160,000	98.70%
Product Sales, Net	$18,505,000	34.14%	$11,456,800	19.26%	$ (7,048,200)	-38.09%	$ 900,000	1.30%
Net Sales Revenue	$54,210,000	100.00%	$59,494,321	100.00%	$ 5,284,321	9.75%	$69,060,000	100.00%
Costs of Sales Revenue:								
Direct Product Costs	$11,040,000	20.37%	$ 7,392,000	12.42%	$ (3,648,000)	-33.04%	$ 500,000	0.72%
Wages, Burden, & Other Direct Costs of Sales	$12,882,000	23.76%	$14,374,000	24.16%	$ 1,492,000	11.58%	$19,247,500	27.87%
Total Costs of Sales Revenue	$23,922,000	44.13%	$21,766,000	36.59%	$ (2,156,000)	-9.01%	$19,747,500	28.59%
Gross Profit	$30,288,000	55.87%	$37,728,321	63.41%	$ 7,440,321	24.57%	$49,312,500	71.41%
Gross Margin Analysis by Sales Revenue Type:								
Software Platform & SAAS Sales, Net	63.92%		72.32%			8.40%	71.76%	
Product Sales, Net	40.34%		26.07%			-14.27%	n/a - Immaterial	
Operating Expenses:								
Corporate Marketing, Branding, & Promotional	$16,093,575	29.69%	$18,517,500	31.12%	$ 2,423,925	15.06%	$15,351,400	22.23%
Research, Development, & Design	$ 5,692,000	10.50%	$ 7,139,000	12.00%	$ 1,447,000	25.42%	$11,687,000	16.92%
Corporate Overhead & Support	$ 6,473,625	11.94%	$ 6,771,272	11.38%	$ 297,647	4.60%	$ 6,767,140	9.80%
Depreciation & Amortization Expense	$ 1,571,429	2.90%	$ 1,642,857	2.76%	$ 71,429	4.55%	$ 1,750,000	2.53%
Total Operating Expenses	$29,830,629	55.03%	$34,070,629	57.27%	$ 4,240,000	14.21%	$35,555,540	51.48%
Operating Income (EBIT)	$ 457,371	0.84%	$ 3,657,692	6.15%	$ 3,200,321	699.72%	$13,756,960	19.92%
Operating Margin (EBIT Margin)	0.84%		6.15%			5.30%	19.92%	
Other Expenses (Income):								
Other Expenses, Income, & Discontinued Ops.	$ 0	0.00%	$ 50,00,000	8.40%			$ 100,000	0.14%
Interest Expense	$ 339,000	0.63%	$ 407,000	0.68%			$ 277,500	0.40%
Total Other Expenses (Income)	$ 339,000	0.63%	$ 5,407,000	9.09%			$ 377,500	0.55%
Net Income (Loss) Before Income Taxes	$ 118,371	0.22%	$ (1,749,308)	-2.94%			$13,379,460	19.37%
Income Tax Expense (Benefit)	$ 41,000	0.08%	$ 0	0.00%			$ 4,682,811	6.78%
Net Income (Loss) After Income Taxes	$ 77,371	0.14%	$ (1,749,308)	-2.94%			$ 8,696,649	12.59%

Confidential - Property of QW Example Tech, Inc.

EXHIBIT 15.2—ALTERNATIVE ENDING – BALANCE SHEET COMPARISON

Unaudited - Prepared by Company Management

Balance Sheet as of the Fiscal Year Ending	Actual 12/31/2022	Actual 12/31/2023	Forecast 12/31/2024	Financial Strength	Amount
Assets					
Current Assets					
Cash & Equivalents	$ 775,161	$ 2,851,747	$10,340,749	Net Working Capital	
Accounts Receivable	$ 6,776,000	$ 8,009,000	$ 8,632,500	FYE 12/31/22	$ 5,083,050
Inventory	$ 3,822,000	$ 206,000	$ 250,000	FYE 12/31/23	$ 3,726,600
Prepaid Expenses	$ 600,000	$ 625,000	$ 650,000	Change, YOY	$ (1,356,450)
Total Current Assets	$11,973,161	$11,691,747	$19,873,249	FYE 12/31/24	$14,123,249
				Change, YOY	$10,396,649
Long-Term Capital Assets					
Property, Machinery, & Equipment	$ 4,000,000	$ 4,500,000	$ 5,000,000	Current Ratio:	
Accumulated Depreciation	$ (1,571,429)	$ (2,214,286)	$ (3,964,286)	FYE 12/31/22	1.74
Net Property, Machinery, & Equipment	$ 2,428,571	$ 2,285,714	$ 1,035,714	FYE 12/31/23	1.47
Other Assets				FYE 12/31/24	3.46
Intangible Assets, Net	$ 2,000,000	$ 6,000,000	$ 5,000,000	Debt to Equity Ratio:	
Other Assets	$ 100,000	$ 100,000	$ 150,000	FYE 12/31/22	0.86
Total Long-Term & Other Assets	$ 4,528,571	$ 8,385,714	$ 6,185,714	FYE 12/31/23	1.09
Total Assets	$16,501,733	$20,077,462	$26,058,963	FYE 12/31/24	0.42
Liabilities					
Current Liabilities					
Accounts Payable	$ 1,405,000	$ 1,459,000	$ 1,750,000		
Accrued Liabilities	$ 1,084,000	$ 1,758,000	$ 1,500,000		
Short-Term Loans Payable	$ 3,390,000	$ 2,400,000	$ 500,000		
Deferred Revenue & Other Current Liabilities	$ 1,011,111	$ 2,348,148	$ 2,000,000		
Total Current Liabilities	$ 6,890,111	$ 7,965,148	$ 5,750,000		
Long-Term Liabilities					
Loans Payable, Less Short-Term Portion	$ 750,000	$ 2,500,000	$ 2,000,000		
Total Liabilities	$ 7,640,111	$10,465,148	$ 7,750,000		
Stockholders' Equity					
Capital Stock	$ 7,500,000	$10,000,000	$10,000,000		
Dividends & Distributions	$ 0	$ 0	$ 0		
Current Earnings	$ 77,371	$ (1,749,308)	$ 8,696,649		
Retained Earnings - Carryforward	$ 1,284,250	$ 1,361,621	$ (387,686)		
Total Stockholders' Equity	$ 8,861,621	$ 9,612,314	$18,308,963		
Total Liabilities & Stockholders' Equity	$16,501,733	$20,077,462	$26,058,963		

expense of $438,000. While stopping at this point with our alternative ending would be convenient, as the differences in our alternative ending income statement and balance sheet have been explained, it is important to remember that our financial report is not yet complete as it goes without saying that our executive management team and BOD better present a damn good overview of what happened, why these decisions were made, and what positive impact it will have on the company moving forward. Rest assured you can bet that the company's lenders and new investors (as remember, $2,500,000 was raised during the year from the sale of capital stock) will be paying close attention to the company's financial performance and condition as the net loss of roughly $1,749,000 was a bit of a "surprise," raising significant concerns with the external capital partners.

With a seasoned executive management team and BOD in place, the financial statements presented in Exhibits 15.1 and 15.2 were also accompanied by an informative and credible MDOR drafted to not just relay the company's struggles with the product division during the FYE 12/31/23 but more importantly, to clearly relay the logic associated with the business decisions made and why 2024 and beyond hold such great promise for our example company. You will notice that our example company provided additional financial information in the financial statements attached and more specifically, forecast operating results for the FYE 12/31/24. Why were forecast financial statements included? Well, the company's financial story would not have been complete without including this vital information.

It should be noted that the financial forecasts for the FYE 12/31/24 are not the same as the financial forecasts presented in chapter 10 for our example company. The reason for this is that the FYE 12/31/24 financial forecasts completed in Chapter 10 for our example company were based on the assumption that the product's division would be continuing to operate in 2024 and beyond. In our alternative ending, the FYE 12/31/24 financial forecasts have been adjusted to reflect that the product's division has been terminated as of the FYE 12/31/23. This is why the financial forecast figures differ between chapter 10 and what is presented in Exhibits 15.1 and 15.2.

The revised MDOR was provided to external parties to assist with their evaluation of our example company's financial performance, both from a historical perspective as well as forward looking:

To Our Investors, Lenders, and Critical Business Partners:

Attached are QW Example Tech, Inc.'s (the "Company") unaudited quarterly financial statements and associated financial analyses for the fiscal years ending 12/31/23 and 12/31/22 as prepared by our internal executive management team. We are providing this financial information to you as part of our quarterly financial reporting compliance requirements to all Company investors, lenders, and critical business partners.

To start, we would like to acknowledge that the Company incurred a net loss of approximately $1.75 million for the FYE 12/31/23 which compares to our original forecast net income of roughly $2.9 million (representing a negative variance of $4.65 million). This negative variance is centered in the decision made by the Company to close down its product division that had exceedingly become uncompetitive in the hardware segment of the market. In total, the Company realized an added charge of $5 million during the FYE 12/31/23 to account for all division terminated related expenses anticipated to be incurred in late 2023 and early 2024 including establishing an inventory valuation reserve of $3.5 million to account for obsolete finished goods and setting aside an additional $1.5 million to account for lease, personnel, professional fees, and related expenses anticipated to be incurred with the decision to discontinue this business division.

While our decision to close down the product division was difficult and one which involved significant discussions, financial analyses, and assessments, it has also paved the way for the Company to dedicate our financial, technical, and personnel capital toward much more promising, and faster growing, market opportunities centered in our software/SaaS and services business unit. To this point, I would direct your attention to the financial forecasts included for the FYE 12/31/24 and highlight the Company's significant financial upside as measured by the following KPIs:

- *Sales revenue is forecast to increase from $59.5 million for the FYE 12/31/23 to $69.1 million for the FYE 12/31/24, an increase of $9.6 million or 16%, all centered in the high gross margin software/SaaS business unit.*

- *Gross profit is forecast to increase from $37.7 million (63.4% gross margin) for the FYE 12/31/23 to $49.3 million (71.4% gross margin) for the FYE 12/31/24, an increase of $11.6 million or roughly 31%. The increase in gross profit and gross margins is the direct result of focusing on the high-profit software/SaaS business unit and eliminating the costly and low-profit margin products division (which represented a drag on the Company's operating performance in the FYE 12/31/23).*

- *Net income after tax is forecast to reach a Company record of $8.7 million for the FYE 12/31/24 compared to a net loss of $1.75 million incurred during the FYE 12/31/23. Further, EBIT is forecast to reach almost $13.8 million for the FYE 12/31/24 producing an EBIT margin of almost 20%, again both records for the Company.*

- *The Company's financial strength is forecast to improve across the board as measured by its current ratio, forecast to increase from 1.47 as of the FYE 12/31/23 to 3.46 as of the FYE 12/31/24 and its debt to equity ratio, forecast to improve from 1.09 as of the FYE 12/31/23 to .42 as of the FYE 12/31/24.*

The Company's outlook for 2024 is exciting, as while tough decisions had to be made in 2023 related to the products division, the Company has successfully executed its restructuring, allowing for internal resources to be focused on the software/SaaS business unit. Supporting this business pivot, we would direct you to the following financial operating summary for the FYE 12/31/23 compared to the prior fiscal year ending 12/31/22 as highlighted by the following key operating achievements and financial trends:

- *Net sales revenue increased by $5.3 million year over year representing a 9.75% increase in total net sales revenue. More importantly, the Company achieved sales revenue growth of roughly $12.2 million or 34.2% in its software and services division, which substantiates the Company's strategic business pivot shift into new markets that offer higher growth potential and gross margins. Net product sales revenue decreased by approximately $6.9 million year over year, which is in line with management's expectations and directly the result of the Company electing to close down this business division.*

- *The Company's gross profit increased on a year over year basis by approximately $7.4 million (a 24.6% increase), generating a gross margin of 63.4% compared to a gross margin of 55.9% for the prior year. The improvement in the Company's gross margin is the direct result of a.) a sales revenue mix change toward higher profit software and services sales (increasing from 65.9% in 2022 to 80.5% in 2023) and* *b.) improving gross margins being realized in the software and services segment of the business as a result of economies of scale (from 63.9% in 2022 to 72.3% in 2023). While the gross margin in the products segment of the business decreased from 40.3% in 2022 to 26.1% in 2023, this was largely expected and a direct result of more aggressive sales discounting strategies used to move older product (in coordination with closing down this business division).*

- *Selling, general, and direct operating expenses increased from roughly $29.8 million in 2022, representing 55% of total sales revenue to approximately $34.1 million in 2023, representing 57.3% of total sales revenue. Increases in selling and research & development expenses were incurred as a result of implementing a more aggressive selling and support program associated with the launch of new software products, again within management's expectations.*

- *The result of the Company's efforts, including increased sales revenue and improved gross margins, provided for an increase in its annual EBIT from less than $500,000 in 2022 representing less than 1% of total sales revenue to approximately $3.66 million in 2023, representing 6.2% of total sales revenue.*

- *The Company's financial strength remains on sound footing as net working capital and liquidity remain at levels that are more than adequate to support on-going operations. Further, the Company's successful debt and equity capital raises completed during the FYE 12/31/23 have provided added financial capital to execute its long-term business plan.*

The Company's executive management team and board of directors are satisfied with the fiscal year ending 12/31/23 core operating results and encouraged with the direction of certain financial operating trends and KPIs. We also understand that the Company's pivot into pursuing new opportunities with the software and services division is just getting started but came at the expense of making a difficult but necessary decision to close down the products division. As such, we anticipate that the operating results for future years will continue to strengthen as we execute our business plan.

As always, feel free to reach out to me with any questions, feedback, and/or additional information needs as it relates to your assessment of the Company's operating results and financial condition. We appreciate your continued support and look forward to working with each and every one of you in the years to come.

Sincerely,

———————————
(signed)
CEO/President

As you can see, the revised MDOR prepared for our alternative ending is one that is more expansive and informative, which in this case is sorely needed to help build confidence and credibility with external parties. You can see that the financial report proactively acknowledged the poor FYE 12/31/23 financial operating results, its causes, and how the company was going to pivot toward new and more promising business opportunities in 2024 and beyond. Oh yes, here is a perfect example of the art of financial reporting. If the FYE 12/31/23 financial operating results were presented without the MDOR and forecasts for the FYE 12/31/24, you can imagine that the external parties (which in this case are debt and equity capital sources) might have drawn a negative conclusion and become somewhat stressed over the direction of the company.

Finally, I will also let you in on another little secret that is especially important to understand (and emphasizes again how important it is to know your target audience). More than likely, the executive management team of our example company had already communicated and "telegraphed" (for lack of a better term) the company's financial operating results to certain key parties including its lenders (that have provided loans) and new investors that purchased $2,500,000 worth of capital stock in 2023 well before this financial report was provided. This was done to prepare the external parties for the unwelcome news but also relay that greener pastures are on the horizon. Trust me when I say that there is nothing worse than delivering unexpected negative surprises that are empty, incomplete, and let the external parties' imagination run wild, envisioning the worst possible downside situations as opposed to understanding the best upside operating scenarios.

A Very Short and Concise Conclusion

As I close this book and help you reflect on all the content, material, concepts, and exhibits presented along the way, I would like to emphasize three underlying concepts that you should be keenly aware of by now.

First, always, always know your target audience. As should be crystal clear with our alternative ending presented in this chapter, having a clear understanding of who you will be communicating with and what needs to be communicated is absolutely essential to write an effective financial report.

Second, early in the book, I introduced you to the concept that accounting is just as much of an art form as it is a science. As you can tell from the exhibits provided and especially with our alternative ending, I applied some basic accounting "art" to a company that changed its financial statements and operating results significantly. But if you think accounting is the only art form, well think again as drafting financial reports is a next level form of art that is essential to master to ensure both external and internal parties can efficiently and effectively decipher financial statements and financial information, to ensure critical business economic decisions can be made with confidence and in a timely manner.

Third, if it hasn't occurred to you yet, let me enlighten you as this entire book represents one big financial report. That is, I clearly understand my target audience, am knowledgeable with the subject matter, understand what financial information and topics need to be communicated, and have done so in a complete, accurate, reliable, and timely manner. Thus, this is the art and essence of writing financial reports as there is no hard science or web-based AI platform that you can quickly access with a click of the mouse or stroke on the keyboard to produce the desired output. You must be able to think, understand, and communicate, skills that will always retain their value in the business world!

In closing, I should note that the financial report illustrations provided for our example company don't really even scratch the surface of the vast types of financial reports that are produced by businesses on an hourly, daily, weekly, monthly, quarterly, or annual basis. Rather, the idea with this book was to provide simple and basic introduction to the concept of writing financial reports and then let your imagination and energy run wild, but kept in check via coordinating with your knowledge and experience. In the end, there's nothing more gratifying than writing a financial report that is clear, concise, focused, understandable, timely, well received, and contributes to increasing the value of a business. This is the essence of writing a financial report.

ABOUT THE AUTHOR

Tage C. Tracy (Anthem, Arizona) has operated a financial consulting firm focused on providing executive-level accounting, financial and risk management, and strategic business planning management support to private businesses, on a fractional basis. Tage specializes in businesses operating at distinct stages, including startups and launches, rapid growth, ramp-up and expansion management, and strategic exit. He also has expertise in acquisition preparedness and management, turnarounds, challenging environments, and survival techniques.

In addition to authoring *How to Write a Financial Report*, Tage was the lead author of *How to Read a Financial Report*, 10th Edition, *Business Financial Information Secrets*, and *Accounting Workbook for Dummies*, 2nd Edition. Further, Tage has co-authored a total of five books with his late father, John A. Tracy, including *Accounting for Dummies, 7th Edition, The Comprehensive Guide on How to Read a Financial Report, Cash Flow for Dummies, Small Business Financial Management Kit for Dummies*, and *How to Manage Profit and Cash Flow*.

Tage received his baccalaureate in accounting in 1985 with honors from the University of Colorado at Boulder. Tage began his career with Coopers & Lybrand (now part of PricewaterhouseCoopers) and obtained his CPA certificate in the state of Colorado in 1987 (now inactive). (His first name, pronounced *tog*, is of Scandinavian origin.)

You can find Tage online at: http://financemakescents.com/ or reach out directly to Tage at tagetracy@cox.net.

INDEX

Page numbers followed by *e* refer to exhibits.

A

Accounting for Dummies, 7th edition (Tracy), 130
Accounts payable, 83, 101
Accounts receivable, 95, 103, 160, 163, 184
Accrual-based accounting, 90–91, 130
Accrued liabilities, 101, 188. *See also* Current liabilities; Liabilities; Long-term liabilities
Accumulated depreciation, 78, 103. *See also* Depreciation expenses
Accuracy, 31, 50, 51, 52*e*, 56, 126, 131–134. *See also* Complete, Accurate, Reliable, and Timely financial reports (CART)
Amortization expenses, 9, 68–69, 79, 90, 94, 103. *See also* Depreciation expenses
Apple, 20
Arm forecast model, 115
Artificial intelligence (AI), 11, 195
Audited financial statements, 21–22, 24–25, 45, 55, 66*e*, 70, 76*e*, 80, 88*e*, 140, 141*e*, 142*e*, 152, 169, 181, 182*e*. *See also* Unaudited financial statements

B

B2B (Business-to-business), 10
B2C (Business-to-consumer), 10
Back of the envelope (BOTE), 110
Balance sheet comparability, 133
Balance sheets, 24, 28, 40, 41*e*, 43, 45, 53, 64, 73–83, 76*e*–77*e*, 81*e*, 86–89, 91, 92, 94, 98, 99*e*, 100*e*, 101, 102*e*, 103, 104, 109, 113, 116, 119*e*, 122, 133, 141, 143, 147*e*, 148, 154, 156, 159*e*, 160, 161*e*, 162, 177, 182, 185, 190*e*, 191
Black-Scholes model, 128
Board of Directors (BOD), 162, 164, 166–167, 183, 187, 188, 191
BOTE (Back of the envelope), 110
Bottom line, 8, 31, 32, 67–69, 87, 91, 92, 109, 122, 168, 169
Bottom-up forecasting models, 113–114, 122. *See also* Financial forecasts; Top-down forecast models
Breakeven, 8, 116–117
Budget-to-actual-variance analysis, 31
Budgets, budgeting, 57, 109, 110–111, 153, 167, 170, 174
Buffet, Warren, 25, 135
Burn rate, 10

Business forecast models, 109. *See also* Financial forecasts
Business-to-business (B2B), 10
Business-to-consumer (B2C), 10

C
C Suite executives, 130, 154, 156, 166, 167
Caddyshack (film), 7
CAGR (Compounded annual growth rate), 10
Capital expenditures (Cap Ex), 9
Capital sources, 9, 17, 19, 21, 47, 54, 57, 131, 138, 140, 141, 166, 177, 181, 194
Capital stock, 68, 79, 92, 103, 191, 194
CART, *See* Complete, Accurate, Reliable, and Timely financial reports
Cash flow from operating activities, 87, 91, 104
Cash flow from profit, 87, 93, 104
Cash flows, 9–10, 23, 24, 28, 40, 44, 45, 57, 64, 85–96, 88e, 98, 100e, 101, 103, 104, 109, 114, 116, 118–119, 121e, 122, 134, 142e, 144, 154, 156, 160, 169, 177, 182, 185
Certified Public Accountants (CPAs), 18, 21–22, 25, 44, 54–55, 105, 133, 134, 140, 181, 188
Chief executive officers (CEOs), 24, 93, 130, 139–140, 153–154, 164, 183
Chief financial officers (CFOs), 93, 127, 130, 139, 154, 164, 181, 183
Chief operating officers (COOs), 16, 130, 154
Chief technology officers (CTOs), 16, 154
COGS (Costs of goods sold), 8
Company equity transactions, 133
Compiled financial statements, 21–22
Complete, Accurate, Reliable, and Timely financial reports (CART), 11, 37, 39–59, 108, 112, 122, 126, 131, 135, 187. *See also* Accuracy; Completeness; Reliability; Timeliness

Completeness, 31, 37–48, 51, 111, 172, 177. *See also* Complete, Accurate, Reliable, and Timely financial reports (CART); Consistency
Compounded annual growth rate (CAGR), 10
Confidentiality, 28, 29, 31, 152–153
Consistency, 109, 111, 152–153. *See also* Completeness
Contribution margin, 9, 32. *See also* Gross margin
Cost of sales (COS), 8, 67. *See also* Costs of sales revenue
Costs of goods sold (COGS), 8, 67, 69
Costs of revenue, *see* Costs of goods sold (COGS); Costs of sales revenue
Costs of sales revenue, 67–69, 101, 109, 174, 177. *See also* Cost of sales (COS); Sales revenue
CPAs, *See* Certified Public Accountants; Certified Public Accountants (CPAs)
Cruise, Tom, 166
Current liabilities, 79, 83. *See also* Accrued liabilities; Liabilities; Long-term liabilities
Current ratio, 116, 163, 184, 192
Customer relationship management (CRM) systems, 11, 172

D
Data in, garbage out (DIGO), 11–12, 56, 128
Debt service, 9, 10, 94, 96, 116
Debt service coverage ratio, 116
Debt to equity ratio, 144
Depreciation expenses, 9, 68–69, 90, 94, 95, 103, 111. *See also* Amortization expenses
Direct to consumers (DTC), 56
Distribution of earnings analysis, 53
Dividends, 32, 43, 94, 117–118, 188, 191

E

Earnings before interest, taxes, depreciation, and amortization (EBITDA), 9, 94

Earnings before interest and income tax, 68

Earnings per share (EPS), 68

Employee turnover, 58

Enron, 131, 134

Enterprise resource planning (ERP) systems, 11, 126

External financial reporting, 17, 19–22, 28, 35, 44, 55, 131. *See also* Primary external reporting drivers

External users, 4, 6, 15–25, 45, 64, 65, 67, 70, 75, 80, 137–149, 152–153, 164, 166, 180, 181, 183

F

FCF (Free cash flow), 9

Federal Reserve, 134

Financial Accounting Standards Board (FASB), 31, 129, 133

Financial condition (of a business), 74, 75, 79, 83, 92–93, 140, 144, 152, 156, 160, 163, 164, 181, 183–184, 187

Financial forecasts, 9, 32, 39, 45–47, 57, 98, 107–122, 156, 160, 162–163, 168–170, 172, 174, 183–184, 187, 191–192. *See also* Flash reports

Financial report audience, 6

Financial report range, 6

Financial variance analysis, 174

Flash reports, 9, 28, 31, 32, 34*e*, 56, 153, 166, 168–170, 172–173. *See also* Financial forecasts

Formality, 152

Forward twelve months (FTM), 10

Free cash flow (FCF), 9

FTX, 134

G

Garbage in, garbage out (GIGO), 128

General and administrative expenses, 8, 68–69, 101

Generally accepted accounting principles (GAAP), 6, 21–22, 31, 44, 129, 130–134

Greenspan, Alan, 134

Gross margin, 8, 31, 67, 140, 143–145, 156, 162, 167, 170, 174, 177, 183, 192–193. *See also* Contribution Margin; Gross Profit

Gross profit, 8, 31, 45, 47, 66, 67–68, 156, 167, 170, 174, 182, 192. *See also* Contribution margin; Gross margin

H

How to Read a Financial Report, 10th edition (Tracy), 16, 24, 134, 160

I

Income statements, 5, 8, 9, 24, 28, 29, 31, 32, 33*e*, 40, 42*e*, 45, 46*e*, 51, 52*e*, 63–71, 66*e*, 71e, 74, 75, 78, 80, 86–87, 91–94, 98, 99*e*, 101, 103, 109, 113, 116, 117*e*, 119, 126, 130–131, 133, 138, 142*e*, 143, 146*e*, 154, 155*e*, 156, 157–158*e*, 160, 162, 177, 182*e*, 185–186*e*, 189*e*, 191

Income tax expenses, 40, 68, 69, 188

Initial public offerings (IPOs), 59

Intangible assets, 9, 69, 78–79, 90–91, 94

Interest expense, 68, 69, 133

Internal consumers, 16, 27–35, 64, 80, 94, 96, 138, 151–164, 166, 172, 180, 181, 183

Internal financial information, 25, 28, 29–33, 35, 39, 45, 55, 56, 94, 110, 111, 122, 153, 174

Internal Revenue Service (IRS), 16, 19, 23, 29, 54, 70, 80, 131

Internally prepared balance sheets, 80, 81*e*, 159*e*, 161*e*

Internally prepared income statements, 30*e*, 33*e*, 42*e*, 70, 71*e*, 155*e*, 157*e*, 185*e*

International financial reporting and accounting standards, 18

Internet securities markets, 18

IPOs (Initial public offerings), 59

K

Keep it simple, stupid (KISS), 20, 94

Key performance indicators (KPIs), 31, 45, 53, 111, 138, 140, 153, 156, 160, 162, 168, 170, 172–173, 192–193

L

Liabilities, 25, 69, 74, 75, 77–79, 83, 92–93, 98, 101, 104, 160, 175, 188. *See also* Accrued liabilities; Current liabilities

Long-term liabilities, 79

M

Madoff, Bernie, 134

Management discussion & analysis (MD&A), 21, 24

Management discussion of operating results (MDOR), 21, 24–25, 138, 143–145, 152–153, 156, 183, 191

Margin, *see* Gross margin

Matching principle, 131

Materiality, 50, 131–132

Metaverse, 11

Microsoft, 6, 21, 67, 105

Middle management, 167

Month to date (MTD), 9

N

Nasdaq, 18

Nearness to cash, 75

Net income, 67–69, 75, 79, 87, 91, 92, 103, 104, 160, 163, 182, 184, 188, 191–192. *See also* Net profit

Net profit, 8, 28, 51, 53, 67, 86, 114, 140, 156, 177, 181. *See also* Net income

NetSuite, 35, 126

New York Stock Exchange, 18

Nonoperating cash flows, 104. *See also* Cash flows

O

Operating expenses (Op Ex), 8, 29, 51, 68–69, 109, 177, 193–194

Operating income or earnings, 68

Operational pivots, 115

P

Periodic presentation, 141, 145

Pirates of the Caribbean (film), 129

Primary external reporting drivers, 19–20. *See also* External financial reporting

Private companies, 18, 21, 44, 55. *See also* Public companies

Profit, *See* Gross margin; Gross profit

Profit and loss (P&L) statements, 28, 65, 68, 98, 122, 174

Public companies, 18, 19, 44, 55. *See also* Private companies

Q

Quarter to date (QTD), 9

QuickBooks, 11, 35, 126

R

Rank-and-file employees, 167

Reliability, 17, 19, 21, 22, 29, 38, 40, 44, 48, 50, 51, 52e, 53, 56, 59, 111, 128, 131, 177, 195. *See also* Complete, Accurate, Reliable, and Timely financial reports (CART)

Report notes, 21–22, 24–25, 40, 44, 79, 140, 152, 172, 174

Research and development (R&D), 68, 143, 163, 164, 184, 193

Retained earnings, 79, 92

Reviewed financial statements, 22, 40

Rolling forecasts, 115. *See also* Financial forecasts

Runway, 10

S

SaaS, *See* Software as a service

Sage 50 accounting system, 35

Sales revenue, 8, 10, 32, 34e, 43, 45, 47, 51, 64, 65, 67–69, 92–93, 95, 98, 101, 109, 113–115, 122, 126, 139, 140, 143–145, 154, 156, 162, 167, 170, 172, 174, 177, 181, 183, 192–193. *See also* Costs of sales revenue

Salvation Army, 22

SAP/Oracle, 11

Scientific wild-ass guesses (SWAG), 110

Securities and Exchange Commission (SEC), 18, 19

Segregation of duties, 126, 131

Selling, general, and administrative expenses (SG&A), 8, 68

Software as a service (SaaS), 32, 34e, 47, 71, 156, 162–164, 172, 174, 180, 183–184, 192

South Dakota v. Wayfair, 20

State and local taxation (SALT), 20

Statements of cash flows, 23, 24, 28, 40, 44, 45, 64, 85–96, 88e, 98, 100e, 101, 103, 104, 109, 116, 118–119, 121e, 142e, 144, 154, 156, 160, 177, 182, 185

Stockholders' equity, 75, 79, 92, 101, 104, 160

Stories, storytelling, 4, 7, 10, 16, 53, 59, 74, 86, 110, 131, 138, 140, 144, 149, 152, 153, 156, 164, 166, 167, 175, 181, 183, 187, 191

Story clarity, 152

Strengths, weaknesses, opportunities, and threats (SWOT), 113

Summary of key operating trends, 154, 156, 162, 164, 183

Sustainable growth rate, 10

SWAG (Scientific wild-ass guesses), 110

T

Tangible assets, 9, 54, 69, 78, 79, 87, 89–91, 94

Taxable income, 40, 69

Taxation, 19–20, 54

Taxation and compliance, 19

Tesla, 131–132

Timeliness, 17, 22, 28, 31, 38, 50, 51, 54–57, 59, 132, 168, 195. *See also* Complete, Accurate, Reliable, and Timely financial reports (CART)

TLM&E expenses, 114

Top-down forecast models, 109, 113–114, 122, 177. *See also* Bottom-up forecasting models; Financial forecasts; What-if analysis

Top Gun (film), 166

Top-line sales revenue, 8, 122, 140, 181. *See also* Sales revenue

Trailing twelve months (TTM), 10

Trend and ratio analysis, 70

Trump Organization, 134

U

Unaudited financial statements, 23, 35, 55, 70, 80, 143, 191. *See also* Audited financial statements

Unpaid expenses, 79

W

WAG (wild-ass guesses), 110

Wall Street (film), 174

What-if analysis, 114–115, 119. *See also* Top-down forecast models

Wirecard, 134

Y

Year-over-year change (YOY), 10, 116, 154, 156

Year to date (YTD), 9, 170, 172

Learn how to read, write and analyze financial reports with our full suite of titles

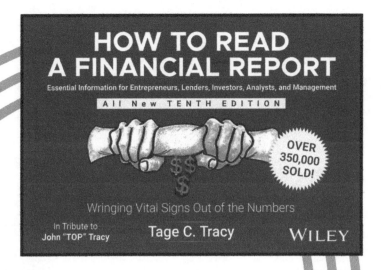
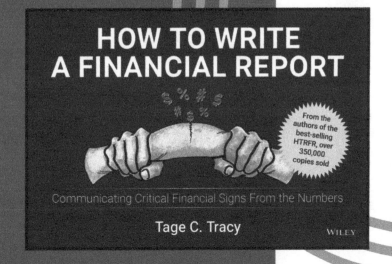
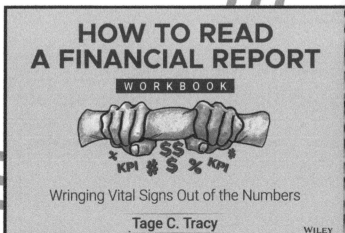